CAPTAIN PROFESSOR

Captain Professor

The Memoirs of
Sir Michael Howard

continuum
LONDON • NEW YORK

Continuum UK
The Tower Building
11 York Road
London SE1 7NX

Continuum US
80 Maiden Lane
Suite 704
New York, NY 10038

www.continuumbooks.com

First published 2006

British Library Cataloguing-in-Publication Data
A catalogue record for this book is available from the British Library.

ISBN 0–8264–9125–1

Typeset by YHT Ltd, London
Printed and bound by . . .

Contents

Acknowledgements   VI

Foreword   VII

Prologue: Family   1

PART 1 *Captain*

  1 Prewar   11

  2 Wartime   38

  3 Italy I: Salerno   61

  4 Italy II: Naples to Florence   81

  5 Italy III: Florence to Trieste   103

PART 2 *Professor*

  6 Peacetime   123

  7 War Studies   140

  8 Strategic Studies   153

  9 The USA   166

10 Whitehall   182

11 Oxford   194

12 *Fin de Siècle*   212

Acknowledgements

My thanks are overwhelmingly due to Max Hastings, who read the manuscript with an expert eye and persuaded me to seek publication; and, as ever, to Mark, for his lifelong – and now legal – support.

Foreword

My old Regimental Headquarters used to address me in their letters as 'Captain Professor M.E. Howard'. I rather liked the title. It sounded like a rank in Cromwell's New Model Army, one whose task it was to hammer sound doctrine into the heads of the buff-coated soldiery. (Indeed, when many years later the British army decided that that it needed a military doctrine, those responsible did actually consult me about it). I chose this as the title for these memoirs since it well expresses the dual nature of my life. In the first part, although I did not fully realize it, I was being prepared as a member of what were then called the 'officer-producing classes' to fight in a war whose inevitability was becoming clearer with every year that I lived. Once that was over I was able to pursue the profession of my choice, but in an area still largely determined by the experiences of my young manhood. I admired the dedication of those of my academic contemporaries who were able, after long and searing war service, to turn back to studying the min-utiae of medieval kingship or the social structure of sixteenth-century Lincolnshire, but much as I tried I could not imitate them. The Fates had marked me out for something rather different, although it took me some time to realize it.

This book is a straightforward account of my life. The first part is based largely on weekly letters written home between the ages of 9 and 23, sup-plemented by fuller accounts of wartime experiences written in hospital or on convalescent leave. (Some of these have already appeared in an anthology, *No Dishonourable Name*, edited and privately published by David Quilter in 1947, and I am very grateful to him for allowing me to reprint them.) I have not reflected more deeply on my immense good fortune to have been born into a prosperous family, received an elite education of a kind that today would be regarded with deep disapproval, and survived through a war in which so many of my friends were killed. Indeed, when I take a historian's perspective and consider the turbulence of Europe between the wars; the catastrophic nature of the war itself (and what would have befallen my own family if we had lost it); the miseries of the postwar years; and the nightmarish possibilities presented by the Cold War, the odds appear heavily weighted against my enjoying a life so happy, and so long. The least I can do by way of recompense is to try to give some account of what that life was like.

Michael Howard
Eastbury, 2006

Prologue: Family

There was nothing in my background to suggest that I would become either a captain or a professor. I was the youngest son of Geoffrey Eliot Howard, a director and later chairman in the family firm of Howards & Sons, manufacturers of pharmaceutical and industrial chemicals. The firm was well known between the wars if only because one of their products, Howard's Aspirin, was advertised with a hilarious cartoon by H.M. Bateman: THE MAN WHO DOUBTED IF HOWARD'S ASPIRIN WAS THE BEST. (There was much dispute in the family as to whether 'if' was correct or if it should be 'whether'.) The firm had been founded at the end of the eighteenth century by my great-great-grandfather, Luke Howard; a remarkable autodidact typical of the great years of the Enlightenment, better known as the founder of the science of meteorology, and hailed as such by Goethe. The names that he gave the clouds – *cumulus*, *cirrus*, *nimbus*, *stratus*, and their various combinations – remain a legacy to mankind in which his descendants take a justifiable pride.

When I joined the army, many years later, the regimental lieutenant-colonel enquired whether I belonged to the Norfolk branch of the family or 'the Carlisle lot'. Shamefacedly I had to admit to neither. We could trace our ancestry no further back than the end of the seventeenth century when Luke's great-grandfather, Stanley, arrived in London from Ireland, where he had been brought up by a Quaker family and had himself become a member of the Society of Friends. Family tradition has it that his forebears lived in the Vale of the White Horse in Berkshire, just over the hill from my present home in the Lambourn valley. Another and more appealing legend connects him with a Catholic kinsman of the Norfolk family, Edward Howard, who followed James II into exile in Ireland and who may well have sired a son when he was there. The dates certainly fit. This theory is reinforced by a well-attested story of visits paid to Luke's uncle, Thomas Howard of Stockwell, by the Protestant eleventh duke of Norfolk in a desperate effort to persuade him to establish his own claim to the title to prevent it from lapsing – as it ultimately did – into the hands of the Catholic branch. The temptation was firmly quashed by Thomas's staunchly Quaker wife. I am afraid that when I learned that even if the claim had been substantiated the title would go not to my branch of the family but to a very remote cousin, I rather lost interest in the subject.

The family was anyhow quite distinguished enough in its own quiet way without going scrabbling after strawberry leaves. It was a branch of an enormous connection, largely Quaker – Howards, Eliots, Frys, Foxes, Hodgkins, Lloyds, Tucketts, Sturges, Somervells – who had intermarried and given in marriage for well over 200 years: a devout, prosperous, cheerful cousinage, excluded until the nineteenth century from access to the universities or participation in political life, but active as bankers, businessmen and manufacturers, and well content with their station. Sometimes they purchased small estates for recreation or prestige. My own ancestors had acquired the small manor of Ashmore in north Dorset in the mid-eighteenth century, of which we shall hear more. But they were prominent above all in good works. Luke Howard himself visited Germany after the Napoleonic Wars to undertake relief work on behalf of the Society of Friends. My grandfather Eliot did the same on the grisly battlefields around Metz in 1870. My Aunt Elsie (Elizabeth Fox Howard) did relief work during the First World War on the Western Front and paid heroic visits to Germany during the Nazi regime in the 1930s, and again after the Second World War to help the Quakers there with their relief work. Secure in their faith and in their income, intelligent, fecund and benevolent, these people seem in retrospect to have inhabited a golden age.

The family had its problems with religious affiliation. Luke Howard himself, plagued by doubts about the place of the sacrament (or the lack of it) in their worship, left the Quakers to join the Plymouth Brethren. My grandfather Eliot Howard, a civil engineer and magistrate deeply interested in social reform, left the Brethren to join the Church of England, which my Aunt Elsie left to rejoin the Quakers. My elder brother Tony was to cause the greatest fracas of all by becoming a Roman Catholic. None the less, all remained on friendly terms.

Eliot and his wife Charlotte lived in a house, 'Ardmore', on the outskirts of Epping Forest, which they had acquired from the famous philanthropist Dr Barnardo, the improbable father-in-law of Somerset Maugham. There they entertained an enormous circle of cousins and friends and celebrities, including, on his visit to London for the All-India Conference of 1931, the Mahatma Gandhi. And there my father was brought up and resided until 1914, when he left at the mature age of 37 to marry Edith Julia Emma Edinger.

The marriage must have provoked much comment in the Howard cousinage, even in a year when there were far more important things to comment on. The Edingers were not Quakers: they were Jewish, albeit non-practising. Worse, they were not even English: they were German, which in

1914 was not a good thing to be. Further, they were rich and fashionable, lived in Cadogan Square, kept a carriage and a butler, rode in Rotten Row, and in the winter months took the train out to Leighton Buzzard to hunt. My mother's father, Otto Edinger, had been born in Worms in 1856. His father Markus was a highly respected citizen, active in business and political life and (so I am told) a deputy in the Frankfurt parliament of 1848. But his grandfather had passed his life in the ghetto and is described in the local records simply as a '*Trödler*', or pedlar. Otto first came to England in 1875, and like so many other Jewish emigrants of the time made very good indeed in the financial world of late Victorian England. I never knew him, but by all accounts he was a peppery little man and an insatiable social climber, highly cultivated, well-read, intensely musical and a keen horseman. Much of his piano music and library came to me: most of it remains, alas, unplayed and unread.

Otto's only daughter, Edith, was born in 1891 and received the best possible English upper-class upbringing. She went to a fashionable girls' day-school near Sloane Square and to finishing schools in France and Germany. She was presented at court to Edward VII and was able, through a school-friend who married the financier Sir Max Waechter, to gain access to the court society of prewar Berlin as well. She was presented to the Kaiser on his yacht *Hohenzollern* (he spoke English, she reported, a great deal better than did Edward VII). She danced with his officers, flirted with the King of Norway, attended the Berlin premiere of *Rosenkavalier* and in general basked in the last genial rays of the *belle époque*. She was lively, witty, wealthy and, as portraits by Brough and Glyn Philpot show, very beautiful. Her parents may have hoped that she would make a better match, socially and financially, than in fact she did; but in 1914, when Germans were far from popular in London, even the middle-class Geoffrey Howard must have seemed like Bacchus rescuing Ariadne from Naxos. He was handsome, kind, reasonably well-off, and above all thoroughly English. At 37 he was too old to be accepted as a volunteer for military service, though he served throughout the war in London in a territorial regiment, the Artists' Rifles. The common interest that brought the two together was mountaineering. They met at a dance at the Alpine Club and married shortly after.

Geoffrey could thus provide his wife with the kind of security that at the time she badly needed. She was to need it still more when within the next decade she was to lose in quick succession her father, who died in 1917 from a cerebral haemorrhage after falling from his horse in Rotten Row; her brother Val, killed on the Western Front in August 1918; and finally her mother, who died of cancer in 1920. She was happy enough in the 1920s with a growing family and a wide circle of friends that she entertained in London

and the country. She collected pictures and jade with enthusiasm and dis-
crimination – her collection included work by Sickert, Laura Knight,
Duncan Grant, Epstein, Paul Maitland, Mary Potter, Marie Laurençin and
Matthew Smith – and kept up with all that was new in music, theatre and
literature. These tastes she shared generously with her children, taking us to
galleries, concerts and opera as soon as we were old enough to appreciate
them. The London Surrealist Exhibition of 1936 inoculated me against the
more outrageous of the absurdities that postmodern artists have since
thrown at us. But in the 1930s, when the international skies began to darken,
she slipped into a decline from which she never entirely recovered. Still
implacably elegant, increasingly neurotic in spite of all that her husband –
and later her children – could do to help her, she spent the rest of her life in
a search for the kind of stability that the world of the twentieth century
proved unable to provide.

Seeing that the only close relatives my mother had left in London were her
remaining brother George and a genial bachelor stockbroker cousin, Alfred
Marx, it might have been expected that my parents would move to the
comfortable Essex suburbs which lay conveniently near the family firm at
Ilford and were already thickly settled with Howard cousins: large cheerful
families living in large untidy houses with tennis-courts and (when they got
round to mowing them) croquet lawns. One such colony was that of my
father's first cousin Helen, who had married a rather grim lawyer, Stafford
Crossman, and given birth to, among others, my formidable but entertaining
cousin the Labour politician Dick Crossman. Another lived just across the
valley from Ardmore at The Pollards, Loughton, where in their large and
lovely garden Bernard and Janet Howard presented charming revivals of
eighteenth-century opera. A third was the Mann family: my cousin William
was to become the music critic of *The Times*, and his sister Pauline would
marry the conductor Norman Del Mar. But my mother detested Ardmore,
and I suspect that Ardmore had little affection for her. Her relations with her
mother-in-law were cool, those with her sister-in-law Elsie sulphurous. This
was sad, because my father loved his family and all associated with it. My
mother, always intimidatingly well-dressed, accompanied him on Sunday
visits to Ardmore and the cousins, but she showed such little pleasure in
these family encounters and spoke of them afterwards – especially of my
father's female relations – with such a crisp lack of affection that these
excursions were kept down to the minimum compatible with my father's
wishes and the demands of family duty. This I always regretted, and the more
deeply as I have grown older. It is certainly an illusion, but I feel that there
were innumerable opportunities for childhood and adolescent happiness in
those genial households from which I was so firmly cut off.

So I was born and brought up not in my father's world, but my mother's: a world not so much of people as of shops. It was the world of Knightsbridge and above all of that great mercantile cathedral Harrods, where my mother went to worship every day of her life, come rain come shine, come war come peace. My parents had settled after their marriage in a small house in Brompton Square, in a highly fashionable area on the borders of South Kensington and Chelsea, where my elder brothers Tony and Denis were born. After the break-up of the Cadogan Square establishment they moved to one of the large houses at the apex of that long cul de sac, with a small back garden that opened on to Ennismore Gardens and up the hill to Hyde Park beyond. There I was born to them on 29 November 1922.

We lived in a style that now seems incredible but was then by no means unusual for the well-to-do upper middle class. There was an indoor staff of seven to look after the five of us, not to mention incoming 'chars' to 'do the rough'. In the basement a cook (known, regardless of her marital status, as 'Mrs') presided over the kitchen, with a kitchen-maid to help her. A parlour-maid of equal status, always called by her surname, reigned over the pantry and the dining-room, saw to the service of the by no means elaborate meals (three-course dinners, only very exceptionally four) and acted as valet to my father. Two housemaids looked after cleaning 'above stairs', the senior doubling as lady's maid to my mother. Finally a nanny reigned supreme over the nursery, with a nursemaid to bring our and her meals up the five flights of stairs from the kitchen. There was also, amazing as it may seem, a man who came in once a week to wind the clocks. To learn how to manage this intricate hierarchy my mother had attended a 'Young Wives Course', whose contents, to judge from the notes she took on it, were roughly comparable in complexity to those of the army Staff College at Camberley towards the end of the Second World War. In addition was the chauffeur George McCoig, son of the old coachman at Cadogan Square, who lived in a flat in Ennismore Gardens Mews above the two family cars: the large navy-blue sedan ('The Big Car') with the family crest on its doors, in which he drove my mother round the West End, and 'The Little Car', a coupé complete with collapsible roof and dicky-seat, for trips to the country at weekends. George McCoig married the under-housemaid Rhoda, and their wedding – or rather their wedding-cake – is one of my earliest and happiest memories. The garage and his flat above it would now probably change hands at seven figures.

As if this were not enough, my parents acquired a second establishment when Eliot Howard died in 1927. The Ashmore estate had long been divided up and the bulk of it had passed to our cousin Arthur Sturge, whose family were pillars of Lloyds of London in the days when it was almost a family firm. But no residence went with it: the manor house was a small farmhouse that was let with the farm itself, and the Sturges had built a large villa residence for themselves some way out of the village. When the Howard family visited Ashmore they always lived in a pretty little house, 'The Cottage', built probably in the early nineteenth century to accommodate about half a dozen people in conditions of no great comfort. This was the property that passed to my parents.

Even in the 1920s Ashmore was still very remote. Its inhabitants were only a generation removed from the villagers of Thomas Hardy's novels. Their thatched cottages had no indoor sanitation. Water had to be fetched from standpipes on the road, which had been installed only ten years earlier by my grandfather. Before that they were dependent on their own wells. There was no electricity. None of the villagers had cars; a bus took them the six miles to Shaftsbury two or three times a week. Motor tractors were beginning to make an appearance to draw the harvesting combines, but otherwise all traction was by the large, friendly horses whose disappearance has left the English countryside so sadly impoverished. Cows were driven out to pasture every morning, and back every evening, lowing protestingly, to be milked. We learned how to do that, snuggling our heads into their warm bellies as the milk pinged into the pail, before running it down a cooler and taking it home to drink. (What the Health and Safety Executive would now say about that I dread to think.) There were four small farms in the village whose economy must have been very marginal but which produced plenty of new-born lambs and calves for us to cuddle in the spring. The most imposing – indeed the only imposing – house in the village was the Rectory, whose graceful Queen Anne stone front faced the village pond, with comfortable Victorian additions behind that looked out on to a large garden with open fields beyond, and a wonderful view across the whole of Dorset to the sea. Since the house proved too large for the succession of elderly and melancholy incumbents who had to live there, and The Cottage was too small for my parents to live in the style they could now afford, a very satisfactory exchange was made. An electric generator and septic sewage-tank were installed, and my mother spent what were probably the happiest years of her life redecorating what had now become The Old Rectory with the help of an architect cousin, Tony Lloyd, in the elegant and comfortable style of the 1930s.

My parents did not confine their redecoration to their own home. The village church was a nondescript Victorian edifice neglected by most of the villagers, who were for the most part staunch Methodists. It already contained some Howard memorials, not least a window put in by my grandfather in thanksgiving for surviving a shooting accident, that depicts Jesus

Christ wearing a full set of mutton-chop whiskers. Now, in memory of my grandparents, my father commissioned the sculptor John Skeaping, first husband of Barbara Hepworth, to carve the corbel stones in the nave with depictions of the deer which roamed the surrounding woods of Cranborne Chase in illustration of my grandfather's favourite hymn 'As pants the hart for cooling streams'. The four corbels in the chancel were given separate treatment. On one Skeaping carved the patron-saint of the church, St Nicholas. But who should be depicted on the others? Obviously, the three sons of the donor: Antony, Denis and Michael. And there we still are. St Antony is garnished with lilies and small children; St Denis bears his head in his hands; and St Michael, with appropriate flamboyance, carries the sword of righteousness. This alone makes it worth a visit.

I shall have more to say about Ashmore later, but I did not visit it until I was 8. Until then home was Brompton Square, or more precisely the nursery on the second floor of that tall and narrow house. There my life began.

PART 1

Captain

1

Prewar

For a long time, I used to wake up early.

Sometimes I was roused by the sound of the landing-carpet outside my room being quietly brushed by the housemaid, Frances. Sometimes it was the jingle of the Household Cavalry from Hyde Park Barracks trotting along the street outside. Until the curtains were drawn I would lie in bed planning elaborate jewel robberies. The headquarters of my gang was conveniently close at hand in the basement of the Natural History Museum. I knew that I was very young to be their leader, but I commanded the respect of my followers by the brilliance of my planning and ruthlessness in execution. Sometimes I meditated about the future. I was already 7, I thought despondently. I would have to live twice as long again before I was grown up and could be my own master. I had a clear image of what life would be like. First I would have to cross the stormy sea of adolescence. Beyond that lay the golden shores of youth, when with any luck real happiness would begin. Then, penetrating inland, I would have to climb the steep, afforested slopes of middle age. In my fifties I might emerge into sunlit uplands. In my sixties I would be on the mountain peaks, white and cold. Then I would disappear into the mists. It would all be very interesting; but what a time it was going to take! Then Nanny would come in to draw back the curtains, and the day began.

Every morning I would be taken for a walk. Poor Proust had only two ways open to him from Combray: Swann's and the Guermantes'. I was more fortunate: I had three.

The first was 'Nanny's way': to the north, up Ennismore Gardens, past the high walls of Kingston House (still a private mansion), across the flat stretch of Hyde Park where the Crystal Palace had once stood and where I recall a parade of Crimea veterans, into Kensington Gardens. There, while Nanny, immaculate in her uniform of grey suit and black cloche hat, talked gravely to other nannies of her station, I played decorously with other children of my station in the area round Watts's lumpish statue *Physical Energy*. At this stage Nanny was the dominant person in my life. She was set as firmly in the classical mould as a warrant officer in the Brigade of Guards, and a splendid example of that magnificent breed. Firm and affectionate, she devoted the best ten years of her life to my brothers and myself. She ate with us, slept with us in the night nursery, exercised us every day, and sometimes took us to visit her friends and relations who ran farms or pubs in her native Essex. I divided my love equally between her and my mother, and when, shortly before I went to my first boarding-school, she left to marry the large, calm bobby on the beat who had been courting her for years, I was so devastated that I prayed every night that I should not survive her by even so much as a second. Fortunately God is very selective in the prayers he answers.

The second 'way' led west to the towers, domes and minarets of South Kensington. (There were towers, domes and minarets to the east in Knightsbridge as well – Harrods, the Scotch House, the Hyde Park Hotel. Indeed, from the roof of our house we looked out on a city from the *Arabian Nights*.) This was my father's way. In that direction he set off every morning with all the other breadwinners, garbed in dark coat, bowler hat and rolled umbrella, clutching his copy of *The Times* in which he religiously did the crossword, to South Kensington station for the train to Barking and the Howards' factory at Ilford. In that direction he would take us on Saturday or Sunday afternoons to visit the Science Museum (working models of steam engines), the Victoria and Albert Museum (a bit bewildering for the young), or the Natural History Museum (skeletons of the dinosaurs that still, I was gravely informed, prowled in the wild lands that lay north of the Park). And it was in that direction that he took us every Sunday morning to church at Holy Trinity Brompton for an hour of docile fidgeting. I was not a very devout child and longed for the moment of release when the congregation surged out past the pitch-pine pews, stood chattering in sunlight on the steps outside and then dispersed; some to sherry, others to a family walk before the ritual of Sunday lunch.

It was then that London seemed at its most Edwardian – almost Victorian. Elderly gentlemen in the congregation still wore top hats and frock-coats. Elderly ladies still modelled themselves on the still-living Queen Alexandra. The tall stucco houses that during the war would become government offices and later student hostels were still in single-family occupation, and the smell of roast beef was wafted deliciously up from their areas as we walked by. The spirit of Victorian London also descended on winter evenings when the pea-soup fogs were so thick that we could not see the gas-lamp a yard from our front-door. It came round in the mornings with the organ-grinder and his attendant monkey to which we threw down pennies from the nursery window; in the afternoons with the muffin-man with his tray and his bell; and at nightfall when the lamp-lighter came with his pole to light the street-lamp. On summer evenings, the melancholy cry of the lavender girls (burly women very different from the fragile ladies depicted on advertisements) evoked a yet earlier age. There was still much horse-drawn traffic in the Brompton Road, and the motor omnibuses had open tops, the passengers being protected only by a vast tarpaulin they spread over their knees when it rained. I protested bitterly if I was not allowed to ride on top.

My father would arrive home from work at six in the evening, when we would be collected from the drawing-room, given our supper of warm milk and 'Playmate' biscuits (sugar-coated, decorated with animals), dosed if we were unlucky with revolting syrup of figs to keep us 'regular', and put to bed. Once we were in bed he came and read to us; *The Pilgrim's Progress*, which I liked, or the Bible, some parts of which made more sense than others. The more bloodthirsty parts of the Book of Kings made so much more impression at the time than the New Testament that I have always understood the reluctance of the Catholic Church to put this disruptive work into the hands of laymen. But as a result of these nightly readings the Bible became part of my consciousness, as it was of my father and his father's fathers; if not all of its doctrines, then certainly the rhythms of its prose. I am grateful to him for that, as for so much else.

Papa was a good man, bred by generations of good people: honourable, devout, understanding, kind. He was in his late forties when I first got to know him, and not very good with small children. It is impossible to visualize him doing the things that fathers today take in their stride – changing nappies, carrying their children in baby-slings, bottle-feeding. I cannot recall ever having kissed him. I remember him, at least initially, as a stern, authoritative figure, which perhaps is what fathers should be. He was a chain-smoker, the brand being dictated by his sons' current choice in cigarette cards. The habit took 78 years to kill him, but emphysema made a misery of his last years. He had been toughened by youthful mountaineering, the great sport of his generation, to which he had been introduced by his uncle, the renowned mountaineer Francis Tuckett. He had explored in the Canadian Rockies, climbed Mount Sinai, knew every peak in the Alps, and through his cousin Howard Somervell was associated with the Everest expeditions of the 1920s. He was a popular member of the Alpine Club and his bookshelves were full of Alpine literature. I was too young, and he too old, for the scrambles in the Alps on which he took my elder brothers, and I inherited the vertigo that compelled him in middle life to abandon his cherished sport. But his *Schwärmerei* for mountains never died. He quoted constantly and happily the text 'I will lift up mine eyes unto the hills, from whence cometh my help', and wanted it carved on his tombstone at Ashmore. It is.

His other great passion was Lambeth Delft pottery, which he collected and on which he made himself an authority. He wrote a pioneering study of early English drug-jars which the Medici Society published in 1931, prefacing it with the dedication 'To My Wife; who gave me my first drug jar and has regretted it ever since'. The bulk of the collection was acquired by the Pharmaceutical Society and is now appropriately housed in their premises at Lambeth. Some were distributed among his children, as was the far more decorative Italian Renaissance-ware that he also collected. In Brompton Square they were housed in an oak-panelled back-room, together with a fascinating collection of curiosa – antique barometers, water-clocks, puzzle jars – and some English and German black-letter quartos from the sixteenth and seventeenth centuries; including an early edition of Foxe's *Book of Martyrs*, whose bloodthirsty woodcuts of Bishop Bonner burning the Pro-testants must have shaped the prejudices of generations of my forebears. But far more interesting to me than all this was a secret passage concealed behind the panelling, activated by a hidden spring in the window-sill. It led nowhere, and must have been built by a former owner of the house as a *jeu d'esprit*.

My father insisted on monthly Sunday visits to his parents at Ardmore. I looked forward to these without much pleasure; partly because of the thunderously bad humour into which they threw my mother, but more because of the long drive through the dreariest streets of north-east London – Camden Road, Holloway Road, Seven Sisters Road, Finsbury Park, Walthamstow – that always made me car-sick and the very memory of which still depresses me. As we drove past the dingy, peeling stucco lodging-houses behind the Holloway Road, I used gloomily to wonder whether this would be where I would end my days, in some squalid back-room, if I made a mess of my life.

Ardmore, once one got there, was a pleasant country-house whose garden bordered on Epping Forest. There was a large playroom, originally built on as a meeting-room by Dr Barnardo, where my brothers and I pulled each other around in a little dogcart and where the young Syrie Maugham may have disported herself before going on to more glamorous if less happy adventures. There were Victorian picture-books to look at and Victorian toys to play with: Japanese paper flowers that bloomed if put in water, cut-outs, pop-ups, a beautifully furnished dolls' house. The whole place breathed the stolid calm of Victorian England. There was no electric light, but ornate gas-mantles downstairs and candles to light you up to bed. The water-closets had their bowls decorated with blue flowers and encased in mahogany thrones, flushed by pulling up a stirrup-shaped handle. My grandfather I remember only on his death-bed in 1927. My grandmother was a little apple-cheeked old lady, dressed always in black with a fine lace shawl, who remembered the Great Exhibition of 1851.

The only other inhabitant of Ardmore was my Aunt Elsie. In appearance Elsie was the archetypical maiden-aunt: diffident, pince-nez on an amiable sheep-like face, hair drawn back in a bun, inconspicuously dressed. Behind this unpromising façade she concealed a keen intelligence, an excellent sense of humour and unflinching moral and physical courage that she was to need in Nazi Germany ten years later. After my grandmother's death in 1932 she moved to a small house a short distance from Ardmore, so our lugubrious Sunday pilgrimages continued until she died in 1957. I no longer grudged these: the older I grew the more I came to appreciate her remarkable quality, although I am afraid that my interest in things military made me a sad disappointment to her.

*　*　*

So much for my father's side of the family. In the 1930s my mother's relations began to come over from Nazi Germany, a sad procession of refugees: Fulds from Frankfurt, Eberstadts from Hamburg, Ehrenbergs from Prague. My cousin Gottfried Ehrenberg was later to become famous as the historian Geoffrey Elton, and far in the future we were to occupy the Regius Chairs of Modern History at Oxford and Cambridge contemporaneously. But in the 1920s my only maternal relations residing in England were, as I have said, my mother's cousin Freddel Marx and her younger brother, my Uncle George.

George and Freddel used to come to supper on Sunday evenings, a meal for which I was allowed to sit up. Sunday supper was a much jollier meal than dinner on weekdays which was always a rather sombre affair, served by a grim-faced parlour-maid and partaken of, even if there were no guests, in evening dress: dinner-jacket, boiled shirt, stiff collar. But on Sundays the servants had the evening off (in principle to go to church), we dressed informally (though always in suits), and supper was a cold buffet. The presence of George and Freddel usually made the evening uproarious. In appearance they might have come out of an anti-Semitic comic-strip. Freddel was large and bulky, totally bald, with thick goggles and an equally thick German accent that a lifetime spent in London as a loyal British subject could never eradicate. George was short and stout, with a mass of untidy curly hair, hook-nosed and blubber-lipped. Freddel was almost totally deaf, so everyone had to shout at him. George anyhow shouted at everyone, everywhere and all the time. They argued, they quarrelled, made it up, joked, and argued again. It was all very exhilarating, and it went on, in one place or another, for the best part of 30 years.

Freddel made himself as British as his appearance and accent permitted. A cheerful, gentle, clubbable bachelor, he was addicted to golf and bridge, and spent as little time stockbroking as he decently could. George was a much more complex character; clever, erudite, undisciplined and, in contrast to my mother's obsessive orderliness, almost pathologically untidy. He and his brother Val had been sent to school at Wellington; probably because, as a Royal Foundation, it was the smartest of the newer public schools and convenient for London. Val was killed on the Somme in August 1918. George, lamed from childhood by tuberculosis, was unfit for military service and so joined the Friends' Ambulance Unit in Italy. After the war he went up to Oxford, where he was something of a star. He founded and edited the undergraduate magazine *Cherwell*, which is still flourishing as I write, and perpetrated one of the great practical jokes of the age. Psychoanalysis was just becoming fashionable: everyone was talking about it very learnedly, but few had much idea what it was really about. George undertook to give a public lecture on the subject and get away with it. He succeeded. Disguised with a false moustache as a Dr Emil Busch of Tübingen University, he hired the town hall and held a house packed with dons, undergraduates and townsfolk rapt for an hour while he solemnly discussed complexes and infantile neuroses. Nobody rumbled him. The lecture was respectfully reported in the local press. George was tempted to extend the lecture to a full course but wisely refrained. Enough was enough. For a few days he was a national celebrity.

That was the high spot of George's life. Coming down from Oxford with a second-class history degree and a sufficiency of money, he did nothing very much. He settled in rooms in Lincoln's Inn where he read in a desultory way for the Bar, collected books, porcelain, glass and furniture, wrote some lightweight history and dabbled in politics, standing in the Liberal interest at successive elections for the consituency of Leominster. Then he lost his money. Apparently he allowed Freddel to use it to cover some unwise speculations, and in the crash of 1929 it all went. Forced belatedly to earn a living, George turned to journalism and rapidly became very successful. For a time he was a favoured protégé of Lord Beaverbrook. Detaching himself from that fell embrace, he then did quite well as a freelance; well enough to get himself accredited in that role as a war correspondent during the Second World War and to be sent both to Normandy and to the Far East. After the war he worked briefly in Singapore as editor of the *Straits Times* before returning to London in the 1950s to do nothing very much; until in the 1960s he suddenly discovered a new *métier*; that of a tourguide around London. This gave full scope to his eloquence, erudition and gift for languages, and provided him with the priceless advantage of a captive audience. He remained thus happily engaged until well into his eighties – indeed to within a year of his death in 1984, at the age of 85.

But back to my mother: 'Mummy' until I came back from the wars, when I began firmly to call her 'Mamma'. I saw her daily, as all children of my class and generation saw their mothers, for an hour after tea, between five and six; a period that became formalized by the BBC as 'Children's Hour'. Down we went from the nursery to the drawing-room, an elegant mauve room that ran the length of the house and was furnished with the Japanese lacquer tables and cabinets my mother had inherited from Cadogan Square and the Chinese jade she collected herself. There she would read to us, taking us through the whole glorious canon of children's literature of the 1920s: A.A. Milne (poor Christopher Robin was an exact contemporary of mine); the fairy-stories of Andrew Lang and George Macdonald; the *Tanglewood Tales*; Edith Nesbit; Arthur Ransome; and finally Richmal Crompton – the last a catastrophic choice, since at the age of 9 I immediately and convincingly identified myself for several years with her horrible anti-hero William Brown.

When Nanny had her day off I accompanied Mamma along my third 'way'. This ran eastwards along the Brompton Road to the towers and minarets of Knightsbridge and The Shops. The butcher, the baker and the fishmonger all of course delivered, and would call to collect orders early in the morning. But that left, in order of distance, Achille Serre the dry cleaners; Rex the florist; Corbie & Eades the tailors; Woolworths, still living down to its name as the 3d and 6d stores; Mr Green, our friendly neighbourhood chemist, who stood much in awe of my father and stocked the whole range of Howards' pharmaceutical products; Owles and Beaumont the drapers, where the change for one's purchases was despatched on an overhead shuttle; Debry *fils*, the French patisserie; HARRODS, towering over all, not yet converted into an Arab souk; Doughty's the bakers and Burkett's the fishmongers, who had to be visited to confirm or supplement the orders placed earlier in the day; Gooch's the boys' outfitters; Coopers the grocers; Truslove & Hanson the booksellers; Jarrolds for leatherware; Harvey Nichols, smaller and more select than Harrods; Woollands for bedlinen; Hammonds the interior decorators; and as we were now half-way down Sloane Street we might as well go on to Peter Jones, slightly more upmarket than Harrods, and finally return via Walton Street and the upholsterers Noller & Harrison. Every one of these dreadful places, it seemed to me, had to be visited every day, like the Stations of the Cross in Holy Week. Harrods was quite fun, with its elevators, escalators and toy department, but even there we dragged round department after department for hours until it seemed I was condemned to spend my life there. Outside in the street, choirs of unemployed Welsh miners sang tunefully but dolefully. I was encouraged to give them sixpence. The social tragedy that I was witnessing did not make as much impression on me at the age of 7 as it should have, but I have detested shopping ever since.

Beyond Knightsbridge lay Hyde Park Corner and St George's Hospital, later to become the Lanesborough Hotel. The hospital was then supported entirely by voluntary contributions, as large hoardings outside it proclaimed, and to this kind of charity my parents were generous. My mother was active in the Invalid Children's Aid Association, whose committee, all ladies in hats, she hosted to tea in Brompton Square. My father was on the board of Queen Mary Hospital in the East End, where I was once summoned, aged about 6, to present a purse to Queen Mary herself; a large lady in a powder-blue dress and toque who *creaked* slightly as she graciously bent to receive it. St George's supplemented their income by erecting stands outside their windows for state events, and a few years later I was able to watch the Jubilee procession of George V in 1935 (bright sunshine, jingling cavalry, royalty in scarlet tunics and cocked hats, open carriages, exultant cheering). Six months later I watched his funeral (foggy January morning, muffled drums, purple drapings, Chopin's funeral march, royalty in grey greatcoats walking sadly behind the gun-carriage bearing the coffin to Paddington Station *en route* to Windsor). The coronation procession of George VI we watched from the first-floor window of a radio shop in Piccadilly, where we could see the ceremony itself on television. The set was a large wooden cabinet with a small screen in one corner like a postage-stamp. A heavy snow-storm was evidently in progress inside Westminster Abbey which occasionally rose to blizzard-force and blotted out the pro-ceedings altogether. Still, we were watching the making of history.

Beyond Hyde Park Corner lay the West End, an unknown paradise of restaurants and theatres. In those days small children were not allowed in restaurants (O happy restaurants! O unhappy children!), but we were taken to theatres. First there were pantomimes, a vague blur of principal 'boys', glittering transformation-scenes and funny men making us bawl out comic songs; much as today, much as 50 years earlier still. But my first adult stage show, in about 1930, was a landmark in my life: *Mr Cinders*, a classic musical comedy by Vivian Ellis, with Binnie Hale and Bobby Howes singing songs that have happily haunted me ever since. A little later came the last great Viennese operetta *The White Horse Inn*, which laid the foundations for an equally life-long *Schwärmerei* for Viennese chocolate-cream music. And after that, when I went to school, there would be a ritual visit on the last night of the holidays, usually to a musical comedy or a revue. The audience, in the stalls and dress-circle at least, all wore evening dress – black tie and stiff shirt for the men, long dresses for the ladies. We boys wore our grey flannel suits, feeling very self-conscious, till we got our first dinner-jackets, when we felt more self-conscious still.

The holidays. In about 1927 my parents took to renting a house on the coast of north Cornwall, and there we passed the most delectable summers that any child – or any adult, come to that – can ever have known.

Glendorgal lay, and lies still, a few miles north of Newquay, on a headland jutting out from a deep bay at the head of which lay the village of St Colomb Porth. The train left from Paddington, which I regarded as the gateway to felicity, and from Newquay station we took little pony-drawn jaunting-cars to complete the journey. The house faced the bay with a superb view over the coast of north Cornwall from a glassed-in verandah running the length of its front. Behind lay a large garden, divided and protected by walls baked in sunshine, where bees climbed in and out of sweet-smelling snapdragons, and raspberries and gooseberries seemed in everlasting fruit. In front of the house a gravel sweep overlooked the bay, whence steps led down through thick banks of sea-pinks to a cove full of rock-pools and caves, whose depths my adventurous brothers explored but I never did. Beyond the cove lay the flat sand of the bay up which the tide came in its long Atlantic rollers twice a day and withdrew leaving the pools full of warm water and colourful anemones, the rocks covered with mussels and wet seaweed whose bladders we used happily to pop. When the tide was out the wide sands invited not only bucket and spade but also more elaborate works: tunnels, dykes, moated fortifications, irrigation-systems. The leading spirit in all this was our cousin Dick Crossman, who spent a summer with us coaching my brother Tony for the Winchester scholarship examination. Dick, just down from Oxford, was then as burly, spectacled and jovial as he remained in public life: eyes gleaming manically behind his glasses, lock of fair hair falling rebelliously over his forehead as he devised ever more elaborate and ingenious sand-castles, all of which were to be swept away by the tide. Poor Dick: he was fated to build such sand-castles, on a more grandiose scale and with undiminished enthusiasm, for the rest of his life.

It rained of course; rained quite splendidly, lashing the glass walls of the verandah, sending the sea boiling and swirling among the rocks. At the end of the headland a cabin had been built into the cliff, from whose windows we could watch the long rollers come in from the Atlantic and break thunderously on rocks below. When the storms abated we would walk along the cliff-tops to watch the water being sucked in and spurted out through the blow-holes. They were good years, and their memories are the most vivid as well as the happiest of my childhood. The feel of the mussel shells sharp underfoot on the wet rocks; the smell of the rubber bathing-caps; the taste of the saffron buns we ate after bathing; the crumbling rusty iron gate with its enormous key on the path down to our cove; the springy turf of the headlands – all this remains fresh in my mind after the best part of a century.

I visited Glendorgal again 25 years later. Rock, sand, sea and turf were as I recalled them, but a rash of little houses threatened the headland from Newquay to the south and from St Columb Porth to the east. The house itself was now a hotel. In our private cove eight or nine families sat around their transistor radios. That of course was as it should be: good things should be shared. But some things, alas, cannot be shared without spoiling them.

Once we acquired Ashmore we stopped going to Glendorgal, and childhood came to an end. I went away to school. Brompton Square ceased to be the focus of my life and became just a base that I touched in transit between school and Ashmore. I was embarked on the stormy waters of adolescence at last.

*　*　*

One morning, when I was about 5, a formidable change occurred in the pattern of my life. While nursery breakfast was being cleared away I was sent down to the dining-room to chat to my mother. When I returned there had been a transformation. A white oilskin cloth had been spread on the nursery table. On it lay pencils, exercise books, pen and ink. At the head of the table sat Nanny with an unusually businesslike expression on her face. Lessons had begun. As I settled down apprehensively beside her to learn to spell CAT, I felt dimly that I was starting out on a very long journey indeed.

Thereafter I briefly attended a day-school in Queen's Gate, where I learned about the migratory habits of the Kirghiz but nothing else that I can recall. Equipped with this rather rudimentary education, I went on at the age of 7 to a serious day-school, Mr Gibbs's in Sloane Street. My daily walk there lay through the heart of the area generally termed 'Pont Street': dark-red gabled mansions built in the 1880s and 90s whose variegated styles were to be crisply designated by Osbert Lancaster as 'Pont-Street Dutch'. At the best of times it is depressing, but as the road to school it was a *via crucis*.

I did not like Gibbs's. Mr Gibbs himself was a genial old boy who must have run the school for at least 30 years past, and its ethos was still the high imperialism of 1900. Maps of the British Empire hung on the walls. Empire Day was still celebrated on 24 May. We learned the more suitable poems of Kipling. Peter Ustinov, who was a contemporary there, has recorded the presence on a wall of a picture of Jesus Christ taking a Boy Scout with one hand and with the other indicating the vastness of the British Empire, and although I cannot myself recall it, it would certainly have fitted in. We were taught to sing patriotic songs by a stout old man with a walrus moustache and a piping voice. On Wednesday afternoons we were conducted, wearing the school uniform of cherry-red caps and grey shorts, to the Imperial

Institute in South Kensington, to gape dutifully at replicas of South African gold ingots, sheaves of Canadian wheat and various artefacts made with Indian jute. There were no working models as in the neighbouring Science Museum, so I found the whole process very tedious. The only relief came when we entered the tunnel that led to the museums from South Kensington station. Like all tunnels, it had echoes, and we became quite skilful at creating them without being identified as the source. But the imperial ethos never rubbed off on me. Half-Quaker, half-Jew, I must have been unpromising material.

About school work I remember rather more, though I do not like what I remember. We were taught arithmetic, Latin and French by teachers who were clearly competent but quite unimaginative. I was a bright child, and I do not think that it was entirely my fault that in ten years I never mastered Latin, and such French as I know remains totally ungrammatical. History was all right: the kings and queens of England with their dates, qualities and defects certainly stuck. As for English, I suppose that I learned some, but by this time I was reading so voraciously that I hardly noticed what was on the syllabus. For games we were bussed twice a week to playing fields at Barnes, and about those I remember nothing except that I mildly disliked and had no talent for them and the bus journey made me feel ill. Neither of my parents had much interest in organized games, and it was a blind spot that I shared with my brothers. But we had been taught to ride from the age of 6. A few hours' terror and misery in a riding school in Belgravia; then trotting on a leading-rein in the Row in Hyde Park; then driving to Roehampton to ride more spaciously in Richmond Park: this was much more fun, and I became quite adept at it.

My recollections of Gibbs's are thus of overall drabness; that, and being bullied for the only time in my life. I must have been a terrible little milksop, and in my last year a gang of older boys picked on me and made my life a misery. Their leader was a boy named Fawcett. Although everyone of that name whom I have encountered since has been perfectly charming, I have none the less always treated them with the wariness one normally reserves for Alsatian dogs. They look amiable enough, but you never know.

All this reconciled me to the prospect of going away to my first boarding-school at the age of 9; a precipice over which I had watched my brothers jumping one by one. Preparatory schools were in those days pretty grim hell-holes, and I suspect that many of them still are. However benevolent the adults who run them, the capacity of small boys to make life a misery for one another is unlimited, and in general I believe that children should not be sent away from home until the onset of adolescence presents them with problems that their parents cannot help them to solve. But I was extraordinarily lucky. My parents had made their mistakes with my unfortunate elder brothers. Tony had gone to St David's, Reigate, whose headmaster had been a school-friend of our father. He had sworn that if he ever himself ran a school there would be no beatings: 40 years on (according to Tony) 'he had put away childish things and enthusiastically enforced the injunction to turn the other cheek – though not in the sense that its author intended'. However, that experience, followed by the rigours of Marlborough, prepared him for the five years he would have to spend as a prisoner of war in Germany during the Second World War. Denis was sent to St Cyprians, Eastbourne, whose horrors have been immortalized by Cyril Connolly in his autobiography *Enemies of Promise*, and George Orwell in his essay 'Such, Such were the Joys'. God knows how I would have survived in such establishments, or what they would have made of me, but I did not have to. I was sent to Abinger Hill.

*   *   *

Abinger was founded by an educational trust consisting largely of parents who believed that it should be possible in the twentieth century to improve on the methods devised for teaching small boys in the nineteenth. It has always surprised me that the school should never have enjoyed the *reclame* of such other experimental establishments as Dartington, Summerfields or Gordonstoun. This may have been because it was so shortlived: founded in 1929, it was evacuated to Canada in 1940, and on its return after the war it merged with other schools and lost its identity. Possibly its news-value was reduced because it lacked the dottiness that characterized most progressive schools of that era. Its teachers were humane and imaginative, but nevertheless ran it with firmness and common sense. Freedom was extensive, but abuse of that freedom brought old-fashioned punishment: usually with a hardbacked clothes-brush wielded by the muscular young headmaster with minimum fuss and maximum force. This seldom happened, but when it did, it hurt.

Three factors went to make Abinger a success: the staff, the place and the system. The staff were young and vigorous, all well under 40 and most of them considerably younger. The headmaster set the tone. Jim Harrison must have been about 30 when I arrived at Abinger in the summer of 1932. Cast very much in the traditional mould – Shrewsbury, Trinity College Oxford, classics and, above all, cricket – he was a lively, humane, energetic young man with an enormous sense of humour, capable of laughing at himself, at the system, and at – or rather with – the boys. Sometimes he treated us as children to be gently teased, but whenever possible he dealt with us as adults to be seriously consulted and reasoned with; never as 'schoolboys' in the traditional sense. He seldom if ever called us by our surnames, that chilling formality which characterized most schools of the period. Either it was our first names or, more likely, an affectionate nickname of his own devising that passed into general use and sometimes stuck to the holder for the rest of his life. His wife Jo was as young, cheerful and handsome as he was. She read us thrillers after supper on Sundays in her comfortable sitting-room decorated with Lalique glass, and in the summer allowed her infant children to scamper naked about the lawns. His second-in-command, Henry Brereton, was a more formidable figure who seldom unbent to the same extent but taught English and history with something like genius and went on to become right-hand man to Kurt Hahn at Gordonstoun. The rest of the staff consisted on the whole of pleasant young men and women whose life was very much mixed up with ours. They had no common-room of their own, only the large panelled entrance-hall whose deep armchairs and newspapers they shared with the boys. It must have been hell for them, but it was lovely for us. It was like belonging to a large friendly family presided over by an adored elder brother.

Secondly there was the setting. The school was established in a stock-broker Tudor mansion on the southern slopes of Leith Hill in Surrey, which with the addition of a wing for changing-rooms and baths, and two small overflow houses, easily accommodated 60 boys. The grounds extended almost indefinitely into the woods around. I never quite knew where they ended, and no one very much cared. So long as we turned up when and where we were wanted, we could go more or less where we liked. The only places formally out of bounds were the local sweet-shops. Sweets were regarded as prohibited drugs. Any brought or sent from home had to be lodged with the Matron who administered them, like medicine, in small doses after lunch. But like all prohibited drugs, they became the object of a thriving black market. Expeditions to distant sweet-shops became exciting and rewarding adventures. The more enterprising boys used to return laden with Mars Bars and Milky Ways like galleons from the Indies. Those with entrepreneurial skills developed substantial networks of supplies and customers. It was all in its way highly educational, but very bad for the teeth.

Apart from that we used to ride through the woods – the school had its own stables – and camp in them during the summer. We learned scouting officially and played games of cowboys and Indians unoffically, as well as conducting rudimentary sexual experiments in conditions of such prickly discomfort that we were not eager to try them very often. Worse, I am afraid, we occasionally smoked there. I doubt whether these peccadilloes did us much harm, and nobody came to a bad end as a result. More important was the absence of any feeling of constraint, and a sense that we could make our own lives for ourselves. Somehow we did not abuse that freedom. The atmosphere of calm, humorous common sense that radiated from Jim Harrison penetrated even to the most perverse and refractory boys.

This sense of self-reliance was reinforced by the third factor: the educational system. Abinger was run on 'the Dalton Plan'. Today this may be very general, but at the time it was so remarkable that it is worth spending a little time describing it. One or two advanced public schools such as Bryanston and Gordonstoun had adopted it, but among prep schools Abinger was, I think, unique. There were no forms, only sets for particular subjects. There were in consequence no form-masters or form-rooms. Each master taught at most a couple of subjects, and his room was devoted to those. There was little formal teaching: we learned almost everything by doing projects, 'assignments', of progressive stages of difficulty. A classroom therefore contained not a master teaching rows of pupils, but tables at which boys worked at their assignments as if in a library. The master presided like a librarian, helped over difficulties, corrected the work and marked it up in units on a chart which the boys carried with them and showed their progress in every subject.

Most important, every boy devised his own timetable. His chart showed the overall standard he had reached. They were colour-coded – buff for beginners, then on through green, blue, red and more remote shades reached only by rare polymaths like Edward Boyle. To remain too long on a buff chart while one's contemporaries had gone on to blue or green was humiliating, but one could not progress until the quota of units in every subject had been completed. The units were themselves colour-coded, red for good work, blue for satisfactory, grey pencil for bad. A glance at the chart thus showed at once not only how much work we had done in each subject but also where our strengths and weaknesses lay. Every day thus began with a session in which we planned our work for the day with a tutor who kept a general eye on our progress. If we wanted to fill in each subject-column on our chart successively we could, but once one was full we had to complete the others; so hated Latin or maths got their share with beloved history or art. Art indeed had to be rationed to two periods a week. The art room, where we learned not only drawing and painting but also leather-work, basket-work, pottery, wood-carving, stage-design and God knows what else, would otherwise have been unmanageable.

The whole system was very relaxed. We were not pushed, and we did not push one another by mutual competition. The teachers concentrated on helping the lame dogs over their particular stiles, and the rest of us went at our own pace. But excellence was rewarded. For exceptionally good work we were given 'credits', and if any boy won five credits in a week the whole school had a quarter-holiday – a practice that gave the academically gifted considerable prestige with their fellows. Conversely, bad behaviour – talking in classrooms, impertinence, general rowdiness – was punished by debits, and if anyone received five debits in a week the headmaster's clothes-brush was brought into play. This did not happen very often, but when it did, as I have said, it hurt.

Very small boys – and there were some, poor kids, who came to us at the age of 7 – were separately looked after by a couple of jolly ladies, and had their meals in a conservatory furnished with brightly-coloured tables and chairs. One then graduated to the dining-room, where we progressed slowly from table to table until reaching the ultimate dignity of the Prefects' Table in the window where we lunched with the headmaster, sharing his jokes and, if he was feeling especially amiable, his beer. Food was ample but unexciting. That more than anything else made us long for the holidays; that, and the lack of privacy. The dormitories were small and cheerfully furnished, but they were unheated – as all bedrooms were in the 1930s. I still recall the horror of being roused on icy mornings by the clanging of the school bell (Oh, if only someone could steal it and throw it into the swimming-pool, would this dismal misery perhaps stop?) and hugging the last seconds of warm comfort before facing the rigours of the day.

The English upper classes traditionally made up for the comfort of their background and the privileges of their station by ten years of misery at boarding-school. Thanks to Abinger I missed half of this, and the second half, at Wellington, was not bad either. But the contrast between home and school was still stark. I went back at the beginning of term with the deep reluctance immortalized by Max Beerbohm: dreading the day, dreading the hour, dreading the drive to Waterloo, dreading the school bus from Dorking station 'through Surrey pines' to the school, dreading the noisome unpalatable supper the first evening, dreading the first morning's wakening by that dreadful bell. Conversely the end of term was ecstatic, especially at Christmas, when we rose in the dark, for once welcoming the morning chill, our heads echoing with Christmas hymns and carols, and crowded happily into the same school bus on the first stage to the anticipated delights of the holidays.

Once the icy shock of term-beginning had worn off, I was very happy. I know that it is too easy to forget the tedium, apprehension and anxiety of which so much school life consists, but a pleasant and friendly teaching staff made for a pleasant and friendly community – and there was so much to *do*. I was no good at games, and was written off as such quite cheerfully. In retrospect I am sorry. I would like to have learned to master one with a reasonable degree of competence. But I was good at work, especially English and history, and in that liberal establishment this was taken to compensate for much. In my very first term I had a piece published in the school magazine, and since it was my first published work it deserves to be printed in its entirety:

The Dreams of a Modern Boy

Slowly as the people of our time struggle up the path of progress they do not dream of the Future. But the future, when you think of it, how marvellous it appears! There are aeroplanes bigger than houses, escalators, cars that can swim, fly or climb Mount Everest. We see new lands opening up, new wonders – airships, free trips to other planets, wonderful telescopes, and Mount Everest in the power of man at last. Also great cities, marvellous lights and education by new and marvellous ways. And man! What of man! Oh, people of 1932, have you no time to think of the man of 1,000,000? No one knows what the man of the future is like. People always think of the Present, sometimes of the Past, but never of the Future. Ah Future, thou art neglected now, but soon thou wilt be at thy greatest beauty. Thou art the end of the path of progress! But what people await us there? Ah! no one knows.

Indeed they don't, and didn't. But my letters home showed a precocious interest in the German presidential elections of 1932 which led to Hitler's assumption of power. Throughout my schooldays, world events provided a menacing ground-bass which suggested with growing insistency that perhaps my generation would not have much of a future at all.

This did not worry me much at Abinger or later, though one of the excellent features of the school was a weekly discussion of current affairs. Another was a flourishing debating society, where Edward Boyle rapidly emerged as a star. Edward was a couple of terms junior to me, and I was appointed his 'Big Brother' (another excellent institution of the place) to look after him when he arrived. On the first Sunday of term I walked him round the grounds while he talked to me, somewhat to my bewilderment, about Elgar's Cello Concerto. He lived near me in London, in Queen's Gate, and we became close friends. Throughout my life (or rather, his, for sadly he was to die long before I did) he was to hold forth to me, modestly and affably, on subjects that I did not quite understand but pretended that I did. Intellectually he was already formidable, and had a preternaturally heavy, statesmanlike air about him. He humoured our childishness by showing how he could fold his capacious belly into a marsupial pouch and fill it with milk which he then lapped up. He was happy to make a joke of his size and referred to our partnership as that of an Elephant and Howdah. And in a school production of *Twelfth Night* in our last term, in which I figured as Malvolio, he gave a superb and quite untypically coarse interpretation of Sir Toby Belch.

The school attracted interesting and intelligent parents, many of whom had interesting and intelligent children. Robert Mayer, founder of the Children's Concerts, sent his sons Philip and Adrian, and welcomed us to his concerts in Central Hall Westminster on Saturday mornings, where Malcolm Sargent dazzled us with his energy and elegance. Montague Norman, the enigmatic Governor of the Bank of England, sent his stepsons Simon and Peregrine Worsthorne. Simon was already an excellent musician and was well advanced in his profession until he changed his name to Towneley and retired to Lancashire to manage his large family estates and raise a comparably large family of his own. Peregrine became – well, he became Peregrine Worsthorne. Professor Julian Huxley sent his sons Anthony and Francis, both as ugly and talented as himself. Oswald Mosley sent his son Nicholas, a thin boy with a terrible stammer, hugely embarrassed by his father's antics but well able to take care of himself. Lord Melchett, the archetypical tycoon of the 1930s, sent his sons Derek and Julian Mond. Derek was to be killed in the war, otherwise he would have become one of the most formidable industrial and political personalities in the country. Already at the age of 11 he dominated his environment. Even the staff were a little in awe of him. One felt that he could have walked into a board-room and taken immediate control: even at that age one sensed a ruthlessness that was slightly alarming. At Abinger he showed his entrepreneurial talents by running a weekly film-show with an imaginative repertoire of hired films. His brother Julian, who ultimately inherited the title, seemed at the time no more than an amiable featherhead, but time was to prove otherwise.

What Derek did for the screen at Abinger, I did for the stage. Every summer there was a school production – Shakespeare usually, but occasionally a pageant. For one of these latter we had a text written by one of our neighbours, the novelist E.M. Forster, and music by another, Ralph Vaughan Williams. (The script can be found in the collection of Forster's articles, *Abinger Harvest*.) My own activities were humbler. Together with two other boys – a vigorous extrovert, Alec Royds, and a gentle scientist, John Maynard – I used to improvise variations on the *Bulldog Drummond* saga, in which Alec played Drummond, I played my favourite character in all fiction, Carl Peterson (having graduated from juvenile jewel-robber to suave international master of crime), and Maynard acted as producer and cameraman. Gradually these improvisations gelled into a scripted play. Jim Harrison found out about it and typically insisted that it should be produced for the whole school. And so the Abinger Hill Dramatic Society was born, presenting a series of thrillers which I wrote, produced and starred in; always as a formidable villain ultimately worsted by Alec Royds's clean-limbed hero.

Meanwhile I read omniverously. First the classic interwar thrillers: John Buchan, Sapper, Leslie Charteris, Dornford Yates. The proto-fascist tendencies that now make the last three so suspect entirely passed over my head. Then, non-stop, all P.G. Wodehouse, who has kept me going ever since. One day I picked up at home Harold Nicolson's *Some People*, and graduated to grown-up literature – and indeed the grown-up world. If any one book set the pattern of my intellectual interests it was Nicolson's account of the Paris Peace Conference, *Peacemaking 1919*, and by the age of 12 I was vociferously engaged in the domestic discussions over the rights and wrongs of the Treaty of Versailles. One of the masters at Abinger – probably Jim Harrison – lent me his copy of Evelyn Waugh's *Decline and Fall*. The English master, rather an advanced young man given to wearing the uniform of 1930s intellectuals – dark-blue woollen shirts, red ties, corduroy trousers – no doubt amused by my precocity, made me read T.S. Eliot, and though I could not make head or tail of it, the haunting lines stuck in my head, and by the time I left I knew most of *The Waste Land* by heart.

By the time I left, in fact, I was an intolerably precocious boy with a magpie imitativeness and acquisitiveness and no voice or feeling of my own. As my English master nicely put it in his final report: 'His cherry trees, always in flower, are horribly apt to come to fruition in maraschino cherries.' I appeared talented. I could now write well if derivatively. I was a passable actor and a fluent debater. But my talents all lay on the surface. For subjects needing hard intellectual application – mathematics, the classics, languages – I had little taste; but since I could perform adequately at them and was good at English and history, Jim Harrison did not try to push me. In a more orthodox school I would have been put into the scholarship form and bullied and cajoled into developing a capacity for dealing with these difficult subjects. If that had happened I might have gone to Winchester, got a first in Greats and ultimately retired from the Civil Service with a well-earned CB and a modest pension. But I was not that kind of boy, and Abinger was certainly not that kind of school. As I have said, it took boys as they were and made them better at doing the things they were good at. It gave me, and I suspect most of the boys who went there, a cheerfulness and self-confidence that would enable me to cope with most of the problems of later life.

It enabled me above all to cope with the next stage: Wellington.

*   *   *

Why Wellington? Well, my Edinger uncles had been there. My brother Denis was already there, and seemed happy enough in his stoical way. But it had the reputation of being a philistine army school, and I was by no means an army boy; and so far from being a philistine I was intolerably 'precious'. Further, the school had just been shaken by a major scandal with the expulsion of two boys, Giles and Esmond Romilly, for spreading seditious if not communistic propaganda; something the press fastened on all the more gleefully since they were Winston Churchill's nephews. There was some talk of sending me to Stowe, which was the nearest equivalent to Abinger among the major public schools; also new, also liberal, its headmaster J.F. Roxburgh being a member of the Abinger governing council. But I suspect that my father thought that Wellington would knock the nonsense out of me, while my mother was put off Stowe because, she said, there was no convenient hotel nearby where they could stay when they came to take me out. And she was reconciled to Wellington by the presence there of that noble figure: R. St. C. Talboys.

Talboys had been something of a family friend ever since my uncles' time at the school. An Edwardian aesthete, tall, grey-haired, dressed always in a blue suit and pearl-grey homburg hat, he would today be instantly recognized as an old queen. But his liking for boys was effectively sublimated, and he never allowed to slip a protective mask of gentle, mocking irony that made him a figure of awe even to the most barbaric of Wellingtonians – and he must have had to deal with some horrors in his time. He at least would be an oasis of civilization; and he was able to recommend another – Benson House, run by Sumner and Barbara Scott.

Scott, an egg-bald man with twinkling eyes, was an orthodox but liberal schoolmaster who might have passed unremarked but for his wife, who was known throughout the school as 'Napoleon'. Barbara Scott when young must have been a Shavian 'New Woman': strong-minded, unorthodox, independent. She had grown into the mould of a Roman matron, strong-featured and formidable. She treated all the boys in her house as if they were her sons, and I suspect that she knew a great deal more about them than she ever let on to her husband. My own mother had the gift of making friends with her sons' teachers: Jim Harrison had become almost part of the family, and Barbara was to become so as well. After a couple of years the Benson seemed less like school than the home of dearly loved family friends, and one a great deal more relaxed than the elegant formality of my own.

But for the Scotts I would have become badly and perhaps irrevocably unstuck in my first term. I have referred to my 'magpie acquisitiveness' and it was not, alas, purely intellectual. By the time I left Abinger I had got into the habit of pinching things; usually books, but occasionally the odd coins from my mother's bag with which to buy books or small items of clothing such as ties (part of my preciosity was an incipient dandyism). No doubt today it would be explained in terms of 'a cry for help', but it was nothing of the kind. I wanted these things. I found that I could get away with it, so I went on taking them. God knows what would have happened if catastrophe had not come early, but thank heavens it did.

On half-holiday afternoons at Wellington we were allowed to visit a limited range of shops in the village of Crowthorne, including a branch of W.H. Smith – the nearest approach to a bookshop within range. There I bought what I could afford, and what I could not afford I slipped inside my coat. About the third time round I was caught. An embarrassed shop assistant challenged me, discovered my loot, and took my name.

There followed a week of mental agony such as Dostoevsky might well have described. If I had committed murder I do not think I could have suffered more apprehension and shame. Scott behaved beautifully. He summoned me and confronted me with the evidence of the shop assistant. I confessed – what else could I do? He was calm and judicial, simply saying that the matter would have to go to the Master and he had no idea what line he would take. Looking at me in my misery he remarked kindly that I had probably suffered a lot already. Thereafter he and Barbara were as supportive as if I had been one of their own sons. The Master, F.B. Malim, a calm, grim man, took his time about summoning me to the Lodge – days in every moment of which I suffered the torments of the damned – and when he did summon me kept me waiting for half an hour that seemed like another week. When at last he called me in he looked at me with cold grey eyes and said that he was seriously contemplating 'sending me away'. I looked out of the window, my eyes swimming with tears, over the woods stretching away to Ambarrow Hill – a view I was so often to see again under happier circumstances when I became a governor of Wellington – and said as calmly as I could that I hoped he would not do that, and that I would never do anything so foolish again. After an eternity of silence Malim said, 'All right. Then I shall do two things. I shall put Smith's out of bounds to you for the rest of the year. And I shall beat you.' Beat me he did, with remarkable precision and strength and a supple rod of bamboo. Afterwards he told me to stand up and shake hands. There wasn't a next time. The catharsis was complete: crime had been purged by punishment. My poor parents were of course deeply distressed and sent me to an expensive psychiatrist in Harley Street. Fortunately they picked a good one, who took the common-sense view that I was simply a naughty little boy who would grow out of it. There was in fact a conspiracy of sympathetic silence, which enabled the psychological wound to heal very fast. Although I have since then committed most of the deadly sins, theft has not been one of them.

This was almost the only interesting thing that happened in my first two years at Wellington. I was far from unhappy, but after Abinger any orthodox public school would have seemed dull. The teaching in the lower forms was uninspired and the work provided little challenge. Intellectually I trod water, while still reading voraciously. One of the great advantages of the school, and one that reconciled me to the idea of going there in the first place, was that almost from their arrival the boys each had a private room: well, not a room exactly, but the dormitories were divided by partitions about seven foot high into cubicles that gave every advantage of privacy except quiet. For much of the day the latest dance-band hits were blared out on wind-up gramophones, and when they weren't being played they were being discordantly sung. But in our cubicles we could be alone, and we were allowed to furnish them according to our own taste. Encouraged by my mother I chose bright green curtains, bedspread and rugs and brought back a couple of cheerful prints by Raoul Dufy. That shows the kind of boy I was.

It says a lot for the maturity and tolerance of my contemporaries that they never tried to knock the nonsense out of me. Most of them were boys with army backgrounds, mainly from the gunners and Royal Engineers: cheerful, noisy extroverts, but friendly and remarkably tolerant. Boys who were good at work were accorded the status of a 'brain' and treated with amused respect. It was a status that excused even my lamentable performance at games, which usually I avoided by hook or, all too often, crook: plodding, when I could not avoid it, on sodden runs round a prescribed circuit through the woods. Whenever I could I spent the afternoon skulking in my room with a book and a bag of apples. When particularly keen prefects were set on flushing out delinquents like myself, I sought sanctuary in the college library, where Mr Talboys was the tutelary deity. Passing through, in his inevitable blue suit and pearl-grey homburg, he would smile benevolently from a great height. 'Ah, Howard', he would breathe; '*Insatiably* bent on self-improvement!'

Two things kept me going during those two drab years between 14 and 16: music and *eros*. I say *eros* because it was not yet love, nor was it actual sex. Love was to come later: deep romantic passions for a succession of boys a couple of years younger than myself. Sex I had learned all about at Abinger. At Wellington the 'tone' varied from house to house. Some had a reputation for total purity, others erupted at intervals in salacious scandals. In the Benson the attitude was comparable to that of the French to the loss of Alsace-Lorraine after 1870: *on y parlait toujours; on ne faisait rien*. At least no one did anything when I was around, but as I suffered hideously from acne this was understandable. Talk was incessant. Some boys had the reputation of being studs, others tarts, but if they actually did anything they were very discreet about it.

As for me, Eros Paidagogos wept on his virginal bed, but I acquired for one boy after another a series of crushes. Usually I never even spoke to the object of my affections. They were faces seen in chapel; not necessarily very pretty faces but ones that I got into the habit of looking out for and about whose owners I found out all I possibly could. Dull little boys for the most part: I did not speak to them because I had nothing to say. I did not even sexually desire them, so what was the point? Eros is odd, especially when one is 14 or so and there are no girls around; and, as I said, it made life more interesting.

So, on an infinitely greater scale, did music. The then Director of Music was W.K. Stanton, a distinguished musicologist who went on to hold a chair at Bristol. He was a gloomy saturnine figure who saw himself as being locked in battles with the forces of Philistia that he continually lost, but a man of rigorously high standards and great force of character. Every boy who could sing was conscripted into the chapel choir, and those who could not were given weekly congregational practice in the quite elaborate hymns and complex pointing of the psalms that Stanton himself composed and designed. As a result, chapel services reached a high pitch of musical excellence. To celebrate the coronation of George VI in 1937, the choir took in their stride the anthems *Zadok the Priest* and *I Was Glad*, while the whole school thundered out Stanford's *Te Deum* with both accuracy and gusto. I doubt whether any boy passed through Wellington without being affected by the music, or by the liturgy, of the chapel services.

Reinforced by masters and their wives, the choir became the Choral Society. I had a fair singing voice and was that rare animal, a natural boy alto, so I found myself a member not only of those bodies but also of various small choirs as well. Within a few days of arriving at the school I was pitchforked into a rehearsal of the *Sanctus* and *Dies Irae* from the Verdi *Requiem*. It was like being thrown into a turbulent sea in which, after the first moments of sheer panic, I became sublimely happy. I learned how to sing what I could, and maintain a prudent silence when I could not. That hour of choral practice on Wednesday mornings atoned for the drabness of the rest of the week. The Verdi *Requiem* was only the beginning – but what a beginning! The Brahms *Requiem*, the *St Matthew Passion*, the *B Minor Mass*, the *Messiah* and many lesser works lay ahead: a sea of joy on which I floated out from childhood into adult life. In the small choirs I learned the intricacies of madrigals and other polyphonic music, and the unique blend of intellectual and sensuous pleasure these complex combinations could give. Further, Stanton persuaded, or rather ordered me to learn the oboe, and after a tough year mastering its recalcitrant reed I could take my place in the school orchestra. Musicians also, like 'brains', enjoyed a certain prestige at Wellington, especially in the Benson. Music competitions between the houses gave the activity the status almost of a team game. From the very beginning, therefore, music, like Tamino's magic flute, kept me unscathed from any ordeals by fire or water – or worse, sheer boredom – that might otherwise have lain in wait.

In 1938 such ordeal as there was came to an end, and I entered into two years that, if not the happiest of my life, were certainly ones of remarkable felicity. I took School Certificate and passed into the Upper School. This meant that I was able to drop all the useful subjects that I found so tedious, such as mathematics and the physical sciences, and concentrate on the useless ones I enjoyed. I made a funeral pyre of my chemistry and physics notebooks and watched useful knowledge dissolve into ashes. Useless Latin of course remained, but under a brilliant teacher, Herbert Wright. At last, after nearly ten years of dismal slogging, I began to see the point. For the first time I was able to take up useful German, also brilliantly taught by Robert Storrar through the medium of easily accessible poetry and song. German was not spoken at home, and we were offered little incentive to learn it as small children. Given the *Zeitgeist* this was understandable: poor Mamma did not want to be reminded of her German ancestry and had anyhow been brought up as *echt* English. But mainly I was apprenticed to the trade of history which I have practised ever since.

That it *was* a trade we were left in no doubt. Talboys, for whom history was a branch of literature and a tool for the civilization of the Philistines, had now retired, and his place had been taken by Max Reese. Reese, universally known as 'the Gaffer', was a large rugger-playing Welshman, and there was no nonsense whatever about him. For him, history was not a tool of civilization but a way of getting scholarships, and he was infectiously determined that his pupils should win them. We were up against the toughest competition in the country, he warned us: slick Paulines and Wykehamists with generations of scholarship behind them, bright working-class boys who had to do their homework on the kitchen table and whose careers depended on success. So we had to work. He rubbed our noses in the Tudors and Stuarts, on whom he was writing a notable textbook, and we loved it. His tools were primitive: Trevelyan's *England under the Stuarts*, Ranke's *History of England*, Keir's *Constitutional History of Modern Britain*, and an inspissated study by his former tutor at Merton, Dean Jones, *The English Revolution*. Using this unpromising material he not only made the past, in the usual cliché, 'come alive', but also inspired us all with a passion for constitutional history in general and the Civil War period in particular. The Gaffer had a Svengali-like capacity for getting the most improbable boys hooked on his subject. As for me, I could imagine no happier a life than one devoted to ever-deeper exploration of the subject, and decided, if I could, to become a don. In retrospect I can see the Gaffer's shortcomings. He turned us into specialists before we knew about generalities. He told us nothing about how history came to be written, and from what sources. His faults and virtues were those of the Oxford which he had only recently left and to which, if he had anything to do with it, we were very soon to go. But in every pupil who came his way he lit a fire that nothing would ever quite put out.

For English we went to Graham Stainforth and Robin Gordon-Walker. Stainforth was in appearance the slightly forbidding headmaster he was later to become: lean, spectacled, lantern-jawed, with a harsh and splendidly imitable voice; but it was this rather stiff figure who was to guide us through the complexities of contemporary poetry, helping us solve the conundrums of the later Eliot and the early Auden, and opening up for us the world of John Donne and the seventeenth-century metaphysicals. From Robin Gordon-Walker we got Elizabethan love-lyrics. Small, dark, bald, restlessly energetic, Robin dragged us along with his own enthusiasms. He was frankly homosexual and flirted outrageously with the more attractive boys, but he was so nice, and so kind, and so funny, and so good at games that no one really minded. If he did persuade anyone to share his bed, they would have been quite old enough to know their own minds, and remained totally discreet about it. In any case, Robin's open affections were infinitely healthier than the pinched pederasty of some of the other masters. His comfortable untidy room, his eclectic library, in which I first encountered the orange-bound volumes of the Left Book Club and his endless supply of chocolate biscuits, were at our entire disposal. Crowded together on the large divan he cheerfully dubbed 'the pash-couch', we listened in thrall as he read to us Wyatt, Philip Sidney, and George Peele, John Donne, Gerard Manley Hopkins and Wystan Auden. 'Since there's no hope, come let us kiss and part ...'; 'With how sad steps, Oh Moon, thou climbst the skies ...'; 'Busy old fool, unruly sun ...'; 'Lay your sleeping head, my love ...' We learned them by heart at an age when we learned easily, and clumsily tried to imitate them. We were discovering love, and were at that Titania-like stage when we lavished our affections on the first object in sight, which, in the absence of girls, was one another. 'My true love hath my heart and I have his ...' All this Robin looked on with benevolent approval.

Finally there was John Crow, later to be a very important figure in my life. Crow was not cut out to be a schoolmaster, or indeed anything else, and but for the war he would never have come to Wellington. In appearance he resembled the Michelin man: globular body, round bald head, round goggles, clad always in a filthy duffle-coat, he brought an exotic touch to our closed world. His last job, so he claimed, had been boxing correspondent of the *South London Press*. He had an endless fund of mildly scatological stories and a huge collection of ludicrous press-cuttings. He lived in the midst of a chaos of books and old newspapers and revolting tobacco smoke, and battened on his married colleagues for domestic sustenance. 'Mr Crow, you must come to dinner with us', said one naïve and well-meaning young wife. Crow consulted an enormous black notebook. 'Wednesdays', he said firmly, and wrote it down. I cannot remember that Crow ever taught us anything. He just was.

But Crow would not have been there and Robin would probably not have survived (and after I left I am afraid that he did indeed come to grief) but for the seismic shift in the school that had occurred with the advent of a new Master in 1937: Bobby Longden. Malim was the last Victorian headmaster. Compact, grey-haired, square-jawed, he was a figure of awe. His last sermon in College Chapel was a scene from an old-fashioned school story. 'Quit you like men!', he announced the text, in the clipped accents imitated by Old Wellingtonians throughout the Empire; then paused meaningfully and looked round in silence on his cowed congregation: 'Quit ... you ... like ... *men!*' he repeated. Deeply impressed we filed out into the summer evening, determined to quit us like men.

But in September there was a very different figure in the Master's Lodge: no longer Jove, but Apollo. Bobby Longden (and at once there was a difference: no boy ever knew Malim's first name) was a beautiful young bachelor, slim and golden-haired. Aged only 33, he came straight to us from Oxford where he had been a distinguished classical scholar, a member of the generation that included Cyril Connolly, John Sparrow, John Betjeman and Maurice Bowra. It was a courageous appointment, masterminded by Talboys (who himself left to teach at Longden's old college, Christ Church, the same year) and by that most eminent of *eminences grises*, J.C. Masterman, another Christ Church don who was probably grooming Longden for the headmastership of Eton. But how would this elegant, slightly epicene young man, Eton and Christ Church to his fingertips, cope with the tough and unimaginative Wellingtonians – or their even less imaginative parents and teachers? As for the governors, still largely a collection of bemedalled generals (including Sir Ian Hamilton, a ramrod figure who still in his eighties radiated gallantry and gaiety on Speech-Day platforms) ... well, it was their decision and they were stuck with it.

Alas, Bobby had all too short a time to show his mettle. He was to be killed three years later, in October 1940, by the only bombs to fall on the college. But his immediate impact was immense. Unlike the cold and remote Malim, he was universally accessible to the boys, especially to the Sixth, with many of whom he established relations of deeply affectionate friendship. These friendships were entirely innocent, but they reinforced the atmosphere of homoeroticism that was becoming prevalent at the top of the school by the end of the decade: a golden Platonic haze that protected us from the intrusions of an increasingly menacing world. This of course affected only a tiny proportion of the school and did no evident harm. Once they left the school, most of the boys concerned immediately took up with girls, married young and are now grandfathers – those, that is, who survived the war. I was not one of them, as we shall see; but even I could sense that this atmosphere, enjoyable as it was, was not really healthy. When eventually I became a governor of the school, I voted for the admission of girls with more enthusiasm than most.

But Longden was to transform the school as a whole by two imaginative appointments to the posts of art master and chaplain. The men who held these offices when he arrived were figures of ripe farce who might have been deliberately chosen to put the boys off art and religion for the rest of their lives. It would be uncharitable even to try to describe them. Their successors were very different. Kenneth Green transformed the art school, previously used mainly to teach perspective drawing to candidates for the Royal Military Academy at Woolwich, into a craft and design centre, decorated with glass, fabrics, pottery and his own designs for the contemporary Glyndebourne production of *Don Pasquale*. The boys were encouraged to paint huge colourful murals to cover the bleak walls. A new world, or rather a whole range of worlds, was opened up, and even the Philistines were awed into admiring approval. As for Geoffrey How, the new chaplain, he was a quiet Anglican priest who radiated a quality of gentle devoutness which gradually penetrated the formal chapel services. Thanks to Stanton, the music was already splendid; now the prayers began to make sense as well. Geoffrey was indeed 'high', but not beyond the reach of the ordinary boy. He believed in 'the Beauty of Holiness' but did not ram it down the throats of those who did not. For sensitive adolescents seeking for a faith he was irresistible. I was one of them.

Finally there was the new music master, Maurice Allen. When he arrived in the autumn of 1937 I did not think much of him. Stanton was not an easy act to follow. But during the following summer holidays we met him staying at the same hotel in Ireland and rapidly became friends. As a musician he might not measure up to the ferocious perfectionism of his predecessor, but he believed that there was no such thing as a totally unmusical boy, and rather than cultivate a musical elite he made sure that every boy in the school who could play or enjoy music at any level should be given the chance to do so. With Stanton music had been a religion; for Maurice it was fun. If Stanton had been Bach, he was Haydn. When we returned to College in September, the holiday friendship continued, and he made me free of his rooms, of his grand piano and of his magnificent radio-gramophone. The following summer he took me to Glyndebourne to hear Fritz Busch conduct *Cosi fan tutte* – a celestial evening, every moment of which is etched on my memory. Maurice was one of those rare schoolmasters who was able to treat boys as his equals without losing their respect; and although he was also, as my mother put it, 'not the marrying kind' (though after retirement he did marry very happily), his relations with them never went beyond affectionate friendship – friendship often extended to shy, diffident boys who needed it most.

So in September 1938, against the background of a world teetering on the edge of war, my life really began: working at things I was good at, soaking up music and poetry like a sponge. As a bonus bestowed by profligate gods, I discovered that I could run quite fast, so for the first time games became enjoyable. In winter I was taken out of the sweaty torment of the rugger-scrum and made wing three-quarter; a position where I rarely got the ball but might either score a spectacular try (*very* rarely) or be brought down gallantly in the attempt. In summer I was let off cricket – a game that I had found to consist, like war, of nine parts boredom to one part terror – and passed the afternoon on the athletics field, performing respectably as a sprinter or hurdler but in the intervals lying gossiping with friends or reading Plato's *Symposium* or *The Shropshire Lad* in limp leather editions that slipped easily into my blazer-pocket, leaving the titles, oh so negligently, exposed. I was in short a shamelessly affected youth. But both in work and play I moved in a cloud of affectionate friends. Within five years half of them would be dead.

2

Wartime

By the second half of the 1930s it was clear that sooner or later there would be another war. With all our German-Jewish connections it was probably clearer to my family than to most, and the realization that time was running out may have accounted for the frequency with which my parents took us on continental holidays – going while the going was good. Once when I suggested that we had seen very little of England, my father replied, 'There will be plenty of time for that when the war comes.'

One such trip took us to the Paris exhibition of 1937, where the vast Soviet and German pavilions defiantly confronted each other across the all too appropriately named Champ de Mars. The British Pavilion was modest and obscure. Its contents consisted primarily, as I recall, of games equipment and an enormous photograph of Neville Chamberlain fishing. But our usual destination was a lakeside hotel in Switzerland or the Tyrol within reach of my father's beloved mountains, where we spent the days boating or stumping off with rucksacks on long mountain walks. A visit to Bavaria had been planned for the summer of 1934, but was pre-empted by 'The Night of the Long Knives', Hitler's massacre of his dissident henchmen in the S.A. that took place on the Starnbergersee just south of Munich. Instead we went to an Austrian resort just over the frontier, within easy reach of Ludwig II's fairy-tale castles. When things had settled down we ventured as far as Mittenwald and eventually Munich. Both were bright with swastika banners and alive with uniforms. As an 11-year-old I was hugely impressed. It is hard now to understand the excitement and attraction of this Nazi 'theatre' to the apolitical masses who did not feel threatened by it: the sense of release from stuffy bourgeois values the excitement of participating in a great adventure. For adolescents it was almost irresistible. My parents were appalled, both by what they saw and by my reaction to it, and we did not return.

My own awareness of war had begun early. The shadow of 'The Great War', as I still think of it, hung even over my infancy. I remember my nurse speaking of 'the Front' to her friends with a kind of sombre horror, and the phrase 'killed in the War' darkened even the most trivial adult conversation. Within the family, the gap left by my uncle Val's death was never closed. In the 1930s came newsreels of battle and bombing in China and Spain. My adolescent reading rapidly devoured Remarque, Sassoon and more popular pacifist tracts such as Beverley Nichols' *Cry Havoc!* The poems of Wilfred Owen I learned by heart. Canon Dick Shepherd with his Peace-Pledge Union was briefly a boyhood hero (I think that I signed the pledge, but am not sure). At the time of the Munich crisis I wrote a hysterical letter home, of which I am now deeply ashamed, saying I regarded war as madness and did not want to die. Little did I realize at the time how much worse it must have been for my parents, having survived one terrible war, to be faced with the prospect of another just as their three sons were approaching military age. It is not surprising that my poor mother slipped into a deep depression from which, as I have said, she was never fully to recover.

The Munich crisis resolved itself during the first weeks of the autumn term, and most of the boys at school, as in the country as a whole, supported Neville Chamberlain if only out of relief. There was a general recognition, however, that this was only a respite; a recognition that Hitler's occupation of Prague the following March turned into a certainty. My parents decided that we should have one last continental holiday, and took us to a plushy hotel at Brissago, at the Swiss end of Lake Maggiore, from which we could slip across the frontier for a glimpse of fascist Italy. There it rained unceasingly, so we moved to Villars, in Switzerland, where my father took one last look at his beloved Alps. It rained there too, so we went on to Geneva to see the pictures from the Prado moved there for safe-keeping from besieged Madrid. Finally we ended up at Cannes for a brief glimpse of high life. I saw little of it, as a stomach-upset kept me maddeningly in bed; but the sound of the hotel orchestra playing sophisticated dance-music – 'Deep Purple', 'Change Partners' – reminded me that out there exciting, exotic, adult life was going on, and I was missing it.

Just as I recovered, banner headlines announced the astounding news of the Nazi–Soviet Pact. No one had any doubts: this was it. Mercifully we already had reserved seats on the train home, for the station was overflowing with young Frenchmen answering their call-up and tourists whose anxiety was brimming over into panic. My poor mother was in a state of collapse. We accomplished the journey safely and saw the white cliffs of Dover, as we had so often before, from the deck of the cross-channel packet *Invicta*. It was the end of an era, and everyone knew it. But I was 16 and found it all very exciting indeed.

At Brompton Square we savoured for the last time the deep peace of the house: the thick carpets, the ticking clocks, the heavy silk curtains. We could no longer see it, as I had for ten years past, as a refuge of calm in a troubled world. We all believed that London would soon be bombed to bits and that we must get to Ashmore as quickly as possible. So all the maids who wanted to remain with us crammed into one car, the family into another, and we joined the middle-class exodus from London. As we drove out past the stucco terraces of the Cromwell Road, golden in the evening light, I wondered what state they would be in when, if ever, we saw them again. At Ashmore we listened on the wireless to the news of Hitler's invasion of Poland, of the British ultimatum to Germany, and, after church on Sunday, to Chamberlain's broken voice announcing the declaration of war. Afterwards, according to my brother Denis, I said defiantly, 'Well: I think I can now have a cigarette.' I was grown up at last. We bustled officiously about the village ensuring that everyone knew about the black-out. One old lady quavered unhappily, 'Oh, it's terrible, isn't it. Do you know this Mr Hitler, sir?' Alas, that is one name I have never been able to drop.

Although we had been at Ashmore for ten years, continental holidays had ensured that my visits there had been confined to a couple of weeks at Easter and a month at the end of the summer. Now it seemed likely to become our only home, and one might have thought that we could not have a better. A large comfortable house with garden to match, in an unspoiled village in a beautiful part of England far from the madding war – what more could one ask?

Perversely, things did not turn out like that. For one thing the family rapidly dwindled to my mother and myself – and when I went back to school, to my mother on her own. Tony had married a few months earlier, and joined the army as soon as war broke out. Denis followed him a year later. My father, running his Ilford factory in the teeth of mounting difficulties, could come down only for occasional weekends. With little petrol and infrequent, crowded trains to a station ten miles away, the isolation of Ashmore became oppressive. In peacetime the house had been full of cheerful parties of house-guests from London, but amid wartime rationing and transport problems these came to an end. Apart from our Sturge cousins, we knew few of our neighbours; sad, because some of them were very interesting indeed. To the south-east lay the Rushmore estates of George Pitt-Rivers, grandson of the great anthropologist; a noted right-wing eccentric who never concealed his sympathies with the Nazis and whose loyalties were understandably suspect. To the west were the farms of Rolf Gardiner, a noted agronomist who had married one of our Hodgkin cousins and whose son John Eliot would become a world-famous musician. Rolf's practices of inviting parties of Hitler Youth over from Germany to attend his harvest camps and celebrating pagan festivals with invocations to the moon were regarded by the neighbours as distinctly odd. Just over the hill to the east lay Ashcombe, the retreat of Cecil Beaton the society photographer, where the goings-on at weekends were reported to be even odder.

(Later Ashcombe was to have an even more exotic owner in the pop-star Madonna.) After the war the *crème de la crème* of the London intelligentsia arrived when Eardley Knollys, Desmond Shaw-Taylor, Raymond Mortimer and Eddie Sackville-West settled in Long Crichel, a few miles to the south. I did come to know them later, initially as co-contributors to the *Sunday Times* and more closely when Pat Trevor-Roper (brother to my Oxford tutor, Hugh) moved in to join them. Then they invited me over for weekends spent largely in playing games of croquet that I invariably lost. But that is to anticipate by several decades.

Further, although beautiful, Ashmore could, like so much of the West Country, be very dismal, and for much of the year it was. In winter thick hill-mists did not lift for days, and when they did the skies were leaden and grey. Trees that in summer were lush and comfortable in winter became stark and threatening. 'Ashmore at its ashmost', my mother used to mutter, looking out on the grimly desolate garden. Her depression deepened, and the elderly female friends or relatives my father found to act as her companions, either brightly chattering or as depressed as she was, did nothing to help. I, thank heavens, had plenty of work to do, as the Gaffer was now grooming me for an Oxford scholarship. I worked in the mornings, went for long solitary walks through the woods of Cranborne Chase or over the downs in the afternoons, and read in the evenings. But meals, their silence broken only by my mother's despairing sighs, were a sore trial. I longed impatiently to get back to school, where my real life now lay.

Like the rest of London, Brompton Square was reprieved for another year, so early in 1940 we crept back. The dining-room, which faced on to an interior well, became an air-raid shelter, its ceiling supported by stout pit-props. The more valuable pictures were placed in store. Back within reach of Harrods, my mother quickly recovered. Life returned to something like normal until the spring. Then all was changed utterly.

*   *   *

At Wellington life went on as usual except for the black-out, the digging of air-raid shelters and the Officers' Training Corps. The latter now began to make sense. I had joined in spite of my adolescent pacifism, partly because of skilful handling by my admirable house-master, and partly because the only alternative, the Scouts, offered only pointless activities and attracted boys who seemed to me utterly wet. It was easier to swim with the tide; and even as early as 1937, when I joined the OTC, I had a dim sense that military skills might one day prove useful.

Most of our training was tedious and time-wasting, but it gave me a feeling of what the old British Army must have been like. There was web-

equipment to be blancoed, buttons and cap-badges and boots to be
polished, puttees to be wound, thick khaki trousers to be pressed, rifles to be
cleaned and oiled. Once all that was done, our energies were devoted to a
complex foot-drill based on 'forming fours'; moving from two ranks into
four and back again. We learned to fire the heavy rifles that made arms-drill
so painful for striplings like ourselves, and there was elementary fieldcraft in
the heather and birch-scrub that then stretched for miles in every direction.
Once a term there would be a field-day against Eton or Charterhouse, when
we were taken in buses and dumped in more distant scrub to march, deploy,
fire off blank ammunition and scramble across the heath. Then we were
retrieved by our faithful buses and taken home for hot showers, a film-show
and sausages and mash. There was an annual week-long camp at Tidworth,
on Salisbury Plain, where I first encountered the army smells of grass under
canvas, of mess-tents and latrines; endured the 'rough male kiss' of blankets
on hard, hard ground, and heard the sad sweetness of 'Last Post' dying away
at sunset. It was all the more romantic, as I was in love for the first time and
spent every spare moment scribbling letters to what Evelyn Waugh once
unkindly described as the 'doughy-faced urchin on whom [I] lavished my
first affections'. I could see how 'soldiering' might be an attractive way of
life to some, though certainly not to me. The main lesson that I learned
from this rudimentary military experience was that discomfort endured in
congenial company can actually be enjoyable. It was not a bad beginning.

On the eve of the war the reforms that Hore Belisha and Liddell Hart
(both men regarded at Wellington with intense dislike and suspicion) were
introducing into the army began to trickle down to us. Drill was simplified.
We now moved everywhere in flexible columns of three, opening out to
single-file when within range of notional aicraft. We learned tactics based on
the Bren light machine-gun instead of the rifle, sections dividing into two
which gave mutual cover as they moved forward. We were shown how these
tactics of 'fire and movement' could provide the basis for platoon, company
and battalion tactics, and how what we were learning would fit into a larger
operational picture. For the first time I realized that military affairs might be
interesting. I began to take pleasure in the good performance of drill. To my
own surprise, and my family's astonishment, I found myself becoming a
reasonably competent soldier.

For all these reasons, as well as those described in the last chapter, the
summer of 1940 was a time of almost ecstatic happiness for me: happiness
only enhanced by the dramatic background of world events, as sunshine is
enhanced by the swelling over the horizon of menacing thunderclouds. In
March I had gained an open scholarship to Christ Church, Oxford (and I
hope that my success did not owe too much to the coincidence that Robin

Gordon-Walker's brother Patrick had been one of the examiners), so such schoolwork as I did was very much up to me. My call-up was deferred by a humane government to enable me to go up to Oxford and gain some sort of degree before I laid down my life for my country. I had been made a house prefect, with all the genial privileges this involved – mainly staying up at night reading for as long as I liked. My friendships, both with boys and masters, were in excellent repair. For reasons that are now obscure I was given the chance to stay on for one more term, and I took it. For my part it was a self-indulgent prolongation of adolescence. The attitude of my adult advisers, I suspect, was that I might as well be happy while I could.

And happy I was, in spite of the hammer-blows that in May began to descend on us almost daily, like a demolition contractor's iron ball striking the walls of a still-inhabited house. We listened to the news on the large radiogram in the House Library. The German attack in the West on 10 May; the breakthrough at Sedan; the trapping of the British Expeditionary Force, with many of my friends' fathers and elder brothers (including mine) in Belgium or France; the tension and relief of the evacuation at Dunkirk; the armistice and surrender of France: all this was exciting rather than tragic. I realized, not for the last time, that if one has to be involved in a war, the important thing is to be young.

There was one consideration to flaw my happiness. My brother Tony was serving with the army in France. A good linguist, he had joined Military Intelligence as a corporal, and all we knew of his whereabouts was that he was somewhere in the Maginot Line. Weeks passed before we learned that he was safe; scooped up by the German war machine and deposited in a prisoner-of-war camp where, poor man, he spent the next five years. His wife Rina was already carrying their child Patrick, who was born the following January. They joined the family at Ashmore, making life there far more tolerable.

The wider tragedy of the fall of France was brought home to us by one sad incident. I was now trying to learn languages seriously and sitting at the feet of Albert Noblet, a grim little nut of a man who had served as a liaison officer and interpreter during the Great War and sported a Légion d'honneur in his button-hole. He spent hours simply reading to us in French and making us read to him, to get the rhythm of the language into our heads and our tongues round its syllables. When the Germans broke through at Sedan he was unworried. 'There will be a *countaire* attack!' he announced confidently. Day followed day and there was no counter attack. At first we teased him gently: 'What about that counterattack, sir?' Then we fell silent, in sympathy with his evident misery. Ironically Maurice Allen had decided to include in the Speech-Day concert, along with Constant Lambert's 'Rio

Grande', a spirited rendering of the 'Marseillaise' with full choir and orchestra. Yet more ironically, Speech Day fell on the very day that the French announced their surrender. Poor Noblet appeared at the concert in full military uniform, stinking of brandy. He stood rigidly at the salute, tears streaming down his face, as we crashed manfully through the 'Marseillaise'. Then he was led away, and we did not see him again.

*   *   *

The Battle of France was over, as Winston Churchill told us in those grinding accents we were all learning to imitate, and the Battle of Britain was about to begin. We now had to mobilize to repel the invader by air and land. Our part in the air battle was to mount a daylight aircraft-spotting post. We took it in turns to sit in one of the college towers armed with binoculars, a field-telephone and a guide to the silhouettes of Spitfires, Hurricanes, Whitleys, Wellingtons, Hampdens, Messerschmidts, Dorniers and Junkers: looking out over the flat landscape of east Berkshire, reading (inevitably) Tolstoy's *War and Peace*. I think I saw a German aircraft once, but could not swear to it. But from Tolstoy I went on to Stendhal, and from Stendhal to Dostoevsky, and became reasonably well read. The war was to produce a highly literate generation.

More important was our Home Guard, hurriedly formed, efficiently organized and, thanks to the OTC, quite well armed. We even received an issue of that most sensible of all uniforms, battledress, and discarded our absurd puttees. A German parachute-landing in our area did not seem at all unlikely; nor did fifth-column sabotage of the railway-line that bordered the southern part of the college grounds. So units composed of masters, staff and senior boys assembled at dusk and patrolled the woods in the soft summer night, breathing in the sweetness of the air, listening to the owls hooting, gossiping quietly ('All the fault of those bloody Jews', grumbled the gym-instructor, a foul-mouthed Glaswegian) before returning to scalding-hot cocoa and Marie biscuits at the armoury and dossing down among the rifles on camp-beds. The rough male kiss of those bloody blankets was to become far too familiar by the time the war was over.

I had no desire to go home when term ended, so I enlisted in a college harvesting camp at Buckland, near Faringdon. We bicycled happily over from Wellington, young men on the *Bummel*. All my closest friends were there, as was Bobby Longden himself, now a gentle, withdrawn, anxious figure briefly escaping from his horrendous responsibilities. The days were exhausting; the wheat and barley-sheaves prickly, heavy, and full of insects that happily transferred their attentions to intimate parts of our bodies. The fields were large, the farmers demanding, the sun hot. In the evenings I was introduced to pipe-smoking, and the insipid liquid that in wartime passed for beer. After closing time we went down to the lake in Buckland Park and lay in punts in the moonlight, reading *The Waste Land* aloud to each other. One Sunday evening we bicycled over to Oxford for evensong at Christ Church cathedral and stayed on for a choral concert: Mendelssohn's 'He, Watching over Israel', Brahms's 'How Lovely are Thy Dwellings', Mozart's '*Ave Verum*', Schubert's 'The Lord is my Shepherd'. The war seemed a long way away.

Eventually the idyll had to end, and I went back to Ashmore. The Germans seemed quite likely to land at Poole, 30 miles to the south, and there was little to stop them driving straight inland. Standing on the highest point of the downs with superb views in every direction, Ashmore could be a significant strong-point. We prepared road-blocks and cleared fields of fire; not that we had anything to fire with except a few shot-guns. People like Tom Wintringham who had fought in Spain were rushing out books full of tips about guerrilla fighting. I scoured the neighbourhood for hollow lanes across which we could stretch wires and decapitate German motor-cyclists. The thought that if we did anything of the kind the Germans would probably shoot the entire population of the village did not enter our heads, or at least my head. Nor did the realization that if we lost the war I would be deported, along with all fit young men over the age of 17, as slave-labour to Germany, and that for my mother, 100 per cent Jewish, an even worse fate might lie in store. I have never had much sympathy for those historians who suggest that Britain would have been wise to capitulate to Hitler in the summer of 1940.

The invasion did not come, but war in the air did. One weekend, when my father was down with us, the news came of the first bombing of London. It was almost exactly a year since we had fled London in fear of the bombs. Now our instinct was to go back there at once. My father had to be at his works at Ilford anyway, while Denis (in his last weeks as a civilian) and I did not want to miss anything. We were able-bodied, adult (well, nearly) and might be able to help. Besides, there were maids again at Brompton Square who could not be left alone. This change of attitude gives a good indication of the change in national mood between 1939 and 1940. Even my mother did not protest. We caught a crowded train at Salisbury and were carried through the twilight towards our first air raid.

We never got there. After about six hours of crawling and stopping, the train reached Clapham Junction and went no further. We spent the rest of the night on the platforms or in the undergound passages linking them. To the east the sky was an angry red where the docks were burning. Elsewhere searchlights waved across the skies searching for the bombers whose irregular drone never quite died away. At intervals came the shuddering detonation of bombs, though mercifully not round us, and once a great flower erupted on the horizon where a gasworks was hit. The night seemed to go on for ever. With dawn, normality returned. A train took us swiftly to Victoria and a taxi (they still existed if one was patient) drove us through an as yet unscarred West End to an as yet unscarred Brompton Square. All was well there, but since there was no gas, there was no hot breakfast or hot baths, only tea and Ryvita biscuits.

I spent the day doing desultory shopping and looking for more signs of war. They were not evident in Knightsbridge, though everyone said 'It was very bad in the East End.' In the afternoon I went to see *Gone with the Wind* at the Empire, Leicester Square. After half an hour the film stopped and a message was flashed up onto the screen: there was an air raid, patrons were kindly requested to leave the theatre in an orderly fashion and proceed to the nearest shelter. As we emerged into the daylight, the sustained notes of the siren were sounding the All Clear, so I proceeded in an orderly fashion back to Brompton Square. I have still to see *Gone with the Wind* to the end.

In the evening my father came back from work, and the three of us went out to dine at an Italian restaurant in the Brompton Road. As we entered, the sirens began to moan on the rising and falling note that was to provide the *leitmotiv* for the Blitz and that I now heard for the first time. With true British phlegm we went on with our dinner (no less phlegm from the courteous restaurateur with whose country, curiously enough, we were now at war) until suddenly there was the howl of an approaching bomb and three massive detonations shook the building. I half-rose, clutching my napkin. Denis dived under the table. My father sat rock-like, gently chuckling at his timorous sons. We sat down again, finished our meal and went home. It was now dark, but we could see the activity round the site where one bomb had fallen on the other side of the Brompton Road. A second had dropped behind the restaurant in Ovington Square. We had been straddled. My father firmly quelled our impulse to explore further and took us home, where we bedded down in the dining-room/air-raid shelter.

It was a bad night. The bombers droned overhead like monstrous mosquitoes, but we were kept awake less by their bombs than by the continuous bark of the guns in Hyde Park. When the bombs did fall they generated a *crump* that could be felt rather than heard, the blast-waves penetrating the building and making it rock slightly. I was wearing foam-rubber ear-muffs to muffle the blast, and over my pyjamas a rather elegant 'siren-suit', a form of civilian battledress later popularized by Churchill, which I had prudently bought at Harrods that morning. Lying on Dunlopillo mattresses, we were not uncomfortable, but there was no sleep till the All Clear went at about 4 a.m., and not much after that.

In the morning we shaved, again in cold water, and considered. There seemed no point in hanging around. There was nothing to do. I was too young to be accepted by the ARP (air-raid precautions) services, and I was anyhow due back at school the following week. It made sense to go there at once: a wise decision, though hardly a courageous one, which my father, who had troubles enough, greeted with relief. I sent a telegram to the Scotts (which never arrived) and presented myself on their doorstep that afternoon.

A week later Brompton Square was hit: not our own house but that next door. No one was hurt – the air-raid shelter stood up most effectively – but all the windows were blown out and the building declared unsafe. The household was once more evacuated to Ashmore, the furniture put in store, and I returned for a last look and to rescue a few treasures. It was the end of an era. The house stood empty for two decades and is now divided into flats better suited to the egalitarian world into which it has somehow survived.

At Wellington life went on much as usual, except that when the siren sounded we made for the air-raid shelters we had dug in the woods a year earlier. This seldom happened by day, though once when it did I saw, high and minute in the blue autumn sky, a cluster of German bombers like silver minnows sailing serenely overhead, presumably on their way to the Midlands. At night the siren went so often that soon we slept in the shelters every night; not uncomfortably, in spite of the damp smell of concrete, on Dunlopillo mattresses in wooden tiers of bunks. It was really quite convivial. Then one night, after we had been in the shelter for about an hour, there came three heavy crumps. My experience of the London Blitz, brief as it had been, told me that these were bombs, and very close. Half an hour later Scott arrived and told us how close. They had fallen along the south front of the college. One had scored a direct hit on the Master's Lodge. The Master had been killed outright. No one else had been hurt.

We could hardly believe the news, it sounded so improbable, but next morning we found the Lodge a pile of rubble and the south front strewn with broken glass. At assembly in Old Hall the Second Master, Edwin Gould, told us what had happened; how when the sirens went, Longden had left his dinner-party to make sure that all was well, and the bomb dropped as he went out of his front door. It was horrible; worse, almost, than if he had been one among a dozen killed. For some time we went around in a daze, too stunned to talk about it much. Life had to go on. Gould took over: a rubicund and genial old buffer not far off retirement who seemed to cope remarkably well. But for me all was now anticlimax. I still enjoyed my work and loved my friends, but Bobby's death signalled the end of an era as decisively as did the bombing of Brompton Square. It was high time to move on.

Ashmore was now our only home, and Christmas there was predictably glum. My mother's depression had returned, but nothing could dampen my father's resilience. He was in his mid-sixties, and had had a terrible autumn. The works had been bombed and the most promising of his young colleagues, my cousin Jim Howard, had been killed. On weekdays he dossed down on the sofas of various Howard cousins who lived nearby, and at weekends he trekked down to Ashmore in slow, cold, crowded trains to console a wife who was now a dead weight on him. But he still ran the business with brisk efficiency and wrote me long, cheerful letters in his firm sloping hand, giving news of family and friends and commenting on the tremendous events unfolding around us. He was sustained by a deep and unwavering Christian faith, and in those months he passed much of it on to me. The works of T.S. Eliot, C.S. Lewis and Charles Williams helped as well, and I began to read John Donne, Henry Vaughan and George Herbert not just as poetry but as guides to devotion. Christianity seemed an anchor of certainty and reassurance in a fast-dissolving world. It still does.

I could now hardly wait to get to Oxford. The village taxi-driver drove me there one bitterly cold afternoon in January 1941, over Salisbury Plain and downland sprinkled with snow, and dropped me in the afternoon twilight outside the massive pillars of Christ Church's Canterbury Gate. My room-mate, Humphrey Leeke, had already arrived. Humphrey was another Wellington historian who under the Gaffer's coaching had won an award at Oxford; a small, neat, fair young man who had become my closest friend. We were to become inseparable, with that totally sexless intimacy possible only between very young men – and, I suppose, young women. In Oxford we did everything together. We were to join the army together and train together. We were to go overseas together and land at Salerno together. We were to be hospitalized and share our leaves in Italy together. Then he was killed on a hillside somewhere in Tuscany. For years afterwards I was to feel very lonely indeed.

All that lay in the future as we set out that January evening to explore our panelled rooms on the ground floor of Peckwater Quad and the grandeurs of Christ Church beyond. The war had not yet destroyed all traces of the *ancien régime*. We were woken in the morning by an elderly scout, a wizened Dickensian figure, with cans of hot water for shaving. The bedrooms were icy, and only the prospect of cold shaving-water forced us out of our warm beds. The sitting-room was heated only by a small coal-fire that we were not allowed to light before midday and took all day to warm the room. But there were baths – huge ones with plentiful hot water – across the quad, and our bedroom slippers crunched on the snow when we visited them. Before the war, breakfast and lunch would have been served in our rooms, but that was now possible only for tea. So clutching little pots containing our sugar and butter rations, we mounted the great fan-vaulted staircase to get into Hall before the doors were shut on us at 8.45. There we ate under the serene gaze of the bishops and statesmen whose portraits covered the walls. Henry VIII glared down on us from above the high table; Cardinal Wolsey prudently averted his gaze. The food did not measure up to the grandeur of the surroundings. The steward was a retired soldier, and sardonic undergraduates who attended his military history lectures suggested that he was so convinced of our imminent defeat that he did not think it worthwhile feeding us. So the temptation to have half an hour longer in bed and breakfast in a workers' café in the market was often irresistible.

My tutor was Keith Feiling, whose reputation rested on his beautifully written history of the Tory Party. Gentle, shabby, wise, cocooned in books and tobacco-smoke, he emanated learning and deepened my passion for the seventeenth century. 'It's a p-p-pity you can't get up to the British Museum, Howard', he would stammer, after listening patiently to my essay. 'You'd find some f-f-f-fascinating stuff in the Tanner Manuscripts about all that.' This may not have been particularly helpful, but it filled me with the determination to get to the British Museum sooner or later, which was probably a good thing. Political thought was taught by the great medievalist Nowell Myres. As the poor man was doubling as a civil servant in the Ministry of Food during the day and could see me only in the evenings, he found it hard to stay awake during our tutorials, but he guided me skilfully through Aristotle. Hobbes spoke lucidly and wittily for himself, and no one could persuade me that Rousseau was anything more than romantic and dangerous nonsense. That it was important nonsense I learned from J.M. Thompson of Magdalen, a withered, saurian little man to whom I was farmed out for the French Revolution and Napoleon.

I was likewise farmed out also to A.J.P. Taylor for nineteenth-century European history. Taylor was not yet the *enfant terrible* he was to become. The impression he gave was mainly one of efficiency. He lectured without a note, taking post on the dais in Magdalen Hall at five past the hour and concluding his last sentence as the clock struck. He listened alertly to my essays and commented on them point by point. The weekly hour I spent with him was exhilarating and fruitful, made all the more pleasant by the fact that he taught me in the summer term and I walked to his house at Holywell Ford down a chestnut avenue breaking into full blossom. That, I reckoned, was what Oxford was all about.

My Latin – then still quite properly regarded as an essential tool for historians – was execrable in spite of ten years' expensive teaching, and I had desultory tuition from Robin Dundas. Dundas was a 'character': a shambling figure with a crumpled grey face, always wearing the same crumpled grey suit, cigarette eternally stuck to his lower lip, mainly notorious for his open interest in the sex-life of his undergraduates, which he quite evidently wanted to share. In summer he frequented the nude bathing beach at Parson's Pleasure, eyeing speculatively any young man rash enough to be seen there. He was regarded by the undergraduates with a kind of affectionate disgust, and the main point in his favour was that he inhabited the rooms occupied 60 years earlier by Lewis Carroll and still furnished much as he had left them. In particular, the fireplace was surrounded by tiles depicting vaguely heraldic animals, the prototypes of the Gryphon and the Mock Turtle among other immortal beasts. These at least enabled us to change the subject when he asked us whether we masturbated, and if so, how often.

Very, *very* different was Tommy Armstrong the cathedral organist, a cherubic-faced, rather episcopal figure who also trained the Bach Choir. A very fine musician indeed, he combined total dedication to his craft with an encouraging openness to anyone, however young and inadequate, who wanted to practise it. Humphrey and I went to him for voice-tests that we happily passed. So we found ourselves singing Haydn's *Creation* in the Sheldonian Theatre, an experience in felicity surpassing even Sydney Smith's eating *foie gras* to the sound of trumpets. But even better things lay ahead. Shortage of male voices for the cathedral choir made Armstrong seek recruits among undergraduates; and since I was, or tried to be, a tenor, could sight-read adequately, and was prepared to return to Oxford at weekends during vacations, I spent the six winter months of 1941–42 as the cathedral's cantoris tenor, singing anything from Palestrina to Vaughan Williams. To listen to the choir had been joy enough: actually to *sing* in it was to dwell in the courts of the Lord.

Also, while on the subject of music, I should mention that I played under Armstrong's baton as an oboist in the Oxford orchestra. I suppose that I was a reasonably competent performer, but I was very surprised indeed to be visited one day by an Old Wellingtonian musician who was talent-spotting for the RAF orchestra. Would I be interested in joining the RAF, he asked, and training as an oboist? Since at that time I had little if any idea which service I intended to join, beyond feeling rather unimaginatively that it would have to be the army, the idea was not unappealing, I went to consult Feiling about it. He listened puffing his pipe, looking like a wise old owl. 'Y-yes, Howard', he said when I had finished. 'I-I can see that it doesn't look a b-b-bad idea. But afterwards, when they ask you w-w-what you actually did during the war, and you said that you spent it p-p-playing the oboe ...' I got the message, and abandoned the idea on the spot. I doubt whether it would have made the slightest difference to my reputation if I had accepted: the odder the things people did during the war, the less it seemed to matter. But my career would certainly have taken a very different turn.

Finally Humphrey and I joined the chorus of an amateur opera group to sing a pleasant sub-Mozartian composition by Vere Somerset, a history don at Worcester College. Armstrong dismissed it as the kind of thing anyone could write if they went to Glyndebourne every day of the season and then set down everything they remembered, but it was fun, and we were trained by very competent professionals, mainly Jewish refugees living in Oxford. The conductor, Karl Rankl, was to become musical director at Covent Garden immediately after the war. More important, we met Girls – not easy in Oxford then – and Humphrey and I dated two pretty sisters, Audrey and Valerie, who, although they were two years younger than we were, seemed so terrifyingly mature that we did not dare to touch them. Eros Paidagogos continued to weep on his virginal bed.

How we found time for any actual *work* heaven alone knows, and the First Class that to my astonishment I was eventually awarded I attributed to the indulgence of wartime examiners rather than to my own merits. It was as if we were determined to exhaust every experience that Oxford had to offer before war claimed us for its own. I acted with the OUDS – or rather its wartime stop-gap – in *Othello*, in which Michael Flanders and I provided grave senatorial foils as Brabantio and Lodovico to young stars whose names, alas, I no longer remember. I edited the student magazine *Cherwell*, which had been founded by my Uncle George, where I was assisted by (among others) a serious young man called Geoffrey Rippon and the poet Sidney Keyes, some of whose best poems I had the honour of publishing and who would be dead within a year. And I became a regular speaker at the Union, usually from the cross-benches.

The Union was in the doldrums. The last star had been Roy Jenkins, and there was to be no other of distinction until Tony Crosland returned from the wars. I was then vaguely Conservative, partly from a romantic Toryism derived from Feiling's interpretation of seventeenth-century England, partly because Derek Mond had reappeared from Eton and had cast his Svengali-like spell over me again. But we all, regardless of party, looked forward to some kind of Brave New World after the war. Marxism made no appeal to me whatever. At school Robin Gordon-Walker, a socialist of a kind, had taught us about Marxism in a decently neutral way, but had never been able to answer the idiot-boy question 'If you create a dictatorship of the proletariat, how do ensure that it remains a dictatorship *of the proletariat*?' Labour for me meant my cousin Dick Crossman whom I liked and admired but could never take seriously. Liberalism was my Uncle George, whom I took even less seriously. Under Derek Mond's influence, Humphrey and I joined and became respectively secretary and president of the conservative Chatham Club. There we entertained R.A. Butler, who convinced me that the Young Tories (as they were beginning to call themselves, rather like 'New Labour' a generation later) had good and clear ideas about the reorganization of society. Impressive in a different way was Alfred Duff-Cooper, a small man with a head as round as a cannon-ball, who arrived on an afternoon train paralytically drunk, sloshed back brandy all evening, and made a splendid speech at the end of it, quite undeterred by an undergraduate being sick all over him. 'Just like old times', he commented happily. Clearly conservatives were not necessarily bores. A visit from Tom Driberg showed that socialists were not necessarily bores either, but he rather spoiled the effect by making a pass at the treasurer of the club, a lanky Old Etonian, in the loo after dinner. On the whole I decided that the world of politics was not for me.

On top of all this was the OTC, membership of which was a necessary condition of the deferment of our military service. This occupied two afternoons a week and a full Sunday every month. We paraded in the narrow alley behind the town hall and marched to Christ Church Meadow where, like the army of Charles I 300 years earlier, we practised our rudimentary military skills. On the lawns outside the Meadow Buildings we learned how to strip and reassemble the Bren Gun, and went through the ritual of 'naming of parts'. Henry Reed hit it off perfectly:

> ... Yesterday
> We had daily cleaning, and tomorrow morning
> We shall have what to do after firing. But today,
> Today we have naming of parts. Japonica
> Glistens like coral in all of the neighbouring gardens
> And today we have naming of parts.*

We attacked assault-courses, pulling ourselves across the Cherwell on fragile ropes. We were lectured on map-reading by Edmund Blunden, then a don at Merton; every inch a poet with wild hair and melancholy blue eyes, wearing a uniform that fitted nowhere. We were lectured on gas warfare by Captain Green, a solid officer from the Oxf. and Bucks. We were lectured on tactics by a cheerful young subaltern in the Rifle Brigade, Jim Wilson, later to become Lieutenant-General Sir James Wilson, KBE, MC. But the main figure in our lives was CSM Reid, a tall Northumbrian in the Coldstream,

---

* Henry Reed, 'Naming of Parts', from 'Lessons of the War', *A Map of Verona* (London: Jonathan Cape, 1946).

who was all that a sergeant-major should be: efficient, implacable, kindly, omniscient. The adjutant was also a Coldstreamer, and schoolgirl-like I swooned over his elegant black hat and the blinding flash of his buttons. When he suggested that I should join the Coldstream myself it seemed an excellent idea. The combination of elegance and efficiency was immensely appealing, and besides, their use of Figaro's aria *Non piu andrai* as their slow march seemed to indicate both civilization and wit.

I went up to London for my interview with the regimental lieutenant-colonel. Evelyn Waugh had not yet published *Put Out More Flags*, but his description there of a similar interview is exact. In the outer office huge guardsmen with hands like hams were pounding at antiquated typewriters. The inner office was furnished with Chippendale furniture and eighteenth-century prints. The lieutenant-colonel, an immaculate figure smelling slightly of Trumper's *Eucris*, received me courteously, but learning that I belonged neither to the Norfolk nor the Carlisle branch of the Howard family and that I neither hunted, fished nor shot, seemed a little puzzled. 'But why do you want to join the *Coldstream*?' he asked. Figaro did not seem the appropriate answer under the circumstances. I stammered something about having always wanted to join the regiment. This was neither true nor an answer to the question, but it was the correct reply. The lieutenant-colonel grunted approvingly. I was in. On the train back to Oxford I hummed happily:

Cherubino alla vittoria
Alla gloria militar!

Many years later I met the regimental lieutenant-colonel at a regimental dinner. He now seemed a great deal less menacing, so I confessed to him about Figaro. He roared with laughter. 'My dear boy, why didn't you tell me?' he asked. 'We would have been *delighted*!'

My parents thoroughly approved my decision. My father's embarrassment about what the Quaker cousinage would think and my mother's natural preference for seeing me safely *embusque* somewhere in Intelligence were outweighed by the social cachet involved. 'It's a great thing to have a son in the Brigade', my father wrote cheerfully. Both of them were now much happier. Ashmore was clearly an impossible base, and they had sensibly decided, bombs or no bombs, to move back to London. In the spring of 1941 they took a furnished flat in Kensington. For the winter of 1941–42 they borrowed a cousin's house in Loughton. In the spring of 1942 they moved back into central London, taking a flat in Ennismore Gardens, a few yards from our old home in Brompton Square. They still had three maids, all so elderly as to be virtually unemployable elsewhere. Back in

London, like the giant Antaeus in contact again with his native element, my mother regained her old elegance and sparkle: shopping in all her old haunts; visiting picture galleries and adding to her small, excellent collection of contemporary British painters; frequenting Heywood Hill's fashionable little bookshop in Curzon Street, then as now the centre of social and literary gossip. In addition she worked in the Red Cross, attending the needs of prisoners of war. Air raids she took in her stride, refusing to go to the shelter at night and next morning, immaculate in twinset and pearls and gaily sporting a Coldstream brooch on her lapel or hat, she crunched in her high-heeled shoes through the broken glass of Knightsbridge and Piccadilly to the Redfern Gallery or Harrods. Admirable or absurd? No question about it: this was her finest hour.

In vacations I shared my parents' life and enjoyed it. Occasionally in the evenings I went out with my father through the black-out to theatre or supper-parties and came to realize that, upright and honourable as he was, Papa had a connoisseur's eye for pretty girls – or rather, handsome women. Perhaps this was an element in my mother's decision to move back to London to keep him company. Sumptuary restrictions imposed by wartime controls meant that hitherto unattainable places like the Ritz, the Savoy and Claridges became more widely accessible. A basic three-course meal anywhere cost no more than five shillings, and though supplementary charges could be levied for music and ambience and the price of wine went through the roof, it was difficult to pay more than £3 for a meal anywhere. Theatre flourished, especially in the form of intimate, witty revues. Oxford friends took me to nightclubs such as The Four Hundred and even lower dives. Further, thanks to the good offices of my Uncle George, I was elected while still an undergraduate to the Reform Club, where the company was distinguished and it was possible to get an adequate and affordable lunch.

The Reform was not then a cheerful place. The glass roof of the central atrium had been painted dark blue as a black-out precaution, so one moved around in subaqueous gloom. The other members seemed very old, which they were not, and very depressed, as they had reason to be: most were Treasury officials grappling with the impossible problems of paying for the war and the subsequent peace. I used my membership, and my editorship of *Cherwell*, to scrape acquaintance with as many of the literary great as I could lay hands on. A remarkable number of them accepted invitations to lunch, even if they did not come up with their promised contributions afterwards: E.M. Forster, like a diffident mole; Raymond Mortimer with his Bloomsbury drawl; Stephen Spender, with his mad, innocent blue eyes and his fireman's uniform; Cyril Connolly, like a compact Silenus, pug-nosed and gossiping (what about Bobby Longden, he asked me to my astonishment;

did he *behave* at Wellington? At Oxford he was *outrageous*!); Cyril Joad, happy with an audience even of one; and above all Harold Nicolson, gentle, rubicund, interested to meet another literate Old Wellingtonian and full of fascinating reminiscences about past and present. Looking back on it, as a literary social climber I really did astonishingly well.

There was, however, another and very different aspect to my London life. I continued to feel guilty about my flight from the Blitz in autumn 1940, and some Quaker altruistic urge told me that I should be doing more in London than just enjoying myself. So in the winter of 1941–42 I enlisted as a helper at the Wellington College Mission in Walworth, south of the river. The Mission was run by a delightful couple, Ralph and Doris Phillips, with whom I lodged in their tiny house in East Street, famous for one of the liveliest markets in London. The Mission dated from the days when Walworth lay deep in the Victorian slums. It did so no more: the area, though poor, was a bustle of small shops and businesses, as noisy and active as a Mediterranean port and to me no less foreign. The clients of the Mission were lively and literate young people of about my own age. My 'helping' consisted largely in supervising amateur theatricals, but it totally absorbed my energies and triumphed over all hazards of black-out and Blitz. Not that the Blitz was very intrusive: the Luftwaffe was fully occupied on the Eastern Front and raids were infrequent enough to be exciting, though familiar enough to be no longer alarming. Large areas around the Elephant and Castle were in ruins; buses and trains were crowded and taxis almost unobtainable. Otherwise, London life went on almost undisturbed.

I find it difficult indeed to remember much in detail about this back-ground, more drab than frightening, of London in the middle of the war. What mattered was what I was *doing*; working in the Reform Club library and lunching eminences there during the day, rehearsing in Walworth during the evenings, returning to Oxford at weekends in slow cold trains full to bursting with troops on leave, to sing in the Christ Church choir. It was all simply filling in time until the historic date of 14 August 1942, when at last I joined the army.

* * *

Military service did not change my life as much as I had expected. Service with the OTC at school and Oxford had familiarized me with much of it, and had culminated with a summer camp on the Berkshire downs in June 1942, when we spent ten days going through the rigours of battle-school training. More important, many of my Oxford friends and I joined up together, a kind of 'pals' battalion', and we all arrived together, after a last defiant lunch at the Ritz, at Mons Barracks, Aldershot – the wartime equivalent (for infantrymen) of the old Sandhurst, which had been taken over for armoured training.

As barracks go, Mons was not bad. Built quite recently, the barrack-blocks consisted of wooden 'spiders', complexes housing both ablutions and barrack-rooms. The beds were hard, with 'biscuit' mattresses and army blankets, but we could bring our own sheets and send them home to be laundered. Food was plentiful and served in a civilized dining-hall. An effort was made to preserve Sandhurst traditions. A special and quite unnecessary flight of steps had been built from the parade-ground to enable the adjutant to ride his horse up them, the customary conclusion of the Sandhust passing-out parade. The huts that served as classrooms were grandilo-quently called 'Halls of Study'. There was a 'band-night' once a week. The NCOs addressed us collectively as 'gentlemen', individually as 'Mr Howard, sir' (though usually followed by 'You're a dozy idle little man, sir'). We were of course 'chased' – roused early in the morning, harassed, shouted at, punished for petty offences. I forgot to lock the door of my cupboard in my first week, and as a consequence 'lost my name', was up before the company commander and confined to barracks scrubbing floors for a weekend. Of course we were drilled to within an inch of our lives. In charge of drill was the legendary RSM Britten, a huge and terrifying figure before whom generations of guardsmen had trembled. Under his aegis, drill parades could often be nightmarish, but eventually we acquired the pride that comes from doing something spectacular very well indeed. We learned, in fact, in a very traditional way, how to be soldiers.

In addition to drill, PT, weapons-training, minor tactics, military administration and motor-transport maintenance, we carried out a number of exercises, usually known as 'stunts', that involved night operations and long wet days of marching or scrambling about Hampshire or Berkshire, and ultimately a freezing wet week in the Welsh mountains, jogging unhappily under the weight of Bren guns and 2″ mortars; again, extensions of school field-days. These exercises were not unrealistic, but they fell far short of qualifying us to fight the *Wehrmacht*. We learned to be soldiers of a kind, but not yet fighters, let alone killers. I think many of us never did. When in December 1942 I put up my ensign's star on my beautiful dark barathea service-dress and fitted on the long-coveted black hat with its braided brim and Coldstream star, I was not remotely ready to command men in action against so formidable an enemy. The panache of the Brigade still camouflaged all too effectively the harsh reality of war.

After a few days of leave spent swaggering round the West End, no longer feeling a pariah in a city now crowded with uniforms – French, Polish, Czech, Dutch, Norwegian, American, Belgian as well as British – I was sent to the Guards Training Battalion at Pirbright, where our ensigns' stars (lieutenants' pips in line regiments} did not save us from further merciless chasing on the barrack square. In the Brigade, officers drilled with other ranks until they reached the rank of captain, which would take me another two years. But we *were* now officers, with rooms of our own, soldier-servants (never 'batmen' in the Brigade) to clean our kit, and members of a comfortable mess, the excellence of whose food roused dark suspicions that the mess sergeant was heavily involved with the black market. We were introduced to the taboos of the tribe, whose power not even a world war and threat of invasion could weaken. Some I have described. It was always 'the Brigade', never 'the Guards'. (This has now changed, to my abiding horror.) It was always 'the Coldstream', never, but *never*, 'the Coldstreams'. One never spoke of 'a sherry' – always 'a glass of sherry'. One never went 'up to town' – always 'up to London'. A friend who had joined his battalion in the immediate aftermath of Dunkirk, when invasion seriously loomed, told us that he was solemnly advised by his adjutant never to wear pink out hunting when the court was in mourning, but I am not sure I believed him. Those who broke these taboos did not belong to the tribe, and the British army consisted of umpteen such tribes. Military specialists will argue for ever whether the undoubted success of such tribes in bonding fighting-men together outweighs their equally undoubted divisiveness – the *Wehrmacht* got on very well without them – but they certainly made soldiering more fun.

Our seniors treated us with distant friendliness. First names were *de rigueur* except for the Commanding Officer who was 'sir' to his face, 'Colonel Billy' behind his back; but informality in the mess was accompanied by rigorous formality on parade and in the company office. For all administration we were dependent on senior NCOs, 'warrant officers'; not the alert, athletic men who had trained us at Mons but Kiplingesque old sweats with medals from Indian and Great War campaigns, steeped in arcane military law and expert in the byzantine procedures that the army had perfected over many years for producing the minimum of output for the maximum of trouble. Few regular officers in the Brigade bothered to understand them. Their function was to fight, and when not fighting to hunt, shoot, gamble, drink and generally engage in traditional warrior pastimes as their forebears had done for generations. Few expected to remain in the army much beyond the age of 40: command of a battalion, at the very most of a brigade, was the summit of their military ambitions. Most had been to Eton, and many were interrelated over many generations. Cowardice or misbehaviour – 'putting up a black' – would thus taint them for life, so it simply did not happen. But anyone who took the army

seriously as a profession, unless he possessed sterling compensatory qualities, was written off as a 'military shit': the kind of little twerp who went on
to the Staff College. General Montgomery's military virtues were reluctantly
recognized, but he would not have been welcome in the mess. Our hero was
the gentle and patrician General Alexander.

The next phase was the Holding Battalion at Regent's Park Barracks in
London, which carried out 'public duties', in particular finding the guard at
Buckingham and St James's Palaces. Our uniform of steel helmets and
battledress could not rival peacetime scarlet and bearskins, but we performed the traditional ceremony meticulously in the forecourt of what I had
learned to call 'Buck House', the regimental band accompanying us with all
their usual bravura and attracting gratifying crowds. The mess at St James's
Palace was stylishly Edwardian, and as in the days of good King Edward we
could invite private guests to meals. The first time I was on guard our
captain decided to have an Allied dinner. He produced two American
officers and ordered me to find some Russians. I did rather well. I rang the
military attaché at the Soviet Embassy, explained with great difficulty what
we wanted and, astonishingly, two officers actually turned up; a gnarled
bemedalled general straight out of Chekhov, speaking little English and
drinking prodigiously, and a smooth major whose English was impeccable
and who ruthlessly teased the Americans about their racial prejudice. Neither the Americans nor we, alas, knew enough about the Soviet Union to be
able to retaliate in kind, but they took it in good part, and an air-raid alarm
cemented Allied solidarity.

Nevertheless, I quickly grew bored in London. When we were not on
guard there was nothing to occupy us but more drill and military administration, mainly signing innumerable forms and paybooks. That took care
of the morning. Then one was free to disappear. For those with plenty of
money and many friends in London it was an ideal life, but I had neither. I
was delighted, therefore, when after a few weeks I was posted to the unit
stationed at the prime minister's country home, Chequers, to protect the
Great Man against a possible German *coup de main*. For most of the time
the Great Man was not there. First he was abroad attending the Casablanca
Conference, and then he was in London recovering from pneumonia. In his
absence we had the run of the place. I made friends with the housekeeper
and explored the house, spending afternoons playing the piano in the great
hall. I penetrated into the Great Man's bedroom which smelt deliciously of
lavender toilet-water and Havana cigars; the smell, I thought, of the *belle
epoque*. For the rest we trained spasmodically in the Chiltern woods, and in
the evening I read: Dover Wilson's *What Happens in* Hamlet, Edmund
Wilson's *Axel's Castle* and, doggedly, Proust. My company commander,

who sought refuge from boredom in gin, and was the only man I met during the war whom I thoroughly disliked, thought me an affected ass and told me so.

The Great Man appeared only once, for a weekend. When he did, we were invited with the rest of the household to his film-show in the Long Gallery after dinner. We assembled at nine. Half an hour later, Churchill strode in, cigar in mouth, wearing his siren-suit. Behind him trailed an exhausted-looking train of ministers and generals. He had had three hours' sleep that afternoon and they had not. 'Good evening, gentlemen!' he beamed happily, and settled in a deep armchair in the front row to watch a couple of gangster films. From the encouraging noises that came from the depths of the chair it was clear that he was enjoying it hugely. 'Go on ... hit him!' he would growl. 'Look out! He's behind the door! Oh you fool!' After it was over, well after midnight, he strode out again – 'Goodnight, gentlemen!' – followed by his somnolent companions, to get on with the serious business of winning the war.

After a month or so of this halcyon existence, I was posted to our sixth battalion which was stationed in the gloomy premises of Royal Wanstead School, on the north-eastern edge of London. Here the regiment ran its own battle school, and here we were seriously prepared for war. Every day we doubled out, six miles or more, into the Essex countryside, laden with weapons and equipment, where instructors chased us, shouting abuse, through bushes and through briars, over hill and down dale. We spent freezing nights in barns and haylofts and learned what it was to be dirty, hungry and sleepless. Veterans from the Western Desert, where our third battalion had fought since the beginning of the war, lectured to us about the realities of that war. For the first time I felt that I was in the hands of people who really knew what they were talking about – and indeed that the whole country was in the hands of people who knew what they were talking about. We were winning. In North Africa the Germans were being beaten back into the Tunisian bridgehead. In Russia they were in full retreat. As for me, I suddenly realized one morning, after I had just run about five miles in full kit, carrying a mortar weighing some 40 pounds, and felt none the worse for it, that I was physically at my peak. After this, I told myself ruefully, there was nowhere to go but down.

It was at this moment, appropriately, that I was warned for overseas service. So were Humphrey and a dozen or so of the Oxford pals' battalion. We all had ten days' leave. I dodged saying goodbye to my parents, dreading the scene that my mother would quite certainly make; leaving only a curt note, the memory of which still shames me. 'Soldiering today', I wrote with ineffable pomposity, 'is even for the intellectual immensely interesting, giving scope for every kind of talent and providing a satisfaction at once intellectual and physical. I am going to a job that I want to do at a time and an age when it is a real joy to do it.' I expanded on my feelings in a letter to Arthur Koestler, who had just written a perceptive article in *Horizon* about the war-hero Richard Hillary and what he called 'the submerged generation' that was fighting the war – i.e., mine. Koestler liked it, persuaded Cyril Connolly to print it – my first appearance on the London literary scene – and asked me to dinner at his tiny house in Chelsea. Also present were E.M. Forster and Eric Linklater. Forster was intensely shy. After asking me whether I knew anything about sardines, he relapsed into silence, and I wondered whether he had given me a password to which I had failed to respond. Linklater, a literary hero from an earlier stage in my life, was gregarious and jolly. 'I've had two cocktails today', he said happily: 'Tunis and Bizerta' (the capture of which had been announced in the evening papers). He asked me to lunch next day at the Savile Club, where I sat next to Ralph Richardson. Both treated me with the deference due to my uniform. This is the life, I thought.

It was a good moment to be going. Ever since leaving Wellington I had been prey to a melancholy expressed in the slow movements of Brahms' symphonies that ran continually through my head and surged intolerably whenever the news came of another friend's death; and during the past year my school-friends had been killed one by one, usually in the air. All this was now blown away. The true poet of my generation was my Oxford contemporary Sidney Keyes, a dry, difficult young man who had himself been killed in Tunisia a few weeks earlier. He got it right:

> The fifes cry death and the sharp winds call;
> Set your face to the rock; go on, go out
> Into the bad lands of battle, the cloud-wall
> Of the future, my comrades, and leave your fear.*

Nothing about laying down our lives for our country. Nothing about destroying the evil of fascism. We were simply doing a job that had to be done.

---

* Sidney Keyes, 'Advice for a Journey', *The Collected Poems of Sidney Keyes*, ed. Michael Meyer (London: Routledge & Kegan Paul, 1945).

3

Italy I: Salerno

My draft left London one evening early in May after tea at Regent's Park Barracks. The ghosts of all the drafts that had assembled there before sailing for India or France were present in force to wish us well. Three-ton trucks took us and our kit (one tin trunk and one valise apiece) to Addison Road station, and we travelled, dozing uncomfortably, through the night to Liverpool, where we embarked on a Dutch cruise-liner, the *Johann van Oldenbarneveldt* – a ship that after the war was to gain a melancholy celebrity when, renamed the *Lakonia*, she caught fire and sank in mid-Atlantic. (I was a Jonah so far as cruise-liners were concerned. The only one on which I had previously sailed had been the *Lancastria* on a visit to Madeira in 1935. It had been bombed by German aircraft while evacuating British troops from St Nazaire in June 1940 and sunk with the loss of over 3,000 lives.)

On board we were absurdly comfortable. For officers the peacetime routine of the cruise-liner continued unchanged. Little Javanese stewards summoned us by gongs to delicately served meals in elegant dining saloons, after which we played cards or read in the equally elegant lounges. The only difference from a peacetime voyage was that the ship was dry, and our personal supplies of whisky quickly ran out. I shared a cabin with three courteous Old Etonians who did their best not to make me feel an outsider. The troops were less comfortably housed, crowded between decks, lining up with their mess-tins for army rations and kept going by the gallons of hot sweet tea that sustained the army through two world wars. The Brigade contingent was responsible for guarding the ship's armoury, so I spent hours in a hold smelling sweetly of rifle-oil supervising the cleaning and issue of weapons. It was an agreeable limbo. The ships of the convoy held station so exactly that we did not seem to move at all. We steamed far out into the Atlantic and back again. The air grew warmer, the stars brighter. Then one night we found ourselves passing through the straits of Gibraltar, the lights of Tangier cheerfully blazing out of the darkness on our right, and next morning we docked at Algiers.

Landing at Algiers was like stepping on to a brightly lit stage to take part in a performance that I had spent years watching from the stalls. The

monochrome of the news-films was brought to colourful life on the docks
bustling with shouting NCOs, clipboard-bearing staff-officers, swarming
native porters, beggars and small boys offering shoe-shines. The sun blazed;
we paraded in marching order and set out on a hot, thirsty, dusty route-
march to our billets 12 miles away in empty seaside villas at Cap Matifou.
That evening we washed away dust and sweat in the placid Mediterranean.
The moon shone gently on the water. The air was scented with thyme and
the night loud with cicadas. Four years ago, I thought, but in another
universe, I swam in the same waters a few hundred miles to the north, where
they washed the southern shores of France.

Next day we moved to a camp where the pals' battalion met up again.
The southern horizon was bounded by mountains; a few miles to the north
lay the sea. In the evening we listened to the melancholy cadences of
'Stardust' played by Humphrey Lyttleton, then a subaltern in the Grenadiers, on the trumpet he had brought with him to the wars. Flies swarmed.
We improved the tedious army diet with the fruit all too plentifully sold by
Arab boys at the roadside. The result was the mild but nasty form of
dysentery known to generations of British soldiers as 'gyppy tummy'.
Modesty forgotten, we shared our discomfort on communal open-air
latrines, the smell of ordure mingling unforgettably but not unpleasantly
with the scent of aromatic Mediterranean shrubs. Humphrey Leeke and I
shared a tent and hitch-hiked into Algiers, wearing the absurd tropical pith-
helmets that had been issued to us on embarkation. No one else seemed to
be wearing them, and a few days later they were withdrawn. Somebody must
have at last told the War Office that they were rather *vieux jeu*.

After a couple of weeks we moved by slow freight-train to a similar camp
near Philippeville, agreeably sited a few hundred yards from a golden beach
where we spent the last summer of our youth bathing happily in the
tumbling waves. The camp, initially vestigial, gradually took shape as the 1st
(Guards) Infantry Reinforcement Training Depot (IRTD), an establishment
in which, either in North Africa or Italy, I was fated to spend the greater
part of the ensuing year. The primitive conditions presented a challenge
to which we all rose. Our khaki-drill uniforms (shorts during the day,
mosquito-proof long trousers in the evening) were bleached, starched and
pressed, our webbing-equipment scrubbed white, the brass blinded us with
its shine. The tents were perfectly aligned, each occupant's equipment tidied
into meticulous rectangles. We were drilled on the dusty sand as if on the
square at Pirbright. Fifes and drums arrived to stir us with our regimental
marches. I grew a rather unconvincing moustache that I kept, against the
advice of all my friends, for another 20 years. We kept fit with PT in the
early morning and long route-marches once a week. We carried out

increasingly realistic training exercises. Above all, we got to know our guardsmen: huge, gentle young men from Yorkshire or Durham, mainly from mining families, whose disciplined wariness thawed into friendliness under the influence of shared experience and common pride. It was hard to maintain a hierarchical distance when we were carrying out the most basic of a platoon-commander's duties – inspecting his men's feet. In the evenings we brightened the drabness of our khaki-drill with silk scarves and sat on the terrace of the mess drinking marsala or thick Algerian wine that gave us inconceivable hangovers, watching the mountains turned crimson by the setting sun. We were kept abreast of the news by BBC Forces Radio and old copies of *Life*, *Time* and *Picture Post*. In one of these I was astounded to come across a news item that my grandparents' house, Ardmore, had been turned into a home for unmarried mothers – an indication of the brave new world that was being prepared for us when we came home.

Meanwhile, what next? There were two Coldstream battalions in Africa. The Second had landed in Algeria the previous autumn and fought in Tunisia throughout the winter, gaining renown on Longstop Hill. The Third had been in the Middle East since the beginning of the war, campaigned in the Western Desert and carried out a spectacular escape from Tobruk when it had fallen to the Germans the previous summer. It fought with Montgomery's Eighth Army in the closing stages of the Tunisian campaign and was now stationed in Tripoli. To my delight this was the unit, suffused with the glamour of the desert war, that I was destined to join, but as luck would have it, when my draft was called forward, I had been posted away to a battle-course at Constantine, a romantic town set in a mountain gorge full of Roman ruins. There I met Americans for the first time, with their excellent coffee and fruitjuice, abundant equipment, energy, kindness and wit. There I learned from veterans of the Tunisian campaign what a difficult and frightening job fighting the Germans was going to be. I experienced the stifling, sand-laden heat of the sirocco. But when I returned to Philippeville I found that all my friends had gone. Strange faces filled the mess, whose owners treated me with respect as a veteran. I felt forlorn and out of it. The Allied forces had landed in Sicily. The next step, we were all certain, would be Italy. My friends would all be there, but what about me?

I need not have worried. Within a couple of weeks I was called forward as well. Another slow train journey took us to Bizerta in some comfort – eight officers sharing a wagon intended for *quarante hommes, huit chevaux*, lying comfortably on our camp beds as Africa jolted slowly past – so slowly that small boys could run alongside begging for cigarettes. There we were decanted into a transit camp where we stayed for several days. I read *Coningsby* while the air thickened with rumours of the Italian surrender. Again other drafts were called forward and disappeared, leaving us apprehensive and impatient. Then at last our number came up. We were ferried to the docks in enormous American trucks and engulfed in the open maw of a huge American tank-landing ship. We were off.

The ship was comfortable enough. We slept on deck under the stars and shared the Americans' excellent rations. We all knew now where we were going. 'Some of the heaviest fighting of the war', the BBC informed us over the ship's radio, 'is now going on at Salerno.' We had no idea where Salerno was, but we found it on a small-scale map in the ward-room. Its main feature seemed to be that it was surrounded by mountains. We looked at the rest of Italy with apprehensive eyes: there seemed to be mountains all the way up that very long peninsula. The following afternoon the Italian coast appeared to starboard, so close that we could see the temple of Paestum. From the north came the rumble of gunfire. Suddenly the ship's own AA guns opened fire as a solitary unidentifiable aircraft twisted and turned in the sky above us. Darkness fell, and we waited in the huge dim cavern of the tank-deck to land. At length there was a bump, a ramp rattled down, and I stepped out on to the soil of a Europe I had left almost exactly four years before. I was tempted, like a later pope, to kneel down and kiss the ground.

*   *   *

Our debarkation was undisturbed, and guides led us inland to a field where venomous mosquitoes and the continuous thump of guns made sleep impossible. When we woke we found ourselves in a region of orchard and meadow among trees laden with ripe apples and plums – a welcome change after the aridity of Africa. But the landscape was indeed dominated by a semicircle of mountains, from which the Germans could watch every move that we made. Overhead, schools of silver bombers boomed comfortingly towards the enemy. All around us guns thumped and cracked spasmodically, while at intervals naval shells roared overhead with a noise like an express train and landed somewhere inland with a crash that shook the entire landscape. We were busy plundering the orchards when transport arrived to take us to our Battalion headquarters, which proved to be a cluster of camouflaged vehicles under a hedge, where the Commanding Officer, Terence Falkiner, was roused from sleep to greet us. Rumpled, dirty and tired, he was clearly in no mood for courtesies, and brusquely sent us to our respective companies. Mine was 300 yards further on, its headquarters a three-ton truck, a jeep, a huddle of stores and slit-trenches in the shadow of a bank. Half a dozen men were sleeping. The company commander, Alan Davidson, was also roused to greet me, and I realized that all these people were very tired indeed and had hardly slept since they had landed six days earlier.

Alan, a cold, competent unsmiling young man, rapidly 'put me in the picture'. The battalion was, with 2nd Scots Guards and 6th Grenadiers, part of 201 Guards Brigade, which itself was part of 56th Division. A brigade of the Queen's Regiment was on our right and one of the Royal Fusiliers on our left. Beyond the Fusiliers to the north lay 46th Division, which had taken the town of Salerno. Beyond the Queen's to the south were the Americans. A long way beyond them was Montgomery's Eighth Army, which had landed in Calabria in the toe of Italy and was allegedly advancing to join us, but seemed to be taking their time about it. We were ourselves part of the US Fifth Army under an unknown and inexperienced general, Mark Clark. In overall command was General Alexander, a guardsman whom we knew and trusted. In truth, the higher structure of command hardly mattered at our level, for 201 Guards Brigade was very much a self-contained entity that passed from division to division, corps to corps, without our really noticing. We did not even condescend to wear the divisional flash, a black cat, on our shoulders; only a scarlet roman III indicated our battalion number.

Our front line still lay well short of the road and railway running south from Salerno that had been our original objective. The Scots Guards had penetrated as far as the small town of Battipaglia on that road, but had been pushed out after a stiff fight for an establishment inaccurately known as a 'tobacco factory' that lay on its outskirts. The Germans had launched a heavy attack on our own position a couple of days earlier and had been driven back, chiefly by a ferocious artillery bombardment. There was now a lull, so Alan took me on a tour of our sector, a track along a canal. A field of eight-foot-high tobacco plants beyond screened all visibilty. A few Bren guns and anti-tank gun-pits were the only signs of defensive positions. Officers lounged about drinking tea and gossiping, in various states of undress. Only the thumping guns, the sigh of shells overhead and the ceaseless activity of aircraft (all our own) betrayed that this was a battlefield.

That evening the illusion of calm was broken. As darkness fell, we were settling down to supper – tinned stew, tinned rice, tinned stewed fruit – when the background noise of guns was supplemented by the casual, efficient rattle of German light machine guns (MG 42s, usually known as Spandaus) away to the right. There was a confused rumbling, rifle-fire rising to a fusillade and dying away; odd flashes and verey flares lighting up the twilight. A German attack was coming in, perhaps against our own right-wing company to which we were in reserve. Alan went off to see what was happening, leaving me and, thank God, the company sergeant-major in charge. I stayed by the telephone, relaying information forward to Alan from Battalion HQ and eventually orders to send up his reserve platoon to help. A guardsman came back escorting a sad-looking German prisoner. The moon rose; gradually the noise died down, and Alan returned. There had indeed been an attack, mainly against the Queen's on our right, but a German half-track troop-carrier had broken into our positions. It had been destroyed, but its crew had to be mopped up. We could at last go to sleep, so far as the ceaseless gunfire allowed, under our inadequate mosquito-nets in our dirty slit-trenches. I had survived my first night of war.

At dawn we 'stood to' and as the light strengthened, giving colour to the dim figures around me, I again realized how tired and strained everyone was: no one had slept properly for four days. The day passed quietly and a bathe in the river restored me to working order; just as well, since that evening I was given my first serious job. Alan ordered me, at 30 minutes' notice, to take out a patrol, ten men strong, to cross the railway-line, lie up on the main road beyond, and send back regular reports on enemy traffic passing along it. I had no time to think: a sergeant and ten shadowy figures, two of them with bicycles to take back my reports, were already mustered, none of whom I had ever seen before. It seemed to me far too many for a reconnaissance patrol – I had already learned on training that the one skill guardsmen could not master was moving quietly by night – but Alan assured me that we were unlikely to run into any opposition, and I had an experienced sergeant to hold my hand. I introduced myself hurriedly to my new command, gave out orders and warned them that this was my first patrol. 'Don't let me make a fool of myself, and we'll do fine', I said bravely. We set out along the lane, white under the rising moon, that led towards the German positions.

It was a fine night and the moon shone placidly on the flat fields that stretched away on either side. The lane grew muddier as we advanced, churned up by vehicles of both sides, and it became difficult to pick a path that would not send us splashing through the great puddles that lay in our way. I clutched a grenade, one finger in the ring, and made sure that my revolver was loose in the holster. (I had not yet learned to get rid of this useless encumbrance and acquire a more serviceable tommy-gun.) Behind me came Sergeant Price, who *had* got a tommy-gun. The rear of the party was brought up by the two unfortunates pushing bicycles who were to take back my reports through the night.

After a mile or so we came upon three or four abandoned German troop-carriers, and a little further on a dead German by the side of the road. My first corpse, I thought without emotion as we went by, and was glad that my duties permitted me to ignore it. The country became closer as fields gave way to vineyards and woods, where every tree seemed to pose a separate threat. Slow-burning flares, giving a vivid light for about ten minutes, pinned us to the ground more than once. Then a large house appeared on the left about a hundred yards ahead. I realized that we had reached the railway we had to cross. Then the railway-crossing itself came in sight. On it stood three large Germans.

Only three, I thought. We are ten. This is the moment to cover myself with glory. But while I was debating the wisdom of doing anything of the kind, about 25 more Germans appeared from nowhere and formed up in a dark mass on the road. After a little they moved quietly away, but it was clear that progress along this route was barred. I tried working round the right flank. Leaving the bulk of the patrol behind, I took Sergeant Price and a guardsman along the railway embankment until we found a convenient crossing-place, and crawled across the metals of the line. Then our guardian angels deserted us. The other side of the embankment was covered with bushy scrub, a great mass of which looked like thick ivy. To go through this would be to advertise ourselves to the whole German army. I was about to look for a gap when Sergeant Price gripped my arm. From the direction of Battipaglia, at a distance of about a hundred yards, we heard the tramping footsteps of an approaching German patrol.

We were nicely caught now. To descend the embankment would make an enormous noise and put the enemy between us and home. To move in any other direction would be to show ourselves to the advancing patrol, which sounded about eight strong. Like hares we stayed frozen where we were. Anyhow, the situation was too much like a bad melodrama to be taken seriously: I had watched it on the movies dozens of times. It couldn't possibly be happening to *me*.

But it was. About ten yards away the tramping stopped and a German voice spoke urgently and quietly. We heard the patrol get down in the bushes on our side of the track. My cue, I thought. 'Come on', I whispered. We dashed back across the line, down the embankment and across a field into the welcoming shadow of the trees. The Germans opened fire. Bullets were kicking up dust all around us, but I still thought of myself as playing lead role in rather a bad film. Anyhow, I reckoned that we had had enough excitement for one night, so I collected the rest of the patrol and went home. I was apprehensive about my reception, but everyone was very kind and appreciative. I suspect that the whole point of the exercise may have been to give me a baptism of fire, which I had survived intact.

Next morning I was sent up to the artillery observation-post in a nearby farmhouse to direct the guns on to the railway-crossing where I had watched the German post. The farmhouse was littered with swollen animal carcasses, the stench of which cast a miasma over the whole building. Indoors we found pathetic evidence of recent occupation: dirty bottles and glasses on the dresser; religious postcards and crucifixes pinned on the walls; bedrooms in disarray from the looting of three nations. In the attic a starved cat had made a nest in one corner and her kitten darted elusively round the room. At a window overlooking the landscape sat a gunner officer, while a corporal at his feet crouched over a telephone. I tried to locate the scene of my adventures the previous night, but it was hidden in the trees, and all we could do was to spray the countryside with desultory shell-fire.

There was still no platoon for me to command, so my time was my own. I learned that Humphrey Leeke, last seen at Philippeville, was only a few hundred yards away on our left, commanding a Grenadier platoon. I borrowed a bicycle and cycled through the tobacco-plants in warm afternoon sun until I found him. He was well, but like everyone else, dirty, strained and desperately tired. We sat and gossiped and drank hot sweet tea out of our rectangular mess-tins, and he told me about the hell he had been through since he had landed with the first wave a few days before. Then we parted and I wondered whether I would ever see him again. In fact I did, frequently. He was not to be killed until the following summer.

When I returned to company HQ, I learned that they now had a platoon for me, so I rolled up my sleeves to take on the responsibility for which I had been training for over a year. I had a pleasant young sergeant, Hurst, who took me round the section posts where guardsmen sprawled in and around their slit-trenches, cleaning weapons, cooking meals, writing letters home. I conscientiously learned their names, ages, peacetime occupations and military records, and generally chatted them up. There were few if any old sweats from the desert. Several had been in the Tunisian fighting during the spring, but for many Salerno was, as for me, their first engagement. They were friendly and efficient, and I only wished that we could have trained together before action. The mood was now, in general, cheerful. We learned that there had been some kind of 'flap' on the American front away to our right (in fact, as we learned later, the egregious General Mark Clark had at one point ordered a re-embarkation), but we were well settled in, and had no intention of being bundled back to Africa again. That afternoon, Alexander, the Army Group Commander whom we in the Brigade regarded as our own property, had visited the beach-head. As good leaders do, he had spread waves of calm and confidence wherever he went. There were rumours of a link-up with Montgomery's Eighth Army. In short, we were ready to go.

It is worth recording at this stage what we were wearing. Regulation dress was steel helmets, angora wool or khaki-drill shirts, khaki-drill trousers tucked into webbing anklets, thick grey woollen socks and tough, comfortable army boots. In our small back-packs we carried wool pullovers, spare socks, mess-tins and eating equipment, a waterproof gas-cape and anything else we could squeeze in. I usually had writing materials and a poetry anthology. For officers, a little elegant variation had survived from the great days in the desert, whether they themselves had been there or not: suede desert-boots, silk scarves and fly-switches, which they sported deep into the Italian winter and were lovingly caricatured in the army newspaper by Jon in his famous cartoon series as 'The Two Types'. Many of us possessed comfortable custom-built linings to our steel helmets. Out of action we wore khaki berets sporting the regimental star. Some, including me, wore corduroy trousers – warmer than khaki-drill but less washable. We were equipped with .38 revolvers, but few of us trusted or used them. We begged, borrowed or stole American tommy-guns or, better, the German Schmeiszer machine-pistol.

Food was plentiful and good. It came in 'Compo' boxes for eight men containing tins of bacon, sausages, steak and kidney pudding, 'M&V' (meat and veg – a kind of stew), tinned fruit, assorted puddings, butter, cheese, jam, biscuits, chocolate, boiled sweets, a vile kind of cigarette called 'V' which put me off smoking for life, and, not least important, lavatory paper. Tea came in sacks ready-mixed with sugar and milk-powder; a brew-up was in progress at most hours of the day. These rations could be supplemented by purchases from the NAAFI – more respectable cigarettes, soap, matches, chewing-gum, writing-paper. Occasionally we got hold of American K rations, with their excellent coffee, candy and – rarest of delicacies – spam. The countryside provided unlimited supplies of apples, nuts, plums and grapes. Mail came regularly, and my parents were able to keep me amply supplied with books and periodicals. All in all we were very well looked after, and best of all, I had brought with me from the IRTD a gentle paternal soldier-servant, Johanson, who devoted himself to making me as comfortable as circumstances allowed.

We stayed where we were for another couple of days and reinforced our supplies from the half-track troop-carriers that the Germans had abandoned in front of our lines when their attack was repulsed on the night of the 13th. These were so full of kit that we wondered how anyone had ever got into them. There was clothing of every kind: green uniforms, socks, stockings, shirts, boots, underclothes, towels, peaked caps, helmets, equipment – all of good quality except the equipment which was of shoddy imitation leather that tore as easily as cardboard and emanated a peculiar smell that gave away the presence of its wearer for yards around. There were medical supplies – field-dressings, first-aid kits, ampoules that may have been morphia or benzedrine. There were grenades, rifles, mortar-shells, mines, verey-pistols and signal cartridges, Schmeiszer machine-pistols (one of which I appropriated), a powerful pair of periscope binoculars, scarlet aircraft identification-signals that opened like large fans, and exquisitely thin waterproof groundsheets. There were letters, postcards, orders, military manuals. And there was food: pumpernickel, biscuits, hard black bread, butter in orange bakelite dishes, tins of stew, long sausages, cartons of sweets. Clearly the Germans did themselves pretty well too.

The people we felt sorry for were the civilians. In all our training no one had ever suggested that there might be non-combatants around on the battlefield, and of course in the desert there were not, apart from the odd Bedouin. But here there were: families shelled or bombed out of their houses; farmers hanging on and trying to work their fields or milk their cows which were bellowing with pain. Dead cattle lay around the fields, their bloated carcasses polluting the air with the sweet, unforgettable smell of decay. Our sentries rounded up wandering civilians and brought them in the first instance to me. I spoke no Italian except what I had gleaned from opera libretti, and even if I had had a better grasp of the language I could not have understood their thick Neapolitan dialect. How were these sad, bewildered peasants to be treated: as enemies, neutrals or friends? The Italian government had announced its surrender a few hours before the landings, but its juridical status had still to be clarified. Lacking guidance, I could only send them back to some Higher Authority who might accept responsibility for them, but where they would find one in the few hundred yards between us and the beaches, heaven knows. Contact with these luckless people confirmed my conviction that war was a thoroughly Bad Thing.

On 20 September we moved on. Alan took me in his jeep to reconnoitre our new positions. The road was busy with men: signallers laying wires; intelligence officers checking maps; files of guardsmen moving along the verges on either side; while in the blackened fields other troops, huddled and urgent as in a Breughel picture, dug graves for the dead. In one ditch lay the blackened wreck of a Churchill tank, like the carcass of some prehistoric monster. As we approached the town of Salerno, the roadside villas thickened into a knot of warehouses and buildings high and gloomy as those of a city. The railway had been torn up and telegraph wires leaned drunkenly from side to side, trailing their severed cables across the line. The buildings were bleak and empty save for a few scavengers creeping about their doorways. The road zigzagged among piles of rubble where Sappers were cautiously searching for mines. The advancing files of guardsmen met and passed a contrary stream of civilians bearing bundles or wheeling bicycles, returning to see what was left of their homes. We passed the ruins of the famous tobacco factory, where the previous evening we had watched a formation of Kittyhawk fighter-bombers pass over, peel off one by one from their high pattern of specks in the sky and plummet on to their target, wheeling and returning in a wide circle. Their bombs had shaken the air. All that night the blaze of the factory had reddened the sky. The grave-diggers were at work there as well.

We spent that night and the following day in the southern suburbs of Salern. I slept in a barn, the first time I had a roof over my head since leaving England, and the following night we passed through the dead streets of the city to take up positions in steep vineyards immediately to the north. We relieved 46th Division, which was side-slipping leftwards onto the Sorrento peninsula. They had obviously had a very bad time. The unit we relieved was nervous and insubordinate, and the young platoon commander only maintained control with difficulty. 'If you don't do what you are told I'll shoot you!' he hissed in exasperation – and sounded as if he meant it. Next morning we saw why they were so unhappy. We were out of sight of the enemy, but not out of range of their mortars. Their bombs came crashing down with a frequency that made it unwise to stir for long from the very inadequate slit-trenches scraped out on the terraced hillside. Not for the last time I wondered whether we ourselves used our mortars with the skill displayed by the Germans. Our companies further up the hill were even more exposed and suffered heavy losses. There was a grim contrast between the danger of our situation and the spectacular beauty of the Bay of Salerno spread out below us: the deep, deep blue sea and clear blue sky framed by vines laden with bunches of grapes, like a third-rate stage-set.

That night I was again sent out on a reconnaissance patrol, and again performed indifferently. I quickly became aware of how poorly I had been trained to move quietly at night. The two enormous guardsmen I took with me had not been trained at all. We blundered around the steep mountain paths in bright moonlight, alarmingly conspicuous on the paths and horribly noisy off them. Eventually we approached a farm where dogs began to bark and nervous German sentries opened up with machine-gun fire. Although we were still far short of our objective, I saw no way of reaching it and every prospect of getting horribly lost in the attempt, and so turned back with such information as we had. Next morning I reported it to the suave, desert-booted, silk-scarved Brigade Intelligence officer – a Balliol man, as it turned out – who kindly said that I had told him exactly what he needed to know and gave me breakfast in the battle-scarred but still comfortable villa which Brigade HQ occupied at the foot of the hill. Then I returned up the mountain path to learn from Alan what was expected from us next.

It seemed quite a lot. That night 46th Division would attack on our left to open a way across the Sorrento peninsula towards Naples. We would support them with an attack to pin the Germans down on our front. Since this was a feint, only one company would be deployed – ours – but with heavy artillery support. Our objective was a small hill – the 'Pimple' – beyond the large hospital that dominated the town. Securing it would straighten our own lines and give us a view over the valley below. Little opposition, said Alan in an alarmingly deadpan voice, was to be expected.

This all sounded simple enough, though I would be lying if I pretended that I looked forward to it with anything except rather sick apprehension. In practice the whole affair proved so wonderfully illustrative of Clausewitz's 'friction of war' that it is worth describing in some detail.

First we had to find our way to the starting-point, which meant leaving our scattered slit-trenches after dark, still under spasmodic mortar-fire, shaking out into single file, and moving in the correct order over steep mountain paths to line up along the perimeter wall of the hospital. That took far longer than expected. The files lost one another, the platoons somehow got into the wrong order. We eventually arrived at the start-line long after H hour, almost too late to catch up with the artillery barrage. Two out of my three sections had disappeared altogether, and turned up only as the attack began. From the dark hill facing us, streams of tracer bullets were already zipping over the low wall behind which we eventually formed up. Once again I had an absurd sense of *déjà vu*. This was just another B movie, and I was playing the David Niven role as the gallant platoon commander. All right, I thought, if I was cast as David Niven I had better behave like David Niven; so I hissed 'Right – over with me!'

Everything thereafter became so confused that it is hard to make any coherent narrative out of it. We stumbled down the slope, dodging under the fixed lines of enemy fire, and began to climb the opposite hill. The first obstacle was a terrace-wall about six feet high, up which the faithful Johanson pushed me. There were flashes and ear-splitting detonations as the Germans lobbed down grenades. Fire was coming from a dark patch of trees in front, into which we plunged, firing blindly. There were only four or five men still with me and I roared abusively, summoning the others. Once the wood was clear, we pushed on shouting like madmen and shooting at the dim figures we saw scuttling away ahead. By the time we reached the summit, the hill seemed clear. My training clicked in: as the rest of the platoon came up, I disposed them in good positions of all-round defence, our fire-power considerably increased by the capture of half a dozen Spandaus and a good quantity of grenades. About four of my men had been wounded, one of them, alas, my precious Johanson. More had somehow, by accident or intent, 'got lost' – this happens quite often in battle – but turned up in time to share the triumph. Alan came chugging up the hill, under-standably delighted, and spoke kind words. I had done all right.

There was no time to relax. Almost at once the Germans started shelling us with great vigour, and we sheltered gratefully in their trenches. (One of the many military virtues of the Germans we did not share was that when they dug trenches they dug them very fast and very deep.) Shortly after-wards, our own guns opened up an enormous barrage. The hills behind Salerno rumbled and flashed and shells whined swiftly over us like lost souls. Moan, moan, moan, they wept, and up the valley we heard the crump of their explosions. For ten minutes or so they fired unopposed; then three immense crashes on the hospital signalled the German reply. Our own hill rocked under a stunning double punch from heavy guns, and we heard the German shells mingling their whines with ours in the air above us. I was caught in the open by one such burst. As the hill shook, I fell into my slit-trench and tried to burrow deeper into the ground while the shell-fragments above me buzzed in strange circles, like malicious insects. One seemed literally to circle above me as if waiting for its chance to strike. I lay there for an hour or more, watching the pale moon shining through a bare tree above me and listening to the howls and groans and screechings in the air in this monstrous witches' sabbath.

We stood to at dawn, In the first grey hints of light we buried the German dead. These were the first corpses I had handled: shrunken pathetic dolls lying stiff and twisted, with glazed blue eyes. Not one could have been over 20, and some were little more than children. With horrible carelessness we shovelled them into their own trenches and piled on the earth. The scene still remains etched on my mind: the hunched, urgent diggers, the sprawling corpses with their dead eyes in a cold dawn light that drained all colour from the scene, leaving only mournful blacks and greys. When we had finished, we stuck their rifles and helmets above the graves and scuttled quickly back under cover. It was a scene worthy of Goya.

*   *   *

We remained in these positions for a couple of days. Reinforcements arrived, in whose eyes, I realized, I must seem a seasoned veteran. Among them was a new platoon sergeant to replace the admirable Sergeant Hurst, who reverted to his normal command of a section. I asked him about his experience and training. 'I'm afraid I haven't had any infantry training at all, sir', he replied. 'I have been a mess sergeant at Pirbright for the past three years.' 'Then at least you'll see that we're properly fed', I replied with gallant wit, but my heart sank. Meanwhile, we had an excellent view over the road in the valley beneath us, and I witnessed two very significant events. The first was a couple of German aircraft slipping in and dropping a stick of bombs on Salerno harbour before a squadron of Spitfires roared over to chase them away. These were the first enemy aircraft I had seen since I had landed, and they proved to be the last. Our command of the air was complete. Had this not been so, the huge cumbrous columns of the Allied armies would have been barely capable of moving, let alone fighting, up the Italian peninsula. The other was a troop of British tanks probing up the valley road and being laid out almost at once by German gunfire. This was no country for tanks: it was to be an infantryman's war, and until the hills on both sides had been cleared, the road remained barred to further advance.

Sure enough, the following night we were pulled back into Salerno, reorganized, and sent up the Avellino road to take up new positions a few miles further north. It sounds simple enough, but again I was made to realize the difference, as Clausewitz put it, between war in reality and war on paper. Half my platoon lost itself in the vineyards on the way back to Salerno and the other half when we tried to find our new positions on a strange, steep hillside in pitch darkness. There we spent most of the night trying to dig into what was virtually solid rock. Next morning we found ourselves with neither fuel nor water and had to breakfast on cold sausages, biscuits and jam.

Meanwhile, rumours flitted among us like bats. The Grenadiers, we learned, were occupying positions further up the hillside and had attacked the hill beyond – later to become generally known as Point 270 – the previous day. For some reason they had then withdrawn, and the Germans had reoccupied it during the night. Our own battalion was to attack the hill at midday and hold it. Alan gave me a warning order, which I passed on to my men. 'Fucking Grenadiers' was, I am afraid, the universal comment.

This was to be a battalion attack *en régle*: Nos 1 and 3 companies leading; No. 2 (us) in second wave; No. 4 in reserve. If all went well, the Grenadiers would take over the position during the afternoon and we would then sweep round to the left and attack the village beyond Point 270 next day. We were to attack in two hours' time. I gave out my own orders. The platoon would attack with two sections 'up', one in reserve. Small packs would be stacked by ... hrs. Haversack rations would be eaten by ... hrs. Signal arrangements would be ... Meanwhile we could rest. I curled up under an olive tree and tried to catch up on the sleep I had missed during the night.

Our advance into battle was leisurely, almost dreamy. Over the wooded crest of our hill we found the Grenadiers busily improving their positions. Signallers were laying wires or tinkering with their radio sets, stretcher-bearers were checking stores, officers were frowning over maps and conferring earnestly with their sergeants. Infantrymen were burrowing even more deeply into the deep banks beside the path. Then we were through the Grenadiers, striking left on a sunken track that led along the side of the hill. In caves in the banks where they had taken refuge, terrified old Italian peasants peered out at us, or sat in the straw muttering over their beads. No sound came from the Germans on the hill opposite. A few birds sang and the sunlight filtered through the leaves. Eventually the path bent round to the right, skirting the valley just below us. It was terraced with vineyards, and in its centre lay a cluster of houses round a towered church; from hillside to hillside about half a mile wide. We were now in dead ground from the summit of Point 270, and on our right we looked back across the vineyards to the slopes from which we had come. We paused, sat down, smoked, and waited for the forward companies to move on. I remember wishing, with great intensity, that I was not there.

At length there was movement at the head of the column. Almost at once the chattering of Spandaus broke the afternoon peace. For a long time the firing was Spandaus, only Spandaus, rattling and barking in harsh counterpoint, weaving complex patterns of black sound. For an age we waited, listening urgently for the comfortable sound of our Brens to begin. Eventually we heard it – one sedate reply, an unhurried tock-tock-tock, one splash of colour against the casual, ubiquitous rattle of the German fire. We moved more urgently and came to a farmhouse where Alan had established company headquarters. 'Right, Michael', he said. 'Your turn.'

Good training again kicked in. 'Battledrill formation', I told the platoon. 'Number one section point-section. I'll be right behind you. Sections two and three behind me and watch for my order to deploy. OK?'

Sergeant Hurst was point-section commander, and he turned on me a look of combined protest, resignation and – yes, it has to be said – *contempt* that I shall never forget. 'Won't you be leading us, sir?' he asked. That was what young officers were supposed to be for, especially young Guards officers. That is why they died like flies. But at battle-school at home we had been taught that it was not our job to get ourselves killed. It was to kill Germans, and to control our corner of the battle so as to kill as many as possible. When we bumped the enemy, we were to get down, fire, and try to outflank them. But somehow this had not yet caught on in the Mediterranean theatre; and after all, had I not just led a bayonet charge? Well yes, I had, but I was damned if I was going to lead another one in a hurry – at least, not just yet.

We quickly left the protection of dead ground and moved through the terraced vineyards to the wooded hillside in front of us. The terraces still provided cover from direct fire, but snipers' bullets brushed the air above us more than once. Our line of attack must have taken the Germans by surprise, for the full force of their artillery and mortar-fire was crashing on to the houses of the village in the valley below us. In a very short time we found ourselves struggling through burning scrub up the last stretch of the hill.

The noise and confusion was now immense, and we hung desperately to the last men of the platoon in front of us. Suddenly a burst of Spandau fire broke out from the right, about 50 yards away, its bullets zipping the air inches above our heads. I detached my rear section to deal with it (good battle-drill again) and we continued to advance rather more slowly, crouching as low as possible. At last we reached the top, just in time to fling ourselves down as a cataclysmic roar announced the opening of a new mortar barrage. There were no holes to give us shelter: we could only clutch the ground as crash after crash shook the ground and our eardrums ached with the blast. After a little the storm ebbed. I took stock. We were now on the extreme right of the hill, and I found a blessed stretch of soft soil where the platoon could dig in. The next task was to clear the further side of the hill, so I went forward with my runner to reconnoitre. I flushed out of a bush a terrified German, who assured me that his comrades had all gone, and returned to my own men. They had assembled several docile prisoners whom I sent back, escorted by one guardsmen. It then occurred to me that my platoon seemed remarkably small, so I set out to find the rest of my men and to make contact with the rest of the company – indeed, of the battalion – further to the left.

I can remember now only a series of episodes, most of them unpleasant, though not the order in which they occurred. I found the platoon that had preceded us up the hill dug in on the forward slope, and crouched with its officer, a tall Cornish boy with the improbable name of Hank Tom, in a small slit-trench exchanging information as a new mortar barrage came crashing on top of us. 'This is like a bad American film', I remarked. 'Yes', he replied, 'but not such fun.' The Germans still occupied a high ridge to our left and could see far too much of our positions. On returning to my own platoon I rashly exposed myself and received personal attention from another bloody Spandau and scrambled into cover with no dignity what-ever. I found one of my own guardsmen lying in the blackened gorse, his right arm and leg soaked in dark bluish blood and his face the muddy blue-yellow of the corpses I had buried a day earlier. I comforted him as well as I could, tried to cut away his clothes with my clasp-knife, bandaged his great wounds with my inadequate field-dressing and injected one of the two morphia ampoules that officers carried in action. When I got back to the platoon, I found another wounded man who seemed more cheerful. Although a lot of blood was dripping from his groin, he assured me that he was not in pain, but I injected my other morphia ampoule just in case. There was still no sign of any stretcher-bearers, nor indeed any support from the rear.

The platoon position seemed good enough, well dug in covering a rough arc round the right-hand end of the hill. But we had no water, precious little ammunition and, above all, no idea what was happening. I decided to go on another tour of exploration and set off with my runner across the hill to the left. The bushes still smouldered, their smoke stinging my eyes and throat. Among them, wounded men – ours and theirs – still crawled in agony, some being licked by wicked little flames. Others lay dead, one of them a dear friend from Oxford: Rognvald Gunn. I remembered him as a florid, giggling youth given to wearing velvet smoking-jackets and floppy bow-ties, famous for an outrageously camp performance as Osric in an OUDS *Hamlet*, and an even more outrageous performance as 'Wanda, the Queen of the Wogs' at Philippeville. He had no business to be in uniform at all and even less to be lying on an Italian hillside, his dead blue eyes staring at the sky with a sniper's bullet through his throat. Perhaps it was a mercy: he would not have enjoyed the rest of the war.

Eventually I found another officer, Christopher Bulteel, whom I had not seen since we had been at Wellington together, and between us we tried to sort things out. His company, No. 3, was on the left of the hill, mine on the right, and somewhere in between was what was left of No. 1. This was not much. They had lost all their officers, and command had been taken over by their CSM, 'Misty' Wright, who, as we later learned, had singlehandedly wiped out several German machine-gun posts for which he earned a well-deserved VC. The Germans still occupied the saddle connecting Point 270 with the higher ridge to the west, and their fire still commanded all approaches to our positions. Hence, presumably, the absence of stretcher-bearers and reinforcements. Junior as we were, we seemed to be the only officers left on the hill. We had no working radio-sets. Relief would no doubt come up after dark, but before then a counterattack seemed more than likely, and we were almost out of ammunition. We agreed – or I think we did – that I should go back down the hill to rustle up a carrying party to bring urgent supplies. I returned to my platoon position, handed over to the admirable Sergeant Hurst (his successor was nowhere to be seen), and set out. In retrospect I can see that this was disgraceful behaviour, tantamount to deserting my post in the face of the enemy. I should have stuck it out with my platoon and waited for supplies to come up. But at the time it seemed to make sense and no one reproached me for it, then or later.

Obviously, I thought, it would take too long to go back along the roundabout track by which we had approached the hill: much quicker and simpler to cut straight across the valley, and not much danger from snipers if I kept moving. So I set out across the vineyards, cramming bunches of grapes into my mouth to quench a very great thirst. The way was further and more complicated than I had thought, and though I was right about snipers, I was wrong about other things. I was nearly across the valley when there was a whizz and a terrific detonation as a shell burst about 20 yards away. I hit the ground about the same time as the second shell which landed two seconds later and five yards nearer. Where the rest fell I did not see: I instinctively grasped a vine branch for cover (it was about as thick as my wrist, but I clung to it as if it were twelve foot of concrete), shut my eyes and prayed – less for preservation than out of a desire to die properly. There were about a dozen shells in all, and the last I really believed to have done its job. It threw me in the air and everything went black. Then the black turned to dark brown, and gradually I found myself in a cloud of dust through which I could see about five yards. I picked myself up, too astonished to be grateful for my preservation, and ran to the shelter of the hillside as fast as I could. I learned then the valuable operational lesson that though it takes very few shells to scare the living daylights out of people, it takes a lot to kill them.

I found myself on the Grenadiers' sunken track and eventually reached our battalion headquarters, where they put together a carrying party of a dozen guardsmen and Basuto pioneers (where on earth had they found these? I wondered), laden with boxes of ammunition and grenades and water-cans. I started back at a fair pace, as dusk was already beginning to fall. 'What have we got in front – a fucking greyhound?' someone grunted further back, so I slowed up to check the party. Our dozen had dwindled to about five: the Basutos at the rear had disliked the corpses and the shelling and had refused to come any further. That left me with two cans of water, two boxes of grenades and a box of ammunition – not much to show for my efforts. I had to coax and threaten the rest of the party like mules up slopes that seemed twice as steep as they had been that morning, dodging fixed lines of enemy fire, and reached the summit long after dark.

No sooner had the carrying party dumped their load and disappeared than the silence was broken by sudden close-range Spandau and rifle-fire. Here comes the counterattack, I thought; and then found with some surprise that I was running very fast down the hill, obeying the orders of a nerve-centre somewhere near my stomach. 'Where are you off to?' someone called softly. 'I . . . I'm just alerting Company HQ', I lied. 'There's a wireless-set here, sir', came the reply. You can get through on that.' I blessed the man for preventing me from totally disgracing myself, and scrambled into his slit-trench where there was indeed now a large wireless-set. 'Who's in charge here now?' I asked the signaller. 'You are, sir', he replied. 'Me?' I asked; 'In charge of the whole hill?' 'You're the only officer here, sir', he replied. Now this was total nonsense, as I discovered later, but it made me pull myself together, call up battalion HQ and ask for artillery support. Within seconds it came crashing down, frightening me even more than did the Germans.

When the noise died away, I went in search of my platoon, to discover that someone had moved them to better and deeper positions. Only two men now seemed to be missing. I doled out ammunition, placed mess-tins of water beside the few wounded I could find, and then found myself a good deep trench. I am damned if I am going to keep awake, I said to myself. I am damned if I am going to make a round of the sentries. I will sleep though the heavens fall. Across the valley to the east came the distant flash and rattle of fire as the brigade on our right pushed its way up the mountain, but otherwise all was at last quiet. I wrapped a groundsheet round me and slept.

I was dimly conscious of voices and footsteps during the night, as they at last brought up supplies, but I shrank all the more deeply into my hole and reckoned they could do it without me. Shortly after dawn I rose and wandered about, to find Alan and a party of Basutos bearing welcome supplies. I met Christopher Bulteel again and we agreed rather mutinously that we should not have been left on our own for so long, and it was a good thing that there had not been a serious counterattack during the night. But now plenty of people were beginning to come up, including our commanding officer bringing congratulations and a gunner officer with a serious wireless-set. The Germans were now quiet. In fact they had pulled right back, and a few days later 7th Armoured Division entered Naples.

After breakfast we buried the dead. The six platoons now on the hill divided the task between them, but even so we had about a dozen bodies in our sector. Some were horribly burned, some mangled by grenades. At the time, as I took their personal belongings and supervised their burial, two things made a deep impression on me: burning scrub and wasps. The smell of burning stung our nostrils and throats, while wasps – hundreds of them – crawled over the bodies, into and out of their wounds, having to be brushed away but always returning.

The morning was spent on this gloomy work. At last we had cleaned up the hill, and I went back to my silent platoon for lunch. The rest of the afternoon I spent sitting in deep depression, looking out at the mountains and thinking how much more enjoyable it had been in Africa when nobody had been trying to kill me. At the same time I felt obscurely that I was now paying back for all the happiness of my life up until then. Much had been given me, and it was only fair that much should be asked in return. But I still didn't like it.

At tea-time some Scots Guards subalterns came to look over our positions, preparatory to relieving us at dusk. When it grew dark, their platoons came up and Chris Bulteel led us back. It was the darkest night I have ever known, and raining hard. The only way of keeping contact was to hold the belt of the man in front, and even then you could not see him. We took hours to get back to the field where we had formed up for attack the day before (several centuries ago), and there we rolled ourselves in our soaking blankets, and slept the sleep of utter exhaustion.

Next morning there was a rum issue. I doled out such generous tots that Alan was a little annoyed. Then we filed down to the road and back into Salerno. We were exhausted and dirty, with four-day beards, but cheerful at the prospect of a rest. We must look, I thought, as we marched into the town past the timidly emerging civilians, like a shot from British Movietone News. Billets had been found for us in a hideous fascist block of workers' flats. I settled the platoon in, scoured Salerno for my own kit, and having found it, went to bed. With a feeling of incredulity I lay in a real bed in a real room in a real house. It was the first time I had done so since leaving England five months earlier.

I felt not only tired, but also muzzy and unwell. Within a couple of hours I knew that I had a high fever. After that, consciousness faded into delirium and, together with several hundred other malarial casualties, I was transferred to a hospital ship and taken back to Africa.

4

Italy II: Naples to Florence

I spent the next six weeks in a tented hospital on a beach near Philippeville. Casualties from malaria had been heavy. Although we had been taking Mepacrin – a bitter pill that turned us all bright yellow – since arriving in the Mediterranean, this did nothing to protect us against the breed of mosquito that infested the beaches south of Salerno. Further, an epidemic of jaundice was sweeping the Allied armies in the theatre, and no sooner had I recovered from malaria than I was struck down by that. It rained incessantly and the tents were repeatedly flooded. Invalid food consisted of stodgy fish and local fruit, oranges and dates; but the latter were forbidden to sufferers from jaundice who were fed on dried prunes instead. Mercifully my old home, the IRTD, was only just up the road, and yet more mercifully my faithful servant Johansen was there, having been only lightly wounded, and he kept me supplied with clean clothes as well as the toiletries, books and magazines that my dear parents were sending out to me in abundance. Christopher Bulteel was in the next bed, also with malaria and very ill indeed, but was still excellent company until they sent him home as permanently unfit. Nor could I entirely regret, however guilty I might feel about it, that I was not with the battalion as it tackled the rain-sodden mountains north of Naples. I was really very lucky. The malaria, though not malign, was recurrent, and kept me out of action for six months. Less fortunately, I was not to shake it off entirely for another ten years.

When eventually I emerged from hospital, lean and yellow, and returned to the IRTD, I found that Johansen had procured for me a tent to myself, unpacked all my heavy baggage, pressed my uniforms and polished my buttons. I was still too weak to 'go on the square', so I did office duties. The mess was as jolly as ever, brightened by legendary figures from the SAS who had a training camp just along the road. At night I sat in my tent, listening to the rain lashing the canvas, and by the light of a hurricane lamp tried to get through Gibbon's *Decline and Fall of the Roman Empire*. (I never did.) As soon as I was well enough I was given a week's leave and hitch-hiked to Tunis with Ian Fraser, another member of the pals' battalion. He too had been at Salerno, where he was taken prisoner, escaped and then was badly wounded. Tunis was a totally French metropolis, full of smart shops, restaurants, bookshops and concert-halls, and we enjoyed ourselves immensely. On the drive home, sheltering under a tarpaulin in the back of an open truck as we drove through the dripping cork-forests, I remembered that this was my 21st birthday.

On our return to the IRTD I found waiting for me a letter with the news that I had been awarded a Military Cross for the attack on 'the Pimple' at Salerno. This gave me a surge of happy pride so intense that it has never completely died away. I understood exactly why I had got it. The planned attack had, as we have seen, threatened to disintegrate into a shambles, and it was my burst of manic energy that had, in the words of the official citation, 'been responsible for straightening out the situation'. But I had, as ever, been extraordinarily lucky. First, my charge had been simply a *fuite en avant*: there was nowhere else to go. Second, my seniors had watched me doing it – people whose reputation depended on my success and who were generous in giving me the credit. Most important of all, it was my first action, and any fool can be brave in his first action. It was not to happen again. There were occasions, as we shall see later, when I was downright cowardly. I still feel that I had done no more than earn good points, and that no award for gallantry should be made until, after a sufficient period in action, the good points can be balanced against the bad. When I think of my friends who endured years of hard slog, showing consistent courage of at least comparable quality but still ended the war undecorated, I feel an enormous fraud. But I have never tried to give it back.

I was now judged fit enough to return to the battalion, so after organizing a Christmas concert graced by a superb choir of Welsh guardsmen, I marched a draft to the Philippeville docks and boarded a ship for Naples. That evening I was preparing a repeat performance of the concert for New Year's Eve when malaria struck again. On New Year's Day 1944, with a temperature of 103, I landed in Italy as I had left it three months earlier – on a stretcher.

*   *   *

For the next six months I was to oscillate between hospital in Naples, convalescence on the Sorrento peninsula and the IRTD. This had moved to Italy hard on my heels and established itself with its drill-sergeants and all its beautifully painted regimental insignia in Rotondi, a dirty, sprawling village a few miles east of Caserta. Of Naples itself I was to see little. Much of the city was in ruins, and continued to be ruined as cunningly placed time-bombs planted by the Germans went off at unpredictable intervals. What was not ruined was largely out of bounds. The misery depicted by Norman Lewis in his wonderful book *Naples 1944* was thus largely concealed from us, but the funeral processions clogging the streets bore witness to the virulence of the typhoid epidemic that was decimating the civilian population. We were comfortable enough: we had our well-appointed officers' clubs; there were black-market restaurants where we could eat unimaginably well (far better than in England: the exchange-rate for the lira was daylight robbery); the shops bulged with confectionery, fruit, silk and leatherware that we sent home to families who had seen nothing like them since the war began; and best of all, our enlightened occupation-authorities revived the San Carlo Opera and mounted increasingly impressive performances of Verdi, Rossini and Puccini to audiences consisting not just of officers but of all ranks. I was not the only one who saw his first *Barber*, *Bohème*, *Rigoletto* and many others in those splendid settings performed by young singers who ten years later would be starring at Covent Garden, There may have been misery in the streets outside, but when, I asked myself callously, had there not been misery in the streets of Naples?

My only contact with the civil population resulted from an invitation by a fellow-officer to a dinner he gave for some Italian cousins, aristocrats who were trying to survive in an unheated wing of the vast Royal Palace. It was hard to know whether it was more difficult to sympathize with or to despise them. They were elderly, cold and hungry. Politically they were well to the right of Genghis Khan. They complained angrily about the damage done by Allied bombing. They praised the correct behaviour of the German troops with an implied unfavourable comparison with our own. They spoke contemptuously of the vulgarity of the fascist regime, but praised it for keeping the communists at bay – and who, they asked, was going to do that now? The moment the Allies left, the communists would take over, just you see. But what really shocked me, woolly liberal that I was, was not so much to hear such sentiments on their lips – what else could one expect? – as the outspoken agreement with which they were received by my friends, charming young Etonians who made it quite clear that they were not fighting for a Brave New World, and that the sooner they and their friends could get back to their world of aristocratic privilege the better.

This unpleasant experience was counteracted when I was sent to convalesce in Sorrento. There an officers' convalescent home had been located in the Hotel Tramontano, a comfortable establishment with a wonderful view across the bay to Vesuvius. Its furnishings and staff had changed little if at all since the early years of the century and the kitchens did miracles with army rations. Immediately opposite the hotel was the Villa Tritone where lived the historian Benedetto Croce and his daughters. I knew about Croce and had tried to read him at Oxford, struggling with some difficulty through *History as the Story of Liberty*, so I knew that he was a Good

Liberal. He was also very approachable, or at least his daughters were – Elena, Alda, Lidia and Sylvia. They were generous in inviting young British officers to tea and to play their grand piano. It was not easy to communicate with Croce himself, who was in his eighties, very deaf, and spoke little English, but the girls kept us abreast of his efforts, in association with Count Sforza, to create a serious democratic party in Italy. Further, he had a son-in-law in the Resistance who spent most of his time in the north. Through him we learned that disagreeable as one might find the communists, they were the only people doing any serious damage to the Germans. It was clear that postwar Italian politics was going to be a very complicated affair.

Apart from continuous winter rain that maddeningly delayed my return to health and kept me for long days in the hotel lounge listlessly reading bound volumes of Punch, Sorrento was a delightful place to be. It was made more so by the presence of Humphrey Leeke, who after ten filthy weeks of mountain fighting had succumbed to jaundice and joined me in hospital. Other members of the pals' battalion also surfaced, emerging from hospital or sent to rest from their units, and we thoroughly enjoyed ourselves. We wandered round the town paying homage to Tasso, to whom there was some little memorial at every street corner. (I swore to read him some day, but never have.) We shopped, sending home coral brooches, inlaid boxes, silk scarves and cases of lemons. We ate calamari and pasta and drank Lacrima Christi in the little restaurants; we visited Pompeii and the San Carlo opera; and as our health and the weather improved, we walked in the hills behind the town. As we grew stronger, we became increasingly bored, longing for the summons to our units that in my case did not come until the beginning of February 1944. By then most of my friends had left in time to be shipped off to Anzio, whence all too many did not return.

My own battalion had no room for me, so I returned to the IRTD. There I remained for another five months, living with scarlet majors at the base and shipping glum heroes up the line to death. Candid friends told me that I seemed to be having a very cushy war. I knew this was true, and only wished that I regretted it more than I did.

Rotondi was a dreary village at the best of times and the presence of a thousand or more troops trampling the surrounding fields into glutinous mud did not improve it. It was bitterly cold. The village was full of hungry dogs and near-starving children, to whom at midday we distributed a stew made up of our left-overs; probably their largest if not their only meal of the day. I was billeted with five other officers in two rooms of a smallish house whose owners had been crammed, with all their children and furniture, into the ground floor. They possessed a vast pianola draped in crimson velvet, on which, when in my cups, I would play the Radetzky March. The officers' mess was in the Municipio; reasonably comfortable, selling a disgusting local gin to which most of us preferred the regional liqueur, Strega. The wireless was tuned to British Forces Radio which gave us the news, but in the evening we unpatriotically tuned in to a German station that provided excellent classical concerts. Friends came and went. We were visited by our Guardsman generals. Alexander, small, polite, intelligent, asked shrewd questions about the welfare of the men, and made an excellent impression. Oliver Leese, Montgomery's successor in command of Eighth Army, did not. A burly, overpromoted Coldstreamer, he rapidly lost respect by trying to imitate his predecessor, touring units distributing cigarettes. ('I see they've got another bloke doing this job', one sergeant muttered sardonically). We had the battalion drawn up for him in a hollow square with loudspeakers in the trees behind, so that he could drive his jeep into the middle and address us through a hand-held mike. He did so drive; stood up; threw away his mike and chummily invited us to gather round. We did, and as a result nobody heard a word that he said. Just as well: he assumed that we were all fresh out from England and would join his Eighth Army (in fact most of us were bound for the Anglo-American Fifth Army), and congratulated us on our good fortune in following in the footsteps of our historic predecessors from Alamein, and our privilege in being able to have a crack at the Hun, who was on his last legs. Most of his audience had been fighting the Hun for four months and had good reason to know that he was nothing of the sort. It did not go down well.

In general there was little criticism of our High Command and their conduct of the campaign as a whole. We took it for granted that once Italy surrendered, the Allies had been bound to occupy it and seize as much as possible from the Germans. We also accepted that our role in Allied Grand Strategy was to draw off as many German troops as possible from the Eastern Front and from north-west France, where everyone knew that the main Allied thrust was due in a few months' time; and that this could not be done without hard fighting. Our own objective was Rome, and we blamed our delay in getting there not so much on Allied generalship as on the appalling terrain and enemy skill in defending it. The failure of the Anzio landings to achieve their objective and lever the Germans out of their defences on the Gustav line certainly received unfavourable comment, especially from the convalescent participants in the campaign who passed through the IRTD, but their criticism was levelled at the American corps and army commanders responsible, Lucas and Mark Clark. In spite of the hardships of the winter campaign, morale remained good. That it did so, however, was due as much to the achievements of the supply services that kept our armies so remarkably comfortable and well fed, as to the operational skill of our military leaders.

Desertion rates were admittedly high. They were to be even higher the following winter. By then a lot of men felt that they had had enough, and found it very easy to find friendly shelter among peasants whose own men-folk were prisoners of war. I found myself called on to act as defending officer in courts martial, usually trying to get charges of desertion reduced to absence without leave. I had some sympathy with my clients, but their comrades in the battalion had none whatever. There might have been more if the death-penalty had been reintroduced, as the High Command at one stage seriously considered. Wisely, in my view, they decided against it.

On my return to the IRTD, after a brief and very necessary toughening-up course, I was appointed training officer to the Coldstream company. This involved promotion, albeit local and temporary. Captain M.E. Howard, MC, looked pretty good, and I was treated with awed respect by subalterns fresh out from England. With two Coldstream battalions in Italy, there were quite a lot of these to be speeded up the line to death. I was given a very free hand, and the facilities were excellent. From the village a steep woodland path climbed up the mountainside to wide alpine meadows studded with shepherds' huts which we attacked or defended, whenever possible using live ammunition. Most of my pupils had already had their fill of this kind of thing at battle-school at home, but what they had *not* had, as I knew to my cost, was experience in finding their way around, silently and in unknown country, by night. I gave them a lot of that, but was not thanked for it – at least, not at the time. Officers returning from the horrible fighting on Monte Camino and the Garigliano approved, but pointed out that nothing could really prepare troops for the cold, the wet and the sheer endurance needed to fight on bare mountains where the only protection against enemy mortar-fire was rock sangars you had to build for yourself, where it took eight men four hours to carry a stretcher down steep slippery paths to the dressing-stations; nothing except the sheer bloody-minded determination to ensure that the Germans should suffer worse than we did. Today, of course, they would all need counselling, and would probably sue the army for neglecting its 'duty of care'. Then nothing mattered except defeating the Germans and getting home.

There was one glorious diversion while I was at Rotondi. Vesuvius erupted. The mountains cut off a direct view of the eruption unless one climbed up further than seemed altogether reasonable, but the sky burned a fiery red and ash was carried by the wind to make the village even filthier than it already was. I was able to get into Naples to see an enormous cloud hanging over the volcano that dwarfed the mountain itself. Ankle-deep purple dust covered the streets, drifted into the buildings, and hung around for weeks in spite of all attempts to clear it. For the Neapolitans it was a nuisance, but a minor one after all they had been through; and it would be a bumper year for the vines that grew on the mountain slopes.

February yielded to March, and March to April. It grew warmer. The mud in the village dried into dust. The woods became thickly carpeted with wild crocus, the fruit trees covered with pink and white blossom. We changed from battledress back into khaki-drill shorts and welcomed the sight of our knees white from their winter hibernation. And I went down with malaria again.

This time it was complicated by a huge goitre that the medical officer said was caused by iron deficiency, itself a byproduct of malaria, so I not only felt rotten but also looked grotesque. Back to hospital for a couple of weeks, and then another week of sick leave. This time I was able to go to Ravello, where we had taken over the exquisite Hotel Palumbo. Providentially, Humphrey, who had returned to the IRTD after several weeks of hell in the mountains, was able to come with me. It was our last leave together, and a good one. It was pleasantly warm and the gardens bloomed with wisteria and roses. From the hotel balcony we looked down on the crawling azure sea, the Salerno coast-line veiled in mist beyond. We revisited our old battlefields and the cemetery outside the town where our friends were now decently buried. Crown Prince Umberto, heir to the Italian throne, was residing in a neighbouring villa while the fate of his dynasty was being decided. We made friends, guardsmen to guardsmen, with the officers of his suite, pleasant young men from the north who detested the Germans and felt themselves as much foreigners in Naples as we did ourselves. In the background rumbled the thunder of our guns as we launched our final, and successful, assault on Monte Cassino.

When we returned to Rotondi, I found that my job as training officer had gone to someone fitter and more experienced, but since I was still adjudged convalescent I became second-in-command of the company, with mainly administrative responsibilities. I was encouraged to apply for an intelligence course at Algiers, and while waiting for this to come through, I was made Battalion Entertainments Officer, with the task of keeping boredom at bay. This was fun. I discovered enough local talent to make up our own concert party, and scoured the neighbourhood to recruit others. With the help of ENSA and the Americans, who were endlessly generous with their 'big bands', I was able for a time to provide almost nightly entertainment. For this it was necessary to build an open-air stage, and find someone to design it. Exactly the right man was to hand – Captain C.R.S. Buckle, Scots Guards – better known in the world of theatre as Dicky Buckle.

For some 25 years after the war, Dicky was to brighten the London scene as a balletomane and designer of fantastic exhibitions, and even more by his colourful personality. He was something of an anachronism: dandy, aesthete and wit, he bridged the worlds of Ronald Firbank and Andy Warhol. Understandably he was regarded by the army as a distinctly odd fish, but the Brigade rather prided itself on its tolerance for odd fish, so long as they made up for their oddity by physical courage and what General Lyautey had once defined as the first requirement in an officer: *gaiety*. Dicky possessed both in abundance – the latter in every sense of the word. His gaiety was indeed such that his friends sometimes wondered which would befall him first: court-martial for indecent behaviour or a posthumous Victoria Cross. An anecdote, *ben trovato* if not strictly *vero*, was current when I first knew him, of his being despatched on a particularly dangerous patrol behind the German lines, from which his companions returned to report that he had last been seen attacking a German strong-point with grenades in face of heavy machine-gun fire. A week later he reappeared with an exact plan of the enemy positions and a digest of Italian partisan reports. 'But my dears, you really must go', he informed his interrogators: 'They have the most *marvellous* violets!' Camp of this kind was not to the taste of every commanding officer, but even the most unimaginative appreciated the contribution to morale that could be made by such a licensed wit so long as he behaved himself. Anyhow, I was able to recruit Dicky on to my team and began a friendship that lasted well into the postwar years. Since Humphrey had now returned to his battalion and I was never to see him again, I was particularly glad of Dicky's company.

Meanwhile, in quick succession, Rome fell and the Allies landed in Normandy. The mess opened a book on who would get there first – Alexander to Vienna or Montgomery to Berlin. As the weeks passed and the latter seemed badly stuck in Normandy while we raced north towards Florence, the odds seemed pretty even, and Alexander's plans to crack through the Alps and reach Vienna that autumn did not seem so ludicrous at the time as they do in hindsight. What we did not realize was that the French forces serving with us, the only units which showed the slightest skill at mountain warfare, could not possibly be retained in Italy while their own country was being liberated, and were already being prepared to land in the South of France. This I learned when, in mid-June, I was whisked back to Algiers to take up my place on the Intelligence course for which I had applied a month earlier.

I was flown back to Algiers on an American aircraft in company with a Russian general and his staff – the first Soviet troops I had yet seen. They were not friendly: the genial rays of the Mediterranean sun could make no impression on their Siberian permafrost. But on arrival at the airport I was met by a fellow Coldstreamer, Ralph Anstruther: a man of infinite charm and generosity, later to devote his life to the service of the Queen Mother and at the time on the staff of the Allied Supreme Commander in the Mediterranean Theatre, General 'Jumbo' Wilson. Ralph had a car and a villa covered with bougainvillea above the town, both of which he put at my disposal. He took me for a drink at the Aletti Hotel where the first person I saw was Ian Fraser, still unfit and serving in some liaison capacity. Between them they introduced me to everyone who was anyone in Algiers – British, American, above all the French, who had once again re-established their social and political dominance in the city. In one of my few solitary moments I was having a midday aperitif in a café, when a French officer at the next table recognized my Coldstream shoulder-flashes and introduced himself as a former liaison officer with our battalion in France during the Dunkirk campaign, and took me home to lunch. We were joined by a group of his fellow officers, where, over the best *omelette fines herbes* I have ever eaten, they argued bitterly about politics, which was virtually the only topic of conversation anywhere. It was taken for granted that there would be landings in the South of France, and no attempt was being made to conceal their preparations: the more German troops that could be pinned down waiting for them, the better for the Allied armies fighting in the north. But what would happen after they landed? Who would take charge?

After three hectic days in Algiers, I made my way to a dusty village a few miles outside, where I spent a further two weeks learning everything that was to be known about the German army: its organization, uniforms, doctrine, personnel, tactics, weapons – everything except why it was so *bloody good*, which still, after half a century, remains something of a mystery to me. The course was run and largely attended by Americans, with their excellent food, generosity, friendliness, and overwhelming *joie de vivre*. A little too overwhelming, if truth were told: they made me, at the age of 21, feel as old as Tiresias. But I worked hard and flew back to Naples hoping that I might have the chance to put my new-found knowledge to good effect. The chance did come, but not for another decade and not in the way that I had expected: only when I began to learn my trade as a military historian.

*   *   *

Shortly after returning to Rotondi I received the long-awaited summons to rejoin the battalion, some nine months after I had left it. My adventures for the next few weeks I recorded in a letter home, which I reprint, lightly edited, below.

My convoy drove up the Appian Way to Rome, and until the Alban Hills the country was dull or bleak, or both. Formia and Gaeta were two long piles of rubble – about five miles of ruin beside a sparkling blue sea, as vivid and improbable as a picture by de Chirico. Then came the horrible scrub-coloured bareness of the Aurunci range, relieved by the occasional skeleton of a tank overturned on a hillside. Increasingly the hillside was littered with all the messy debris of war: ammunition-boxes, tins, ration-cartons, steel helmets, German respirators and other equipment, wrecked guns, abandoned rifles, weapon-pits and charred tanks. The scenery on top of the Alban Hills was like an English park with great old trees, rolling turf, heather and bracken. For the first time I felt that we were getting nearer home after the vineyards and olive trees of the south. Rome we hardly entered. The convoy swung right at the city wall, went past the San Lorenzo railyards, where we saw the first signs of bombing, and crossed the Tiber north of the Flaminian Gate. What we could see of the city was lovely even beneath the scum of traffic signs, and my men in the back of the truck who had been singing bawdy songs for the past hour were uplifted enough to change to 'Jerusalem' and 'Land of Hope and Glory'. We then drove up the Flaminian Way in a landscape that did more to explain Italian painting to me than a lifetime of lectures, until at twilight we reached Terni and turned off along a bumpy track to the unpromising collection of tents where we were to spend the night. In the darkness the confusion of sorting out the men, reporting to the authorities, receiving orders, finding the men again, seeing them fed, giving them orders, finding a tent for oneself – all this was nightmarish. In the army, once you are shaken out of routine and find yourself in a no man's land of transit camps and strangers who care nothing for you, life can be very disagreeable.

Next day we were collected by a Jewish transport unit. My driver spoke little English but had, I gather, taught mathematics at Frankfurt University. He spent the long pauses on the road studying what I assumed to be calculus out of a large volume. The journey took us over the hills to Spoleto and along the valley to Perugia. There we were stuck in a ten-mile traffic-jam that made me profoundly thankful that we had command of the air (but did we really, I wondered apprehensively, have total command of the air?) through thick dust-clouds to Arezzo – and now the ruins became thicker again behind the dust, the road busier with the signs and vehicles of divisional base troops. Men wore shorts and a beret, a deep tan, and nothing else. At length we turned into a field of dust thinly edged with tents, and that was our night's lodging.

It was a bleak little place presided over by an insolent but harassed sergeant-major and a major whose regiment had obviously got rid of him because of drink, ill-temper and incompetence; but there was a mess where we were given a good meal and a bottle of beer. A few yards away there was a prisoner-of-war compound, and after our evening meal we wandered over to look at it. The prisoners were a dirty and unhappy-looking collection, most of whom, in their filthy uniforms, did not look like soldiers at all. Most of them were probably *Volksdeutsch*, resigned to their lot and settling down mildly enough in the blankets tossed over the fence to them by an English orderly almost as scruffy as they were. But there were a few elite troops who stood apart in a godlike select circle, bare to the waist and displaying the most magnificently bronzed torsos I have ever seen. I asked why they chose to go about half-naked at this mosquito-infested hour. The answer gave me great satisfaction: their clothes were swarming with lice. Evidently the sanitary arrangements of Valhalla were as deficient as its ethics.

The next day after a long wait our transport arrived, but not enough of it, so we had to fight savagely to get our own men on to the trucks and keep the others off. I was among the more successful and we were off again, over a dusty road towards Siena. The countryside was now rolling and shrubbily wooded, and signposted everywhere 'Riservuto di Caccia': the Chianti Hills. The convoy was to take us to our B Echelon – the rear unit of a battalion where, when the battalion is in action, there are left such fundamentally peaceful people as the quartermasters, bandsmen, storemen, transport personnel, drill-sergeants and officers' mess staff. When we arrived, however, we found only empty fields scarred by wheel-tracks, and the information that the whole outfit had moved on a couple of hours before, though nobody knew precisely where. If we drove on to Greve, they told us, and followed Route X from there, we would see the signs of our various units along the way. This was disconcerting, since by a process of erosion I was now senior officer in charge of the convoy and had awful visions of leading it straight into the enemy lines. In fact if I had obeyed these instructions I would probably have done that very thing, for Greve was only half a mile behind our forward positions and anyone advancing beyond it was shelled with violence and accuracy. Fortunately anxiety made my eyes keen and I noticed just in time the small sign with the Brigade colours and our battalion number, pointing, from a village choked with ruin, up a small side-track. We turned off and at length found some tents in a small oak coppice. I saw a large naked major powdering himself in the middle of a bush, and knew that we had arrived.

Dinner was formal and soothing. Candlelight and four courses washed down with good Chianti wine was welcome after the hurried guzzles of the past few days. The powdered major proved to be a rather aloof regular who addressed the newcomers no more than was strictly necessary. But next morning the Commanding Officer appeared: Colonel George Burns, a magnificent person with a breadth and a vigour that seems quite out of place in the twentieth century. He had a vast laugh, a vast appetite, prodigious energy and a wonderful gift for inspiring confidence and cheerfulness in the most depressing situations. He and the powdered major talked with infinite gusto about their strange escapades as peacetime subalterns in a rich and spacious world, while the rest of us listened with awe and envy. After greeting me by my Christian name and asking with real solicitude after my health, he told me that he intended to keep me in reserve until the battalion came out of the line – which, after six weeks' continuous action, was imminent – so that I could then do a lion's share of administration and give other officers a rest. So for two more days I wandered over the wooded hills, and stumped up the hill to find Dicky Buckle who had just arrived at Scots Guards B

Echelon and told me with great excitement that Ronald Firbank's body had been transferred from the Catholic to the Protestant cemetery in Rome – or it may have been the other way round.

...Then came a change of plan. A vacancy had occurred for a platoon commander and I was to take over. Next morning I scrambled on to a truck crammed with stores and was ferried up to the battalion. It was Sunday morning, and church bells were ringing in Greve. The town was not much damaged. The first Allied proclamations had just been posted, and little groups were gathered round reading them. Liberation was new enough for the Italians to cheer us as we went past, but soon there weren't any more Italians. A sinister notice read 'Drive Slowly: Dust is Death!' At length we came to a farmhouse on a hillside, and in the field behind it the battalion transport. This was 'F' (fighting) echelon. I collected my belongings – small pack, satchel with writing material and books, water-bottle, a '38 army-issue pistol, shovel, steel helmet (in addition to the beret I was wearing), Schmeiszer machine-pistol and two grenade-pouches – and, feeling very warlike, reported to the adjutant. A guide then escorted me to my company position further up the hill. On the way I was struck, almost like a physical blow, by a sudden and totally unexpected feeling of panic, like that felt by a patient before an operation as the anaesthetist's mask is placed over his face. It passed as quickly as it had come, and I slipped into a sort of 'front-line' gear that was to function quite well. Although I was to be frightened again often enough, this irrational generalized terror was never to recur.

...Number 3 Company was in a large white villa, behind which was clustered a collection of jeeps, Bren carriers and piles of stores. There seemed a lot of people there, guardsmen, gunners and mortarmen manning OP posts, signallers netting in their sets and maintaining their lines. Water-cans, ammunition-boxes and mortar-bomb containers were heaped against the walls. Broken flowers and creepers trailed on the paths. Tame rabbits lolloped in unaccustomed and bewildered freedom over the uncut lawn. The place was in that state of messy untidiness that is inseparable from war, and far more typical of it than any amount of horror. Think, when you try to visualize conditions at the front, of the debris of a civilian house, perhaps your own, dusty and looted; and superimpose on it the disorder of the army – weapons and ammunition, piles of web equipment, washing and writing materials hanging out of packs, maps and mess-tins and cans of rations; mattresses dragged from beds and carried to the safe rooms downstairs; drawers hanging open; windows barricaded with wash-stands; men sleeping on the floor under dirty mosquito-nets; a strange mixture of newspapers, the *Daily Mirror*, *Eighth Army News*, *Völkische Beobachter*, *Il Popolo*, scattered everywhere; and flies, flies, flies.

...My company commander was Christopher Jansen: dark, thin, and desperately tired. His courage was not in question – he had been badly wounded in North Africa and refused to leave his post until marched off by his platoon sergeant – but when a fearful crash shook the house he started like a nervous horse. 'That happens', he remarked apologetically, 'It's a 15cm mortar a long way back, and sends one over just when you don't want it.' We weren't really in defensive positions, he explained: the company was dug in behind the house with sentries on the reverse slope 'in case he sends up a patrol, which is unlikely. His morale is even worse than ours. But he can still shell the shit out of us.' The same point was forcefully made by the members of my platoon when I went out to find them. They had dug themselves into holes about four-foot deep, lined with straw and sometimes roofed over with boards, from which they crawled out regretfully like animals being dug out of their burrows. They were sadly diminished after a month's hard fighting, and had only one question: 'When is the brigade coming out, sir?' Apart from one, whom I sent back that evening as 'bomb-happy', they seemed fundamentally reliable – one, amazingly enough, came from a village two miles from Ashmore – and Sergeant Smith, my platoon sergeant, was clearly an excellent man.

. . . After a midday meal of bread, cheese and the inevitable but none the less welcome mess-tin of tea, Christopher took me up to the company OP to look at the ground ahead of us. The forward slope of our hill was wooded, and across it ran most conveniently a sunken track that easily accommodated not only our own OP (two men with binoculars and a Bren gun) but the forward observers for the gunners, the medium mortars and heavy mortars, each with a telephone back to their batteries. We crawled up the track and peered gingerly over the edge. Directly ahead was a valley some five miles wide, green and cultivated, flanked on the left by spurs of heathery hills and on the right by the prolongation of our own mountain. Three miles away were the red roofs of Strada, beyond that a crest on which stood the next village, Impruneta. In the background, startlingly near, were the blue mountains beyond the Arno, and in the haze at their foot you could just see, through glasses, what I took to be the white suburbs of Florence. The nearest German positions were in a house about a mile in front, and shortly after our arrival our guns began to shell it.

. . . It was an interesting experience. The OP officer gave the range and the order to fire. There was a silence. The leaves rustled peacefully and the birds twittered. I strained my ears to catch the sound of our own gun amid the miscellaneous, continual bangs that punctured the afternoon. There was the strange swift sighing of a shell rushing overhead. Then came a great brown mushroom of smoke and dust on the green hill opposite, two seconds before the crash of the explosion. The next mushroom was behind the hill, and we could only see the smoke curling up after the explosion. The third shot hit the target, which disappeared in a cloud of yellow dust. It was almost disappointing, when the dust cleared away, to see how slightly the house had been damaged, but almost at once mushroom grew out of mushroom on the house and the crashes became continuous. It was ten minutes before the smoke cleared. Already the Germans had retaliated. I ducked instinctively at the crescendo whistle of a shell that pitched a quarter of a mile ahead of us, shaking the ground and the air with blast. But the casualties from such shell-fire, on both sides, were always astonishingly small, and the Germans, conserving their ammunition, now rarely hit back.

...I stayed for an hour or two in that sunken track, watching the landscape with a hazy mixture of business and pleasure. Insects buzzed and crawled, and if I lay on my back I could see the trees waving slowly against the bright blue of the sky. The soft whine of the shells made the afternoon still more peaceful, and the distant spurts of machine-gun fire seemed unimportant. Then the warning whistle of a shell would rudely shatter my unsuitably pastoral reverie. Our mortars were shooting too, but there you only heard the cough of the detonation and the crump of their arrival. Then I returned to the house to unpack my bag and clean my weapons. It was Sunday, and at five o'clock the chaplain came up with his suitcase of prayer-books to hold a service. The shelling made us nervous of collecting the company in the open air, so we assembled in a cellar. The Italian caretaker and his family came too. I was touched at the devotion of the guardsmen. Drumhead services in the front line are always moving, and who, whatever their creed, can fail to be moved by the magic words: 'Lighten our darkness we beseech thee, O Lord, and by thy great mercy defend us from all perils and dangers of this night'?

...Afterwards we adjourned for pre-prandial drinks – Italian gin but real lemon-juice – and were making cheerful conversation when the house shook with a terrific crash, through whose rolling echoes came the steady drone of planes. We were bombing Strada. Another crash sent a blast through the window that fanned our hair. From the window we saw our planes high up, circling round politely, each waiting his turn to dive on to the target. The bombing stopped for a little and was succeeded by a noise as of ripping calico greatly magnified as they started to machine-gun the town. Then a few more bombs and it was over. We sat down to our prefabricated stew with great relish. Next day delighted Italians told us that 30 Germans had been killed as they were queuing up for their evening meal.

...We did not go unpunished. Next morning, after a night in a slit-trench, I had washed and breakfasted and was chatting up my platoon when the first German shell arrived.

...Where it landed I don't know. There was just a sudden whistle and a crash so loud and so near that I was not conscious of it as noise at all, but as force, as violence, as air suddenly expanding in a great annihilating wave. Everything was dark with dust and cordite fumes and there followed a sinister silence when all the world was still and I felt suddenly released a panic-stricken fluttering inside my ribs that had a second earlier been grasped in a hand of stupefying paralysis.

'That was a near one', said Sergeant Smith.

...I scrambled with what dignity I could muster into the nearest slit-trench. Things were quiet for a moment and I looked around. To shout to people to take cover was hardly necessary. There was nothing to do but stay where I was. Then came another whistle growing louder horribly quickly, culminating again in a crash that could be felt but not heard, in that instant of blind personal paralysis when all thought and feeling – even fear – is frozen, blotted out as vision is momentarily eclipsed by a wink. Then again the release of breathing, the release of fear, the release of the fluttering bird under my ribs. That one was nearer the house and must have caused damage, but should I go to make sure? As I debated the question, I recognized in the far distance the bang of our particular gun and pressed closer, impossibly closer to the ground, fixing my eye on some silly little detail, a blade of grass, a stone, a struggling ant, concentrating desperately on that until the paralysis, the shutter, again descended and reduced me to something with no semblance to a man.

. . . There must have been about a dozen shells all together. In the intervals I lay still and thought how pleasant it would be when it was finished and we could get up and walk about in the sun again. Eventually no more came. I cautiously got up and went round checking my platoon. There appeared to be no damage, except to our collective nerves. At company HQ two men had been lightly wounded, and Christopher had had a fantastic escape. He had been lying on his bed on the ground floor with his head against the outside wall when a shell had hit the wall two feet above him, exploded, knocked a hole three feet square and covered him with bricks and rubble. He was dug out, giggling apologetically and white with dust, and took everyone down to the cellar. The next shell had exploded just outside the cellar door on a jeep that mercifully absorbed the force of the explosion. A third had not exploded, but remained as a witness and example of the size of the things they had been throwing at us – 17 cm, so they told me. A fourth exploded upstairs, totally destroying the staircase and the bedroom in which I had just washed – and had left, I suddenly realized, all my belongings. All that was left was a great pile of rubbish on the floor of the room below. And everywhere was powdered plaster, whose presence and smell always accompanies ruin.

. . . We had barely had time to catch our breath before Colonel George came stumping up to see us, armed only with a stout walking-stick and grasping an unlit pipe, for which he unconcernedly requested a match. He had that essential quality of leadership – calm. He spoke to everyone, not so much cheering us up as convincing us that there was nothing we had to be cheered up about. He left having made us feel like a million dollars. And I went back, rather self-consciously, to reading *Mansfield Park*.

That is where my long letter stopped. Now I must rely on memory.

Next day we moved again. An attack by the New Zealand Division on our left had broken the German defences, and we were to push on to Florence. If the Germans decided to defend the city, we would have to fight through it – a prospect that appealed to nobody. But if, as seemed more probable, they blew the bridges and withdrew into the mountains beyond, we would pull back and reorganize. The news gave the battalion a much-needed second wind. At dusk we withdrew a couple of miles, spent a moonlit night in a steeply terraced vineyard and next morning waited to be called forward. As ever the wait seemed endless, and the call when it came was urgent. The rest of the day I recall only through blurred impressions. Strada had now fallen but was still under heavy shellfire, in the midst of which Colonel George stood magnificently directing the traffic with his walking-stick. We scrambled through the vineyards beyond, up the slopes towards Impruneta, for much of the time under heavy fire. So long as we kept on the move, the fire did not worry us, but once we stopped, as we did when we reached Impruneta, we felt very vulnerable. In Impruneta we found a troop of accompanying tanks from the sixth South African Armoured Division (to which our brigade now belonged), and the troop commander seemed happy to keep watch while I got my men under cover in the cellars, so long as we took over at nightfall. So we crouched in the darkness while the shells crashed on the houses above us, and I tried rather unsuccessfully to cheer people up by telling them that the weight of the shelling showed that the Germans were really serious about withdrawing. I doubt whether anyone was impressed.

Eventually – it must by now have been late afternoon – Christopher squirrelled us out and set us on our way again towards the next village, San Gersole. We were growing tired, and German mortars shelled us with vicious accuracy as we went. Many times I flattened myself to the ground and repeated the magic words of the 23rd Psalm, as so many soldiers had done before me. Miraculously, only one man in my platoon was lightly (but nastily) wounded, and I quite wrongly allowed his mate to escort him to the rear. As darkness fell we cautiously approached San Gersole, to find it already occupied by Andrew Cavendish with 4 Company. Andrew, wonderfully debonair, found us accommodation in a large villa that would have been comfortable if the German troops who had occupied it until that morning had not systematically trashed it and smeared everything with excrement; so much of it indeed that they must have been saving the stuff up for days. We settled down exhausted and, so far as I was concerned, oddly depressed. After only a single day, I wondered how on earth the rest of the battalion had been able to endure six virtually uninterrupted weeks of this kind of thing.

In the middle of the night we were roused by the loudest noise I have ever heard in my life. It seemed as if the heavens themselves were cracking open and releasing a storm of sound that fluttered and reverberated among the mountains for what seemed like hours. This could mean only one thing: the Germans had blown the Florence bridges, and were withdrawing from the city. Next morning my depression had vanished. It was a lovely day, there was no sign of war, and Scots Guards patrols drove through our positions to probe up to the Arno. With them, perched on a Bren carrier, was Dicky

Buckle. 'Shelley's birthday!' he howled cheerfully as he drove past. The local inhabitants clapped and beamed at us; clearly not just pleased but happy with a radiant inner happiness that shone out of their eyes whenever they looked at us. 'To know that we have caused such a feeling', I wrote home, 'makes the whole war seem worthwhile.'

No time was wasted in pulling us out. That evening transport arrived to drive us through the night to billets in a large farm a few miles outside Siena. From the window of my bedroom I looked across flat fields to the towers of the city. The battalion now had a three-week rest which it – though not I – richly deserved. Most of the officers went on leave. Those who remained spent the evenings in heavy drinking and gambling for prodigiously high stakes, so I was relieved to be invited to join a party visiting Rome. Rome was insufferably hot and swarming with military police, so some of us continued south to Positano. The more *mondaine* of our colleagues warned us that while the women there were riddled with clap, the boys could be very obliging, but I was too cautious to sample either. We stayed at a small restaurant on the beach, Il Buco di Baccho, rose late, breakfasted on iced peaches, coffee and fruit-juice, bathed off secluded beaches and in the evening ate omelettes, *fritti misti* and huge plates of pasta to the accompaniment of timeless Neapolitan music. Then we mounted our trucks again and bumped back to the war.

We returned to find that we had missed both the palio and a magnificent parade in Siena's main square at which General Alex had taken the salute. A major reorganization of the battalion had switched me to No. 4 Company under Andrew Cavendish. Andrew, I discovered, had a passion for books and patronized Heywood Hill's bookshop, from which his sister-in-law Nancy Mitford (who worked there) sent him book-parcels even larger than those sent to me by my mother. There reigned a spirit of wild optimism. Montgomery and Patton were overrunning France and the Russians were deep inside Poland. The German High Command seemed in a state of revolt. The end of the war before the end of the year now seemed not only possible but probable. Another winter spent campaigning in the Apennines, which now reared in front of us like a menacing green wall, seemed as unlikely as it was undesirable.

When we advanced again, our movements were leisurely. Our divisional line of advance now ran west of Florence, through Empoli and Montecatini. The flat country south of the Arno provided an excellent killing-ground for the Germans, who were comfortably ensconced on the higher north bank, so all movement had to take place by night. We relieved an American unit by crawling along ditches, over which German machine-guns were firing on fixed lines, and took over positions that seemed crammed with candy and comics to the exclusion of any more warlike material. The Arno lay a few hundred yards ahead, with a few German alarm posts on our side which they occupied only by night and we raided at intervals in hope of picking up a prisoner. It was there that I learned that Humphrey had been killed. It was like a blow in the guts.

But life had to go on, and so it did. After a few days the Germans withdrew again, we crossed the Arno and trudged up towards the mountains. Now we felt like true liberators. At each new village partisans came tumbling out of the woodwork, eager young men wearing tricoleur armbands and brandishing captured German weapons, anxious to join us (which they couldn't) or tell us where the Germans had gone (which they could and very usefully did). Sometimes they had already taken control of the village before we arrived. In one they proudly paraded a group of depressed elderly men in dusty suits, the fascist former mayor and *sindaco*, in case we wanted to use them to clear mines before they were shot. Women and children lined the street clapping us, their eyes shining with happiness. When they could, they lured us into their houses and gave us enormous meals. When they could not, they offered great *fiaschi* of wine to take with us. As I have said earlier, it made the whole war seem worthwhile.

There was only one aspect of all this that jarred. Relations between our troops and the Italians were excellent – so long as the Italians were on the spot. But if they had gone and left their houses empty, our troops systematically looted them, giving a new and sinister dimension to the term 'liberation'. Anything mobile that took their fancy they packed up and sent home. When I first encountered this, I protested to my platoon sergeant, pointing out that the men were robbing people who were probably much poorer than they were. He advised me not to take it too seriously: 'The lads see it as a kind of perk.' My fellow officers took the same line, so I reckoned that this was no time to be priggish. The Germans, we were to learn, had done infinitely worse.

Eventually we reached Montecatini and struck north into the mountains. Andrew installed Company HQ comfortably in the hilltop village of Montecatini Alto, and we began patrolling deep into the wooded foothills, checking up on partisan reports of German withdrawal. This had been considerable. Shortage of troops was compelling them to abandon the formidable 'Gothic Line' for more tenable positions further north, leaving only small rearguards to cover their retreat. So our patrols were relaxed affairs: strolls through chestnut-wooded hills and meadows, plucking red apples and drinking from ice-cold mountain streams, usually returning in time to change and drink a glass of vermouth before dinner. Until this happened.

I was leading a patrol that was wandering peacefully beside a stream in a very attractive Alpine valley when the peace was broken by two devastating explosions of black and orange just by my head. These sent me reeling and, after a moment, stumbling into the stream-bed. As I fell, I noticed with surprise that my tommy-gun was covered with blood from a wound in my head. I assumed that the explosions had been caused by grenades and the next move would be for a German ambush to move in with machine-pistols and either kill or take us prisoner. But nothing happened. Bleeding profusely I scrambled into the cover of the woods, expecting to be shot at any moment. My men had disappeared. But no one shot me. Everything was now quiet again. There seemed nothing to do but apply a field-dressing and find my way home, as eventually I did. There I found that my men had beaten me to it and told everyone that I had had my head blown off.

To this day I do not know what had happened. I found that I was peppered with nasty little pieces of metal, too harmless to have come from a mine. They were more consistent with a hand-grenade, but where was the hand that had thrown it? Perhaps it was some kind of booby-trap. Anyhow, it did me no serious damage, but after having given my report I felt cold and sick and dizzy, so Andrew sent me back.

My progress was then as follows:

1. stretcher across mountain-paths to a road a mile away, borne by six cursing stretcher-bearers
2. medical jeep (stretcher strapped across it) to regimental aid post, a thousand feet below
3. ambulance to Casualty Clearing Station (five miles) where I was given tea and sent on to
4. an advanced Dressing Station (four miles), where I was given anti-tetanus injections and morphia. Knowing that this was where you remained if you had little chance of surviving, I was very glad to get on to
5. the forward Dressing Station in a magnificent Tuscan palazzo, where they dressed my wounds again and sent me on to
6. a Field Hospital, where I was put to bed and slept the night.

Next morning, although a furious storm was raging, I was put on a plane and flown back to Naples.

All this indicated that the medical services had at that moment not much to do with their time rather than that there was very much wrong with me. But I was gazetted as wounded, the regimental lieutenant-colonel wrote my father a nice letter, and in due course I got a wound-stripe. But it was evidence not of gallantry but of culpable carelessness. The only consolation was that neither of my men was hurt.

In the Naples hospital they could do little for me except pick out the larger pieces of metal. (A few still remain and occasionally set off the security bleepers at airports.) In a room down the corridor Harold Macmillan, then British Minister with the High Command, was recovering from a throat infection. I peered at him round the door of his room: he looked cross and busy. Then I was sent back to Sorrento, which by this time I knew far too well. It rained; I knew no one, and I mooched around the hotel until they discharged me with a week's leave before I was due back at the battalion. The first person I saw at the IRTD was poor Andrew Cavendish, whose elder brother Billy Hartington had just been killed in France and who had been summoned home to preserve the Devonshire line. Extraordinary and inexcusable shreds of feudal privilege like this still remained – probably to avoid repeating the massacre of the aristocracy in the Great War – but nobody detested it more than its beneficiaries. Then I went on to spend the rest of my leave in Rome.

In Rome I was taken under the wing of Humphrey Brooke, an Old Wellingtonian and a close friend of Talboys, who was at the time a fine-arts officer with Allied Military Government and was later to become secretary to the Royal Academy. Thanks to him I had a whale of a time. I stayed at the Boston Hotel, the junior officers' leave hotel, and was very comfortable; no hot water and little electric light, but comfortable beds and good food. There was an entirely peacetime atmosphere. The rich Italians were the exact counterparts of the Guermantes set: blind to everything but their own comfort; passionately interested in minor distinctions of fashion and precedence; quite unconcerned with the war except as an intolerable inconvenience; and regarding the Allies simply as a source of extra rations and a bulwark against the communism which they believed would inevitably overwhelm the country as soon as we withdrew. The reaction whenever the conversation turned to the war was universal: '*Comme vous m'embétez, vous Anglais, avec cette espèce de guerre. Je déteste la guerre. Parlons d'autres choses.*'

The distinguished exception was the Doria family. They had been in hiding throughout the occupation with a price on their heads for helping Allied prisoners to escape. Now the Prince was mayor of Rome: an idealistic, old-fashioned liberal trying desperately to reconcile the warring elements in Italian politics. The daughter, who was very tall and Nordic and English – one pictured her in tweeds and pearls with two spaniels, of good county family – worked in a service club. The Princess herself, who was small and Scottish and fluttering and vague, ran the vast Palazzo with one servant, sat on innumerable relief committees, and yet had time to show stray officers like myself over the palace whenever they rang up.

The palace, of course, was sumptuous and packed with treasures of quite fabulous value. We unrolled the standard that flew at the masthead of the great Andrea Doria's galley in the fifteenth century. We saw the famous fourteenth-century battle tapestries. We gaped at the vast state apartments with their silk panels painted by Piranesi and the great gold and crimson curtains of appliqué shaved velvet ('all this is awfully hard to keep clean', the Princess fluttered anxiously); and we wandered in helpless awe round the picture gallery. 'That is a Titian, of course', she said, pointing to a canvas in a dark corner. 'He did a set of five for us. The others are in our house at Genoa. No they aren't. It's the Correggios at Genoa. The Titians are in Venice. I remember because we had to move the Veroneses and the Dosso Dossis to hang them properly. That is my husband's great-grandmother – such a badtempered woman, they say. It's either by Goya or Ingres, I can never remember which but I think it must be Goya, because he *is* rather unkind about the cast in her eye. No, there is nothing in there, only the secret room where we hid when the Germans came. And that room is all Breughels and that is mainly Masaccios. I am trying to recatalogue them, but it is all very muddling and I don't really know very much about it.' Eventually we collapsed, exhausted, in the one inhabitable room, and gratefully accepted a glass of marsala.

There was much, much else, and no one else to see it except Allied officers like me, who drove round the streets in horse-drawn *carozze*. Perhaps most remarkable of all was an exhibition arranged by Allied Military Government in Mussolini's state apartments in the Palazzo Venezia; some 50 master-pieces that had been collected from all over Italy and housed for protection in the Vatican. There was a Raphael from Milan, two Titians from Naples, the Bellini *Madonna of the Trees* and the Giorgione *Tempest* from Venice. Every single item was superb, and I visited it every day.

Finally I was taken to an audience with the Pope (Pius XII). This was not very impressive. There were too many people there who had come, like myself, out of curiosity rather than reverence. We all waited in the audience-chamber above the portico of St Peter's, all white and gold, and eventually the Holy Father was borne in on a litter half an hour late, preceded by half a dozen gorgeous dignitaries, some with ruffs and swords, some in diplomatic uniforms, and some wearing a peculiar kind of fireman's helmet. There was no music, only a kind of shuffling silence. The Pope blessed us in French and English with very great dignity, and then everyone who had not applied for a private audience flocked out chattering loudly. All very badly done, I complained in a letter home: there should have been music, and a better-marshalled procession.

After a week gorged with culture and rich food, I found my way back to the battalion. There everything had changed, and very much for the worse. It was now clear that we were condemned to another winter in the mountains. The Eighth Army was carrying out a flanking offensive through the flat terrain on the east coast, but we were still with Mark Clark's Fifth Army, which was trying to batter its way over the passes between Florence and Bologna. The Germans, as I have said, had withdrawn from their original 'Gothic Line' to more economical positions further north, thus shortening their lines of communication and forcing us to extend ours. Our own divisional line of advance now lay along Route 6620 from Florence via Prato up the mountains to Castiglione dei Pepoli, where I reported to our B Echelon. It was pouring with rain, and with the rain came mist, cold and mud. The battalion had changed back from khaki-drill into battledress, not a moment too soon. The winter campaign had begun.

5

Italy III: Florence to Trieste

By the end of September 1944 the Italian campaign had stalled. Even at my level we realized this. From the perspective of Grand Strategy it had now served its purpose: to pin down as many German forces as possible until the landings in Normandy had succeeded. This we had successfully done. Not only that, but all Soviet territory had been liberated and Russian troops were pouring into Eastern Europe. The hope that Allied forces in Italy might make a lightning thrust to reach Vienna before the Soviets may have been entertained by Alexander and his staff, but once we started fighting in the mountains north of Florence, few of us shared it. Oliver Leese may have believed that his Eighth Army would make better progress in the flatter territory on the east coast of the peninsula, but quickly found that the Germans were as skilful in the defence of rivers and canals as they were in mountains. It was clear that we were in for another winter campaign, and we found the prospect depressing.

I cannot believe that even at the height of an Italian spring Castiglione can look pleasant. The view northward down the valley towards Lombardy was impressive, but the town itself was a straggling collection of mean grey houses sprawled haphazardly across the hillside along a single main street. I certainly saw it at its worst, usually in rain or snow or in damp and icy mist that penetrated to every corner. The village was saturated with troops; civilians were crowded into two rooms of their houses, while gardens, fields and road verges were filled to the last inch with every sort of vehicle from every sort of unit. It was the headquarters of our division (Sixth South African Armoured) and all its heavy equipment was parked here, from light-aid detachments to boot-repair shops, mobile baths, dentists and casualty-clearing stations. Our own B Echelon contained the quartermaster's stores, an MT depot, and a ferocious drill-sergeant in charge of defaulters. I spent a couple of weeks with them until there was a vacancy for me in one of the companies. Our officers' mess was in a large house with no central heating, stone floors and not a single glazed window. But there was a bathroom with a boiler that actually worked and, even more unusual, a water-closet that worked as well: a rare luxury in a region where indoor sanitary arrangements, when they existed at all, usually consisted either of a hole in the floor with two foot-rests beside it, or a damp stone bench with a hole in the middle – both very smelly. Unsurprisingly I caught a heavy cold, which turned into flu, which brought on my seasonal malaria; so my return to the battalion was again delayed, until mid-November.

From Castiglione the road ran down the pass towards Bologna, turning at the village of Lagaro into the broad valley of the River Setta. After Lagaro the valley broadened out with hills dwindling on either side, until we were almost out of the mountains and in the suburbs of Bologna. But the valley was still dominated by the peak, directly ahead, of Monte Sole; and on Monte Sole, with a view straight up the valley and far behind our lines, sat the Germans. By the time we had closed up to their positions, they had mined and wired all approaches, dug themselves and their mortars well into the reverse slopes, and were ready to deal with anyone who might try to advance up the apron-like cauldron that offered the only possible approach to its summit.

Soon after Lagaro the road came under direct enemy observation, and we had to turn off along a muddy jeep-track laid with bouncing wire-netting, on to the railway-line that hugged the side of the valley and was thus in dead ground to the enemy. We had torn up the tracks and sleepers to make the line passable for motor transport, and a lively battle raged between the staff, who ordered us to preserve the rails and sleepers so that the line could be put into commission again later, and our guardsmen, who found that the creosote-soaked sleepers made perfect firewood. On the whole, the guardsmen, with the covert support of their officers, won hands-down.

Jeeps and trucks drove gingerly along the track, and troops stumbled angrily over the stones and mud, to the village of La Quercia, which nestled beneath a huge railway viaduct at the foot of the Sole massif. To a passenger gazing out of a first-class window on the Milan–Florence express or down from the viaduct carrying the Autostrada del Sole, La Quercia must look a delightful place, with its pink and white houses gathered round a tiny church and a stream. Our own reaction varied. When we came back from the forward positions on the slopes above, its houses seemed the height of luxury; but on returning from leave in Florence it seemed an appropriately depressing finish to the dreary journey through the mountains – bleak, cold and muddy. Overall, I retain pleasant impressions. The little church still retained its gimcrack finery. The houses were solidly built, with good big fireplaces, and though an occasional salvo of shells came over, the village was too closely tucked under the mountainside to come to much harm. Our companies were dug into positions on the hills above, while in the village itself the battalion command-post occupied a large upper room suitably furnished with marked maps, aerial photographs, telephones, operational orders, files, and above all, a nice warm fire. We felt secure enough there to make ourselves comfortable; so it was possible to enjoy a good dinner rounded off with Marsala or Strega and perhaps a cigar, before blacking our faces, taking our tommy-guns and creeping out on a reconnaissance or fighting patrol. The American unit that eventually relieved us was horrified at such sybaritic luxury.

Beyond La Quercia muddy tracks climbed the hillside between beech bushes and heather, and after an hour of scrambling and slipping we reached our forward positions. Peering through the narrow slits of observation-posts, we saw Sole about a mile away, its sharp peak flanked by the round summit of Monte Caprara, with Monte Abelle appearing behind to complete the triangle. Below these summits was the grey rubble of Caprara village and the large white farmhouse of San Martino. Below them a broad green slope swept into the valley on our left, dotted with ruined farms where the Germans had their own outposts. We learned this landscape by heart (60 years later I can still draw it from memory), scanned it through field-glasses, interpreted it on the map. One night, we thought, we would have to cross it under fire, clearing the houses, dodging the minefields and climbing the last 50 feet of solid rock.

Our company positions were dug into reverse slopes with little regard for tactical requirements: burrowed into the hillside, roofed with branches and old gas-capes, floored, if we were lucky, with duckboards. So long as we were dry and warm and the rations came up, and we knew what was going on and had as much sleep as we wanted, we were reasonably happy. The guardsmen, dishevelled and gigantic in their crumpled greatcoats and stocking-caps, seemed more content here, if the weather was fine, than in more comfortable billets further back. There were no inspections or parades. Sentry rosters were arranged amicably within the sections and carried on without fuss. For the rest of the time they contentedly slept, wrote letters, read the *Daily Mirror* and drank gallons of sweet tea. Our alarm-posts were on the ridge above, slit-trenches concealed among the trees and heather. These we occupied at dawn and dusk, steel-helmeted with weapons at the ready, feeling dramatic and a little apprehensive as we peered through the mists. I would inspect them during the night and return to my dug-out, lifting the blanket that curtained the entrance and slipping gratefully down into its warm, lamplit snugness. The mail would have come up on the mule-train with the evening meal: letters from home, toiletries and parcels of books. I shared the dug-out with my platoon sergeant and we gossiped happily until it was time to sort out our blankets, hurl our equipment into corners and make a warm, comfortable nest for the night.

Every hour or so we took it in turns to visit the sentries. At three in the morning it was hard to shake oneself out of a warm stupor, adjust wind-cheater and muffler and creep out into the icy night to slip round the frosty paths from section to section. The sentries would loom suddenly out of the dark: silent masses motionless in their trenches. I would stay with them for a little while, feeling the frosty twigs on the parapet slippery under my hands, listening to the wind and the night noises. Sometimes there was moonlight and a spectral panorama of mountains and valleys beneath the brilliant stars in the black sky. Shivering, in spite of several layers of clothes, I would go back to my warm, stuffy dug-out, prod Sergeant Hawkins into wakefulness, sink into the morass of blankets and sleep heavily for another two hours.

During this winter I had two adventures: one minor, the other major and rather horrible.

The first occurred almost as soon as I rejoined the battalion and had been put in charge of a platoon, not one single man of which I had ever seen before. A farm lay on a forward slope some way ahead of our main posi-tions. We occupied it only by night, returning by day to our positions on the reverse slope. The occupation and evacuation of this farm at dawn and dusk was always a slightly nervous ordeal: we could never be sure that the Germans had not got there before us. One morning, as we were preparing to leave after a long night's vigil, a shabby and terrified German suddenly appeared through the dawn mists and warned that an SS company was about to attack us. 'Us' now consisted of myself and a single section, the rest of the platoon having already left. I sent him back at the double with a guide to company headquarters, told the remaining section to stay where it was and to fire like hell if attacked, and went back to rally the rest of the platoon for an immediate counterattack. They had already taken off their kit, were brewing up and very resentful at being disturbed again. I sent them under the platoon sergeant to wait under the crest of the hill until I came up to take command. Meanwhile, I stayed at my command-post by a telephone that kept me in touch both with my forward section and with company headquarters. My company commander at the foot of the hill gave moral encouragement, but was not in a position to do more. The German deserter, he said, was a Czech, and had reported the German intention of seizing our position and using it as a base for an attack that night. Unfortunately for them, our company had occupied the exact position they had chosen for an observation-post, and of this they were unaware.

There was nothing to do but wait for their attack. I was now on my own. The morning was fresh and peaceful. The only fire I heard was a sub-machine-gun in the direction of the next platoon. Suddenly my heart gave a gigantic thump. Two large Germans had appeared in the clearing 20 yards away and stood looking at me.

Speechless with terror, I grabbed for my revolver and found it wasn't there. The Germans approached slowly, one carrying a sub-machine-gun. Then I realized that only one was a German. The man with the gun was a guardsman from the next platoon, whose camouflage smock was indistinguishable from the German pattern. The other, a hulking blond caricature of a brutal SS man, was his prisoner, and had been captured trying to set up a machine-gun post. Gibbering with relief, I sent them both back down the hill, giving the escort quite unnecessary advice not to take his finger off the trigger. Then my forward section rang to say that that the German attack had come in on the neighbouring platoon and been seen off without any difficulty. The enemy could not have been very serious about it, but the incident reminded me that there were real live Germans a few hundred yards away who could cause us a lot of trouble.

The other adventure was more disagreeable; so much so that I still find it painful to write about it.

Shortly before Christmas the battalion was ordered to mount the long-delayed assault on Monte Sole, and I was sent on a reconnaissance patrol to explore a possible start-line in front of the German positions. This involved approaching nearer the enemy-held positions than I – or anyone else for that matter – had yet attempted, but it was ground we had surveyed exhaustively by daylight, and I foresaw no major problems. I took with me an experienced young corporal with the encouraging name of Eager, a couple of guardsmen with a Bren, and one with a tommy-gun. I was given the usual candle-lit three-course dinner at battalion headquarters, declined coffee and liqueurs, and then set out up the dimly moonlit path.

At first all went well. The moon was bright enough for us to see where we were going. The ground fell away quite sharply in front of the German positions, so I was able to explore the little valley before them and make sure that there would be enough room for our companies to deploy and that the slope would not be too steep to assault. Having achieved our objective, we then set off for home.

By now a mist was falling and I became doubtful about the direction. The first indication that there was anything wrong came with a sharp explosion behind me. Grenade, I thought, but I was wrong. One of my guardsmen had trodden on a mine – a schu-mine, a devilish little contrivance that, being made of wood, was immune to normal detectors and simply blew a man's foot off. The poor man began screaming with pain. We quietened him as best we could and applied a tourniquet. There was no reaction from the Germans, so I ordered Corporal Eager and one man to help him back to a point on the road to which I could bring up stretcher-bearers. I set out at a fast pace with the other man, Guardsman Terry (not his real name), to collect them.

Somehow I went in the wrong direction. The mist was now thick. Believing that we were now well clear of the enemy positions, I doubled along with Terry close behind me. Ahead there loomed a hedge that looked familiar. We were perhaps ten yards away when there suddenly came, from behind it, the sound of voices.

This *was* fear – the sudden stop of the rhythm of breath and heartbeat, followed by agonized butterflies in the breast instead of lungs. I stopped. The voices stopped. Then came the challenge '*Halt! Wer da?*'

We got down, and all was still. After a little we began cautiously to crawl away; then cautiously stood up and began to walk. We had gone only a few steps before I felt a stinging blow in the back of my legs and heard again that villainous little explosion – this time just behind me. 'Are you all right, Terry?' I whispered. 'No, sir – it's got my foot.'

At once the German post opened fire. Fascinated, I watched the orange spurt of the machine-gun 15 yards ahead apparently firing straight at us. Pressed close to the ground, I heard the bullets swish overhead, firing as usual too high. Poor Terry began to scream in fear and pain, but the only answer was a flurry of grenades. This is the end, I thought. No good firing back; they are well dug in. I am in the open and in the middle of a minefield. I can't get Terry away – he is almost twice my size. Seriously I thought of surrendering, but that would have been stupid: I had been too well briefed about plans for our forthcoming attack, and they would get them out of me one way or another. I had to get back.

This is the hardest part to write. Deliberately, and fully aware of what I was doing, I left Terry and crawled away. The Germans were only yards away, I told myself; they would find him at daybreak and bring him in. I shouted at them that there was a British soldier here, *schwer verwundert*, but the only answer was a flurry of grenades.

Meanwhile, rifles had joined the machine-gun fire. I found that I had myself been lightly wounded in the legs by Terry's mine, and could only move with difficulty. Terrified of more mines, I crawled on all fours, feeling ahead among the tufted grass as I went. The mist was thick, and I had now lost all sense of direction. Just as I thought it safe enough to stand upright, the firing began again, this time from half a dozen directions. Evidently the German company commander had called down defensive fire, and now machine-guns were sweeping the ground where I lay. I thought of that warm, well-lit room at battalion headquarters with its blazing fire. It seemed the summit of all earthly desires. Pressed into a tiny hollow as the machine-guns rattled round me, I wondered whether I would ever see it again.

Eventually the firing stopped, and I crawled cautiously on. Eventually, forcing my way through briars and brambles, I found the right track and stumbled back as quickly as I could. My mind was not so much a turmoil as a series of quite distinct layers of feeling: a layer of relief, a layer of shame, a layer of anxiety and a layer almost of amusement at the absurd figure I was cutting – dirty, bramble-torn, distraught and peppered in the hams. I had learned a great deal – too much – about myself; not least that I did not begin to deserve a Military Cross. It is easy enough to be brave when the spotlight is on you and there is an appreciative audience. It is when you are alone that the real test comes.

Everyone at battalion headquarters was immensely kind. Corporal Eager and his party had, thank heavens, made it back. They had heard the firing and reported that Terry and I were probably dead. I offered rather unconvincingly to take a party back to find Terry, an offer which Colonel Billy Steele (who had succeeded Colonel George a couple of months before) very sensibly refused. The information I had brought back, such as it was, was considered very useful, or would have been if the attack had ever taken place. It did not, the weather being too bad. I was sent back for another brief spell in hospital and then returned to duty in time for Christmas celebrations. I put up a second wound-stripe, even more shamefully won than the first.

And Terry? Poor lad, he did not survive. Whether he bled to death before the Germans found him, or died in their care, I do not know. I know only that he is buried in the divisional cemetery at Castiglione, at the head of the valley with that wonderful view sweeping down beyond Lagaro. Years later I sought out his grave, and sat beside it for a long time, wondering what else I could have done. I still wonder. I know only that I should never have abandoned him as I did.

*   *   *

Another return visit was to be even more disquieting. Forty years later I was invited to lecture in the University of Bologna, and rented a car to explore the battlefield. I found Monte Sole to be nearer the city than I had ever realized, and was in La Quercia in half an hour. I left the car in the village and retraced the steps of my disastrous patrol. I found the location of the German post that had fired on us, and went on to the farm of San Martino. The interior was bare and burned out, and on the wall was a plaque in memory of a dozen or so civilians who had been massacred there by the Germans in the autumn of 1944. A little further on, at Caprara, a group of elderly men were gathered around another similar memorial. It appeared that the landscape we had watched for so long was the scene of one of the most notorious German atrocities in the whole of the Italian campaign. In retaliation for partisan activity in the region, the Germans had rounded up the inhabitants of all the villages on Monte Sole and either shot them or locked them in barns and burned them to death. Someone on our side must have known about it at the time, but at our level we did not have the faintest idea that this had happened, and it did not occur to anyone to tell us.

That evening my hosts had arranged for me to attend a banquet in Bologna to celebrate the liberation of the city 40 years earlier. Many of the other guests had been in the partisan movement. Hoping to be welcomed as a comrade in arms, I told them how and where I had spent the winter of 1944–45. The reaction was not what I had expected. An uneasy silence fell, and they rapidly changed the subject. Afterwards the situation was explained to me. In September 1944, believing that the end of the war was in sight, the Allied High Command had issued orders for the Italian partisans to unmask themselves and attack German communications throughout the north of Italy. They did so, including those on and around Monte Sole. The Germans reacted with predictable savagery. The Allied armies did not come to their help, and the partisan movement in North Italy was largely destroyed. It was still believed – and especially in Bologna, where the communists had governed the city ever since the war – that this had been deliberately planned by the Allies in order to weaken the communist movement, much as the Soviets had encouraged the people of Warsaw to rise and then sat by while the Germans exterminated them. When I protested to my hosts that this was an outrageous explanation and that there was nothing we could have done, they smiled politely. But I was left wondering, as I wondered about poor Terry, was there really *nothing* that we could have done to help? Were there no risks that our huge, cumbrous armies with their vast supply-lines might have taken if we had known what was going on? – and *someone* must have known what was going on. Probably not: but ever since then I have been sparing of criticism of the Soviet armies for their halt before Warsaw.

∗   ∗   ∗

Snow came at Christmas and mercifully closed down the battlefield. Leave to Florence – four hours' drive away – became more frequent. There was not much to see there. The museums were closed, the churches had bricked up their treasures, the bridges were rubble in the yellow Arno, while between the Piazza della Signoria and the Ponte Vecchio there were now vast piles of rubble through which the workers from the south bank had beaten a dusty path. All the hotels had been taken over by the Allied forces, who were now a very miscellaneous lot: not only British and American but also Greek, Brazilian, South African, Indian and 'free' Italian. ENSA had appropriated the cinemas. The narrow streets were made hideous by notices directing the hapless to transit hotels, canteens, cinemas, officers' shops, and the myriad military formations, depots and headquarters that could be found in and around the city. The final touch of gloom was provided by lurid notices warning of the dangers of VD. The weather was cold and dark. Next spring, when the flowers came out on the hills and the troops left to stream north through the broken front, Florence awoke again with some of its magic; but in winter, with its cold streets full of pale civilians and loitering troops, with the ex-fascists drinking with Allied officers at Lelands Bar, with its cinemas and military convoys and glittering trinket shops, this hardly seemed the city of Lorenzo the Magnificent.

But I was, as usual, immensely lucky. Colonel George Burns had before the war been a friend of Mrs Keppel, the *belle amie* of King Edward VII; and Mrs Keppel had made available to him, for the use of Coldstream officers, the Villa del Ombrellino, the house that she owned on the left bank of the Arno. Its terrace commanded a superb view over the city. Its opulent interior was poorly warmed by smoky lignite fires, and the garden, terraced, cypressed, statued, fountained, was bleak, but in six months' time it would rival the wildest musical-comedy set with its roses and heartrending nightingales. Old photograph-albums recorded an annual succession of house-parties sprinkled with royalty or near-royalty. The luxurious bed-rooms, the wildly vulgar but comfortable sitting-rooms, the pillared hall, the torch-bearing negro statues, the chinoiserie, must have provided the perfect setting for the cloche-hatted, white-flannelled groups in the photographs. Mrs Keppel's butler remained and, assisted by a sergeant and a few guardsmen, ministered to the stream of tired, pleasure-seeking officers who bumped wearily down from the mountains for a few days' leave out of battle. One night they would be lying muddy and cold in a dug-out or stumbling along an icy stream on a reconnaissance patrol, listening fearfully for a change in the note of the German machine-guns. The next they slid ecstatically between linen sheets to be woken with a breakfast of fried spam and the *Eighth Army News*. (Somehow it was always fried spam and fried potatoes, and burnt toast and lukewarm tea, but nobody felt like com-plaining.) The bathrooms were magnificent but out of order: hot water had to be brought up and the lavatories flushed from enormous buckets. The officers dressed carefully. Their trousers had knife-edge creases, their belts gleamed snowy-white, their designations and badges of rank shone with scarlet and gold on newly pressed battledress blouses, Their shoes were brown mirrors. At length, toilet completed, they descended in snowy duffle-coats into the city to begin the day with a glass of sticky, expensive ver-mouth at Lelands', by the ruins of the Ponte Trinita.

Sometimes when one of our battalions was out of the line they would give a dance. Bottles of wine and plates of substantial sandwiches filled the dining-room. In the hall an Italian band pounded out the latest dance music. Girls and their mothers were brought up from the city, rather inelegantly, in the backs of 15-cwt trucks. All, of course, came from very good families, both anglophile and anglophone: Capponi, Gaetani, Corsini, Ricasoli, names redolent of centuries of Florentine history, if a little debased by the nicknames – Poppy, Fluffy, Baby, Dolly – bestowed on all their females, irrespective of age. The mothers ate hard, complained of the atrocity of life under the Germans and the problems of life under the Allies, and watched their daughters with sharp eyes. The daughters were nubile and for the most part very pretty. The officers flirted happily and the band played on till 3 a.m.

The end of leave at the villa was like going back to school. One woke in the morning with the familiar sense of impending doom, spent the morning packing, ate lunch with a mockery of an appetite. The gardens, dank beneath a depressing mist, deepened the melancholy. Then the truck was at the door, the baggage in the truck, the villa left behind. The road, drearily familiar, crossed the Arno, swung left down the valley and ran through the dyked plain to Prato which guarded the approach to one of the main Apennine passes. Up this pass we went, jolting horribly over a road whose surface had been almost worn away by rain and military traffic. It curved and doubled and twisted up the mountains, while guns, tanks, carriers, jeeps, half-tracks, mobile workshops and supply-lorries of every kind ground up and down it, always on the verge of blocking it but never quite doing so. When there was ice on the surface, the situation ceased to be boring, but usually one bumped about helplessly in a state of uncomfortable ennui through villages crammed with troops, past scrawled formation-signs or warnings of mines and craters; on upward, dozing or daydreaming, to the top of the pass and just beyond it, Castiglione dei Pepoli. One expected the school porter to be there when we arrived, looking reproachfully at his watch.

When spring came I fell in love; not with one of the girls I danced with at the Ombrellino but with a charming boy called Franco Corsi. Franco was an art student of good family who spoke perfect English. He had joined the partisans when the Allies reached Chianti, and been co-opted as a guide and interpreter by the Scots Guards. Once we occupied the city, he was in general demand. He seemed to know everyone worth knowing, socially, artistically and intellectually. Dicky Buckle brought him to dinner one evening at the Ombrellino. The gardens were moonlit, the scent of roses and wisteria was overwhelming, the nightingales were singing their hearts out, and I experienced the famous 'thunderclap'. Franco was sympathetic. He escorted me round the city, showing me palazzi and museums that were still closed to the public. I responded by driving him around the Chianti hills to visit his relations. We held hands, but that was as far as it got.

Many years later I learned his middle name: Zeffirelli. When Franco came to London for his first season at Covent Garden, Dicky reintroduced us. Franco flung his arms round me: '*Peter!*' he cried ecstatically. Clearly, I was not the only British officer who had been kind to him. He was later to give his own account of his adventures in his film *Tea with Mussolini*. I do not figure in it; perhaps just as well.

*   *   *

When spring came we left the mountains and concentrated with all the other Guards battalions in Italy at Spoleto, then still an unspoiled hill-town, to be reshuffled for the final phase of the war. The Third Battalion went home, taking all the old sweats with it. As a formation it had been overseas for eight years, though few of its surviving members can have served with it for more than two of them. The rest of us were decanted into the Second Battalion, a convivial unit but one that carried with it none of the now rather shop-worn glamour of the desert. Fly-whisks, Hebron coats and desert-boots disappeared. We were transferred back to the Eighth Army, now commanded by an exceedingly able general, Dick McCreery. (Oliver Leese had been transferred to the Far East, where he rapidly came unstuck.) During the winter, the Eighth Army had been able to make as little progress along the Adriatic coast as the Fifth had through the mountains, but now, under fresh commanders, it was preparing to mount a *coup de grâce*. While the staff officers did their stuff, we relaxed, greeted old friends and made new ones. Dicky and I mounted a slightly louche revue in the delicious little opera house that one day was to become the focus of the Spoleto festival. Then I was set on a trajectory of my own.

A few weeks earlier I had been appointed 'education officer' to the battalion, which had meant nothing when we were in the line and little out of it. I gave an occasional lecture on current affairs, on the basis of the vast quantities of bumf with which I was deluged by the Army Education Corps. But once the war was over this was to be a serious business. The War Office, under the guidance of an extraordinarily enlightened Adjutant-General, Sir Ronald Adam, realized that, however skilfully it was managed, the demobilization of the troops would take a long time, and meanwhile something must be done to occupy them. Resettlement courses should be provided to train them for new skills; and, as responsible citizens, they should be prepared to think seriously about the political, social and international problems that would confront them as voters. It was subsequently alleged that the landslide victory of the Labour Party in the postwar election was due to the subversive influence of the Army Education Corps. It is true that the AEC was recruited very largely from secondary-school teachers who did incline to the Left, but I doubt whether they had much influence on tough young squaddies who only wanted to go home and get on with their lives. Further, however great our admiration for Winston Churchill, few of us saw any reason to be grateful to the Conservative Party for its management of national affairs during the 1930s.

Anyhow, I was sent from Spoleto on a course run by the AEC at the University for Foreigners in Perugia. Like Spoleto, Perugia was a completely unspoiled hill-town, surrounded by a valley now bursting with spring. A few miles away was Assisi, still quiet and tourist-free. It was Easter, and the church bells sounded from every village within miles. My companions on the course were almost all university graduates and highly *simpatico*. We were taught how to organize courses, how to produce plays, how to mobilize musical talent, and above all how to *lecture* – something that no one, in the course of what was to be a long and varied academic career, ever thought fit to teach me. Yes, we were taught about the Beveridge Report and other plans for postwar Britain, and encouraged to regard them as Good Things, as we tended to do anyway. We were told about the United Nations, at that moment being set up in San Francisco. We were encouraged to debate postwar occupation policy in Germany. In other words, we were treated as intelligent adults with minds of our own. It was a refreshing change after very nearly three years of simply being told what to do and having to get on with it.

When I returned to Spoleto the re-formed battalion had already left for the east coast. I had been allotted to a reserve company which was to wait until it was needed at Fano, a boring town on a bleak stretch of the Adriatic coast but with a pleasant hilly hinterland in which it was, at that time of year, a pleasure to train. We did not have to wait long. The Allied offensive began early in April and, after some tough fighting, German resistance crumbled. Our company was called forward, but by the time we arrived at our destination the battalion was 20 miles ahead and the Germans in full retreat. For the next week the battalion chased the Germans and we chased the battalion. We learned over the radio that Hitler had committed suicide and that the war was over. Whenever we stopped we were surrounded by crowds of enthusiastic partisans, whose *feux de joie* created the only serious hazard. Much of the chase I did on the pillion of a motorcycle, rushing past the crowds and the flags and the burned-out German vehicles, zigzagging through enormous convoys of enormous trucks, waving indiscriminately at civilians, partisans, British troops, Italian liberated forces who perched on trucks waving enormous flags, even at dazed Germans left behind by the side of the road. In the fields north of the Po, vast herds of horses grazed peacefully, abandoned by the Germans who had withdrawn with all their motor-transport into the hills.

We eventually caught up with the battalion in Gorizia, near the Austrian border. There I discovered that the speed of our advance had been dictated by the desire not only to catch the Germans but also to reach Trieste before the Yugoslav partisans. The partisans, whom hitherto we had good reason to consider as allies, regarded as spoils of war the territory at the head of the Adriatic which had a largely Slovene population and had been acquired by Italy from the Austro-Hungarian Empire only after the First World War. The Allies recognized that the territory was disputed but believed that its destiny should be settled by plebiscite. Allied generals were concerned mainly with safeguarding their lines of communication into Austria. Their political masters were anxious to prevent further territory slipping under communist control. The Allied armies, led by the New Zealand Division, had beaten the Yugoslavs into Trieste by a whisker, but the partisans controlled the routes northward up the Isonzo valley. A temporary agreement had been reached by which the Eighth Army could use those routes and occupy the key points that controlled them, including Gorizia, but the Yugoslavs continued to exercise political control of the region.

I thus found, when I rejoined the battalion, that rejoicing at the end of the war was mixed with frustration at our present predicament and apprehension about the future. The population of Gorizia itself, as of all the towns in the region, was predominately Italian, and under Mussolini the treatment of the largely Slovene rural population had been brutal. The attitude of the partisan authorities was thus dictated partly by revenge, and partly by a desire to reduce the number of Italian voters before any plebiscite was held, and they seemed to be targeting members of the professional classes on whom most of our officers were billeted. As I wrote home unhappily:

Our instructions are all costs, for obvious reasons of *haute politique*, to avoid a clash with the partisans, which means that we sit still with our hands tied and are unable to interfere with what is going on. And what is going on is not very nice. The Yugoslavs are in complete control and are maintaining something in the nature of a reign of terror. Any Italian is liable to be denounced as a fascist and dragged off to a concentration camp. At night bands of partisans go round with proscription lists, getting their victims out of bed and dragging them off. This we watch in frustration but have to stand helplessly by, even when, as happened last night, partisans force their way into an officer's billet and carry off his landlord. To hear the partisan patrols clattering through the empty streets at night and stopping at a house a few doors away is to know how much 'freedom from fear' would mean to Europe if only we could guarantee it. We are besieged by Italians every day, stopped in the street by wretched little men with wives and children hanging behind them. Crowds clustering desperately around our barrack gates wanting protection or passage back into Italy proper, neither of which we can give them. We have to carry weapons because the partisans do as well, and the guardsmen are not allowed to walk out. All shops, cafés and cinemas are closed by order of the Yugoslav 'Committee of Liberation'. Every morning there are fresh decrees plastered on the walls, condemning the Archbishop to exile for activities 'contrary to the public interest', requisitioning all wirelesses or auto-mobiles, or forbidding the propagation or reception of news or literature which has not been censored by the political commissars. And we stand by and can do nothing.

Such was my introduction to the postwar world.

We did our best to maintain friendly relations with the partisans by reciprocal hospitality – what became known later in the Cold War as 'cocktail-party warfare'. In this form of unarmed combat the partisans won hands-down. Our only weapons consisted of genteel receptions between six and nine in the evening at which we stood around drinking bad gin, eating canapés and making stilted conversation usually in bad French. The Yugoslav parties began at three in the afternoon and sometimes went on for 12 hours: sit-down banquets at which they served sucking-pig and *slivovitz*, and proposed endless toasts – *Zvl Tito!*, *Zvl Churchill!*, *Smrt Fascismo!*, *Slobodu Narodnu!* We found it prudent to take our soldier-servants to these affairs, to stand behind our chairs and shake us awake when it was our turn to propose a toast, and ensure that we got home safely. I went to only one of these and was ill for days afterwards. The mere thought of *slivovitz* still makes me feel sick.

Eventually a *modus vivendi* was found, and the partisans withdrew behind a line that roughly followed the Isonzo river. The bridge over the river was guarded on our side by a magnificent turbanned Sikh with bayonet fixed, his equipment burnished a blinding white, his brass gleaming: the very embodiment of the British Raj. At the other end lounged a grim little old lady with a red star in her crumpled uniform cap, munition-belt slung over her shoulders, handling a sub-machine-gun with the casual confidence of someone who knew exactly how to use it. If it ever came to a showdown, I knew which side my money would be on.

In this unpromising environment I had to get the battalion education programme under way. The senior officers in the battalion disappeared on leave to Austria, or even England, and left me to get on with it. I was upgraded to captain again and allotted an office staff of a sergeant and a couple of clerks. The Army Education Corps provided a list of subjects ranging from agriculture and bricklaying through woodwork to zoology, with instructions on how to teach them: some by correspondence courses; some at central campuses where one applied for vacancies; some by recruiting local talent within the battalion. Everyone was surprisingly cooperative. Graduate officers offered to teach languages or mathematics; those from landed families, agriculture. Technically literate NCOs offered courses on electricity and mechanics. Deluged with informative pamphlets sent out by my thoughtful parents, I offered a course on 'problems of the postwar world', some of which we were already experiencing first-hand. I was negotiating with the Yugoslav authorities for the use of an abandoned school building when the political situation suddenly worsened. We moved back from Gorizia into Italy proper, and then forward again to operational positions in a stinking little village in the hills beyond the Isonzo, whose name I now forget and which I have never since been able to find on a map.

There we remained for six weeks, and my fine plans dwindled to a few lectures given in the open air. Our attention was anyhow dominated by the general election. My long-suffering parents sent me the literature pumped out by all three major parties, which we presented to the guardsmen as dispassionately as we could. The level of interest was high. Almost all our audience consisted of national servicemen who were looking forward to imminent demobilization and were understandably concerned about what would happen to them once they got home. Colonel Billy Steele, a calm sensible man, agreed to take the chair for a debate attended by the entire battalion. A senior officer spoke for the Conservatives, shrewdly down-playing domestic politics and emphasizing the need to keep Churchill in power to help shape the postwar world. I could find no officer in the battalion prepared to speak for Labour, so had to import an earnest Wykehamist from the Scots Guards who was unfortunately a hopeless speaker. I myself spoke eloquently on behalf of the Liberals. Then there was a silence. Colonel Billy invited contributions from the floor, and there continued to be silence. Then a young sergeant got up. 'This is all very well', he said, 'But the likes of us – we're all Labour, aren't we? So we'll vote Labour!' There was a deep growl of agreement. That was the end of the debate, and the beginning of my own political education.

We could occasionally escape to attend open-air opera at Gradisca or bathe – either on the crowded beaches of Grado or, greatly daring, off the rocks below corps headquarters at Maximilian's fairy-tale castle of Miramar. There I swam out for solitude to a raft that proved to be already occupied by the Army Commander. He smiled kindly, but since he was, like me, stark naked, I felt it tactful to swim back again.

By the beginning of August the political situation had quietened down sufficiently for us to move into Trieste. Before that happened we learned of the dropping of the atomic bombs on Hiroshima and Nagasaki and the end of the war in the Far East. My reaction was entirely selfish. We had been warned that at least one Guards Brigade had been earmarked for the Far East, and there was a strong possibility that it might be ours. For me – and indeed all of us – the elimination of that possibility was all that mattered. The number of Japanese civilians killed by the bomb, or how they died, was irrelevant. This reaction determined my attitude to the controversy that was to rage for the rest of the century. But I still believe that, however one looks at it, the war was shortened by the dropping of the bombs, and that more lives (including those of Japanese civilians) were in fact saved than were lost as a result of their use. Further, I believe that it was the shock of their use, and the realization of how even worse would be war fought with thermo-nuclear weapons, that preserved peace between the superpowers for half a century to come.

All that was to be for the future. Our immediate concern was the enormous improvement in our conditions once we moved into Trieste. We were stationed, together with the Second Battalion of the Scots Guards, in a large modern barracks overlooking the town, with an enormous square that made our drill-sergeants drool with delight. My third star had arrived just in time to rescue me from the ordeal by drill that I had endured now for eight years, ever since joining the OTC at Wellington. I was given spacious offices for the educational programme and encouraged to take up the ambitious plans I had suspended when we left Gorizia, though the increasing pace of demobilization made their implementation a great deal more complicated. The presence in the barracks of the Scots Guards, a regiment almost as civilized as my own, meant that I could team up again with Dicky Buckle, who had somehow acquired an apartment in downtown Trieste and invited me to share it, which I very happily did.

In return, I invited Dicky to join me on ten days' leave spent touring Northern Italy: Padua, Vicenza, Verona, Milan, Como, Tremezzo (where we were shown, with great relish, the spot where Mussolini had been captured a month earlier before being taken with his mistress back to Milan and shot), Stresa (Dicky, of course, had an introduction to the Contessa Borromeo who showed us the gardens on the Borromean Islands), Milan, Pavia, Piacenza, Cremona, Mantua and Venice. Apart from Milan, we had these places virtually to ourselves: the military had whisked through them, the tourists had not yet arrived, the natives were friendly and Dicky knew exactly what to see.

It was in the course of that sightseeing that something very remarkable happened. One afternoon we were in a gondola making a leisurely crossing to the Lido, and Dicky was ruminating on his postwar plans. He intended, he said, to revive the little magazine on ballet that he had started up before the war. Would I, he asked, like to join him as co-editor?

Now, I knew quite well that whatever other activities might occupy my life, editing a ballet magazine would not be one of them. But the suggestion opened my eyes. For the past ten years – indeed, ever since emerging from childhood – I had lived under the shadow of war; and although I had not assumed that I would necessarily be killed in it, I had never thought very seriously what I would do afterwards. To make postwar plans seemed a waste of time. But suddenly, half way to the Lido, I experienced a kind of epiphany. It was as if until then my life had been spent, without my realizing it, under a sky of monotonous grey. Now the skies suddenly cleared. The world was bathed in sunlight. I was going to have a life after all.

PART 2

Professor

6

Peacetime

My new life began almost at once.

A few days after my epiphany in Venice, I was recalled to the United Kingdom to be demobilized, under a wonderfully humane provision for those whose higher education had been interrupted by military service. An overnight train took us to Milan, where the dark-blue coaches of the *Société Internationale des Wagons lits et des Grandes Expresses Européennes*, familiar from so many prewar holidays, were waiting to take us home. The continent had been devastated; the Germans were still digging themselves out of the ruins of their cities; nine million 'displaced persons' were homeless after the most terrible upheaval Europe had known since the Thirty Years' War; yet for me it was as if nothing had happened since that infinitely distant September six years earlier, when the same coaches had whisked us back from the Riviera. Nothing on the journey indicated that anything had changed since then: neither the prosperous Swiss towns along the shore of the Lake of Geneva so familiar from childhood – Montreux, Territet, Villeneuve, Chillon – nor the flat, harvested fields of northern France, nor the white cliffs of Dover which I greeted from the deck of the same vessel, the *Invicta*, as I had in 1939. Victoria Station was the same, as was the taxi journey to Ennismore Gardens, where my mother, *soignée* as ever in black twinset and pearls, was just sallying forth to the hairdressers as she had done for 20 years past. It says much about her that although we had not seen one another for over two years she did not cancel the appointment, and about me that I never for one moment expected her to do so.

I had only a few days before demobilization to swank about London in uniform and show off my nice new medals. I had a studio photograph taken that shows a young officer moustachioed, bemedalled and gloved, very pleased with himself but still immature, unmarked by serious responsibility or suffering. In spite of my brief front-line service, my war had been as protected as my childhood. 'Captain M.E. Howard, MC' sounded and looked good and it was a persona that I was reluctant to shake off. But it wasn't me, and I knew that it wasn't me.

Still, the uniform had to go, and with it the gorgeous black hat that I had barely had a chance to wear. I went back to Pirbright, where I had once learned to be an officer, to be turned back into a civilian. I was equipped with discharge papers and a serviceable set of 'civvies': tweed jacket, grey flannel trousers, shoes, shirt, raincoat and green pork-pie hat. Nothing became the army like the efficiency with which it organized my leaving of it. As I said goodbye, I realized to my astonishment that I had acquired not only respect but also affection for an organization that had looked after me, on the whole so well, for the past three years.

And so back to Oxford, an undergraduate again within three weeks of leaving Trieste. The dons welcomed me kindly and gave me a magnificent set of rooms in Tom Quad that I shared with a quiet Welshman, John Maddox – later Sir John, editor of *Nature* and the only person who has ever been able to explain complex science intelligibly to laymen like myself. We each had our own sitting-room and led our own lives, and as I settled in on that first evening, I felt a weight almost literally being lifted from my shoulders. I was now responsible for no one but myself, for no life but my own. I would get no more guardsmen killed. One day perhaps I might once more have the kind of responsibilities that had been thrust on me at the age of 20, but not just yet. I could be young again.

But I did not feel young. I felt old, bewildered and lonely. Humphrey had gone, and with him my boyhood and my innocence. Other friends had returned who, like me, hoped for an academic career; in particular Patrick Gardiner, who was to transform himself from a historian into a notable philosopher, and Julian Brown, later to be a colleague as Professor of Paleography at King's College, for long my closest friend. There were others from an even more remote past. Derek Mond, alas, had been killed, but an even more memorable figure from Abinger days had appeared in the bulky shape of Edward Boyle. Edward, who had spent the war at Bletchley Park, was now very large and very serious, his eyes already fixed on the political heights. He had entirely put aside childish things, and apart from politics had now, so far as I could see, only three topics of conversation: the philosophy of R.G. Collingwood, the economic theories of Maynard Keynes and Victorian church music. It was remarkable how any conversation, whatever its starting-point, ended up with a learned monologue on one of these topics. It was not really enough. Our old intimacy was not renewed.

I made new friends, for the most part gentle, frivolous creatures who were more concerned with getting the war out of their systems than with getting on with their careers. Their company was seductively congenial. Oxford was bleak: full of schoolboys and serious married ex-servicemen. There was even less to eat and drink than there had been during the war; so it was pleasant to relax to the nostalgic strains of Charles Trenet, Edith Piaf or Jean Sablon. I became gently dissipated in the literal sense of the word; not drinking too much, as there was little to drink, not taking drugs (which were unheard of), not even sleeping around as I was still desperately shy with both sexes, but letting my energies trickle away doing nothing in particular. Music was still there. I could not get a note out of my oboe after two years' lack of practice, so that had to go, but I could still sing. I rejoined the Bach Choir in time to perform in *The Dream of Gerontius*, with Kathleen Ferrier singing the Angel; a voice the very memory of which still brings tears to my eyes. After leaving Oxford I joined the London Choral Society and sang in Fauré's *Requiem*, but the discipline of getting to St Pancras Town Hall every Wednesday evening was too much for me, so that also faded away. All that was left was the piano, and that would survive into my seventies.

For a while Oxford life revolved round an amiable young man, tall, thin and spectacled, named Adrian Earle, in whose Oriel Street rooms there was always something to drink and someone agreeable to talk to. Adrian was a consciously old-style Oxford 'character' allegedly researching the *fin de siècle* poet Lionel Johnson. In his company one caught a faint and self-conscious whiff of the Oxford portrayed in Evelyn Waugh's new novel *Brideshead Revisited* – an Oxford infinitely distant from the drab world in which we now lived. I am not sure that he did not have a teddy-bear. Unfortunately, charming as he was, Adrian was immoral to the point of psychopathy. His total lack of respect for *meum* and *tuum* would one day land him in jail, when he disappeared from all our lives, but I was grateful for his hospitality and still am. Together we founded a society, the Palatine Club, consisting of the ten most intelligent men and the ten most beautiful girls that we knew. We persuaded, among others, John Betjeman, Raymond Mortimer, Elizabeth Bowen and Harold Nicolson to come and talk to us and drink claret by candlelight. Firmly we turned our backs on the austerity of Mr Attlee's England and the chaotic world beyond its shores.

I did not ignore the things of the mind. Under the guidance of Edward Boyle I tried to read Maynard Keynes, while Patrick and Julian, who were throughout my life to be my good angels, introduced me to Karl Popper. Between them they – especially Popper – exorcized any inclination to Marxism I might have developed, which was anyhow unlikely. There was no longer much of it about. The Union was dominated by the humane socialism of Tony Crosland, a dazzlingly handsome young officer back from the wars. Another boyish ex-RAF officer, Anthony Wedgwood Benn (as he still allowed himself to be called), expounded a gentle old-world radicalism that gave no hint of his future as Tony Benn, the John Lilburne of our time. I read the fashionable gurus, Gilbert Ryle and Freddie Ayer, whose dry commonsensical philosophy suited the mood of our profoundly unromantic generation. From beyond the water came news of Sartre, Heidegger and Kierkegaard, philosophers of a defeat we had not experienced and a despair that we did not feel. Uncertain as the future might appear, and drab as the present certainly was, as the austerity of national poverty tightened its grip, we were glad to be alive at all in a world where many of the familiar landmarks still remained. We talked about *Angst*, especially when clever men from Balliol like Richard Wollheim, Peter Heyworth and Francis King were around, but we didn't feel any; any, that is, beyond the nagging anxiety of youth: would we, in the jargon of the time, 'make it'?

As for history, I dutifully went to tutorials and wrote my essays. The Final Honours School had been divided into two parts for undergraduates doing national service. The first part I had taken in summer 1942 and been awarded a first, which gave me a totally undeserved reputation for brilliance. It was agreed that I should sit the second part in Michaelmas 1946, which gave me four terms and one long vacation to prepare for it. That would have been enough if I had worked at it, but I did not. Nor was I pushed by my tutors. Christ Church was anyhow far too gentlemanly a college to make its undergraduates work any harder than they felt inclined, and my tutors, J.C. Masterman and Hugh Trevor-Roper, after six years in secret intelligence, must have found it even harder than I did to readjust to the humdrum routines of academic life. In any case, I was being urged by Keith Feiling, who had just been elected to the Chichele Chair of Modern History at All Souls in succession to the octogenarian Charles Oman ('about time too', he grumbled when we congratulated him), to sit for the All Souls Prize Fellowship in the autumn of 1946. Other friends already there: Raymond Carr, a raffish figure from my first incarnation at Christ Church who had spent the war teaching at Wellington, and John Sparrow whom I had met in the Coldstream, and of whom more hereafter, were both encouraging. So I spent a long wet summer partly holidaying with my parents in Donegal and partly on a hilariously disastrous reading-party in Co. Wicklow, 'reading for All Souls': ranging widely over history and philosophy to equip myself for that formidably eclectic examination, rather than focusing (as I should have done) on the English history papers for finals.

Further, in Michaelmas 1946 came a temptation I could not resist. Four centuries earlier, in 1546, Henry VIII had founded, or rather re-founded Christ Church, and the event was to be celebrated by a production of Shakespeare's *Henry VIII* in Christ Church Hall. Would I, the producer asked, play Wolsey? It was an invitation that no serious scholar in his finals term should have even contemplated accepting, but I found it impossible to say no. The prospect of sweeping around in cardinal's robes and proclaiming a long farewell to all my greatness in Wolsey's own hall was too good to miss. I accepted and have never regretted it. I was terrific. My performance attracted the plaudits even of Kenneth Tynan, a skeletal young man whose appearance among us in a purple suit and golden shirt showed that Oxford was getting back to abnormal again. Even if the rest of my life were to be passed in drab anonymity, I told myself, this glorious hour would have made it worthwhile.

My tutors were kind. They warned me that it was unwise, and so it was. I had sat for All Souls at the beginning of the term. The papers were enjoyable and as I wrote them Herkomer's cheerful portrait of Sir William Anson beamed down on me with a confidential twinkle as if to assure me that all would ultimately be well. He was right: ultimately it was. But like hundreds of candidates before me and since, I went to All Souls lodge on that fateful Saturday in early November and saw three unknown names on the list. I had failed.

Christ Church still had enough confidence in me to invite me to submit myself for interview for a studentship (i.e. fellowship) in succession to Masterman, who had just been elected Provost of his old college Worcester, but they wisely chose a far more precise and dedicated scholar, Charles Stuart. A few weeks later, after no more than a scrambled fortnight of revision, I sat my finals. My answers were so brief and mediocre that I was lucky to scrape a place in the then undivided second class.

A long farewell to all my greatness. The news came through in the middle of the Christmas vacation when I was on a skiing holiday in Switzerland. I returned to a cold, grey London wondering what on earth I should do next. My Oxford mentors were still supportive: Masterman and Trevor-Roper wrote kind letters and I was elected a member of Christ Church Senior Common Room – more, I suspect, on the strength of Wolsey than anything else. I could have gone back to read for a higher degree, but some instinct warned me that I had been at Oxford for long enough, and when I returned to visit my friends, the place was so bleak and cold in the horrible winter of 1946–47 that I was glad to get away. In fact, of course, my failure was the best thing that could have happened to me. Had I remained at Oxford with a fellowship, I would have led a dull, useful, comfortable life, not written a line, and never been heard of beyond the confines of my college. At that time this was all that I asked of life. The gods, sensible people that they are, decreed otherwise.

*   *   *

I now entered on an unhappy and troubled period before fortune began to favour me again. Early triumphs had given me exaggerated expectations of what I might achieve, without providing the hard discipline needed for real success. I had acquired a wide range of tastes and interests, not all of them good for me but all of which I tried to gratify. For a time it seemed as if early promise was to be followed by mediocre if any achievement, and it was only through astonishing good luck that it was not.

Part of the trouble was to do with health, and part with sex. The malaria that I had contracted at Salerno recurred at least twice a year, albeit with diminishing intensity, throughout my twenties, sapping my vitality. As for sex, it was now quite clear to me, as it had probably been to everyone who knew me for a long time past, that I was 'not the marrying kind'. In the endemic homoeroticism of a single-sex school I was one in a crowd. At an Oxford where girls were still rare it was still an acceptable lifestyle. But in the great world outside it was problematic, to put it mildly. After a particularly squalid episode I went for advice to our vicar, Bryan Green, who was already making Holy Trinity Brompton a centre of evangelism. He listened sympathetically and sent me to a Harley Street consultant.

In view of the thoroughly unprofessional advice that he gave me, I shall withhold the name of that admirable man. I was his last appointment on a wet winter evening, and he was clearly very tired. As I was ushered into his consulting-room the telephone rang. 'I said, no more calls', he snapped into it; 'Oh, all right.' He then he listened as a hysterical female voice battered his ear for five minutes. Eventually he pacified her, replaced the phone and turned to me. 'And what', he asked wearily, 'is the trouble with you?' I told him. 'And what', he asked, his voice cracking with impatience, 'makes you think that there is anything wrong with *that*?'

So far as I was concerned, that brief question had already earned him his five guineas. Seldom has money been better spent. But, he listened patiently as I unpacked my woes, asked some highly embarrassing questions and took plentiful notes. Eventually he said, 'All right. Now look. There are various things we could try. Aversion-therapy is one, but I wouldn't advise it. Another possibility is a course of analysis, and I know a good man. But it could take years, would certainly cost a great deal, you would have to abstain from any sexual activity while it was going on, and there is absolutely no guarantee that it would work. Frankly I shouldn't worry. There are a lot of people around like you, more than you probably realize, some of them very distinguished. They seem to manage their lives quite successfully. You seem an intelligent and balanced young man, so I don't see why you shouldn't.'

Bless him: he was quite right. I rapidly discovered that there were indeed a lot of people around like me, and some of them were very distinguished indeed. So I stopped worrying, and did manage on the whole quite successfully; successfully enough anyway to meet Mark, with whom I have now lived happily for over 45 years without anyone seeming to mind. There may still be some of my former pupils who on reading this will say with amazed reproach, as did Dante on meeting his old tutor in the seventh Circle of the Inferno: '*Siete voi qui, ser Brunetto*?' To them I can only say sorry, but that's the way it is.

* * *

To return to 1946. I was now back with my parents, which is seldom a good place for a young man in his twenties to be. Miraculously, the family was complete again. Tony had returned from five years in German prisoner-of-war camps, thin but well. He settled down with his admirable wife Rina and started to enlarge his family. Denis was back from Burma and married equally happily a few years later. Both went into the family business and suggested, without great conviction, that I should do the same. I had little difficulty in saying no, and I am glad that I did. A decade or so later, the cosy cousinage that had run Howards & Sons for over 150 years disintegrated. My father, still chairman, died in harness. Reorganization made Denis redundant, and he went on to become a freelance consultant. Then the firm was taken over, and Tony soldiered on until early and welcome retirement.

My parents had found a house in Egerton Crescent, still within easy reach of Harrods. There my mother reconstructed the elegance of Brompton Square and they moved in with their three faithful old maids, maintaining a lifestyle unchanged for half a century. The cook cooked in the basement, the parlour-maid waited at table and valeted my father, the housemaid brushed the stair-carpets, 'did' the bedrooms (though now my mother helped her make the beds) and acted as ladies' maid. They were only too glad to provide a comfortable home for me, and I was very lucky to have it. But it was a melancholy household. My father, now entering his seventies, was deeply saddened by most of the Labour government's reforms at home and the darkening skies of international politics, and suffered increasingly from emphysema; though this did not prevent him from catching the train from South Kensington to Barking every weekday as he had for 50 years past, and would until he died ten years later. As for poor Mamma, she was a sad trial to herself and everyone else. The fact that her three sons had survived the war gave her no consolation. The stimulus that war had provided had gone, and there was nothing for her to do. Her depression returned and she went from consultant to expensive consultant, none of whom could help her. She clung to me, her favourite son, like a drowning woman to a lifebelt. I sometimes thought she would drag me down with her.

Objective conditions did not help either. Food was shorter than ever and the weather was vile. Snow fell soon after Christmas in 1946 and remained frozen and rutted in the London streets until the following March. Industry slowed almost to a halt as coal ran low. I took refuge from the melancholy of home in the gloom of the Reform Club, where the depressing talk of the economists drove me home again. Thanks to persistent malaria my physical resistance was anyhow low. I became dyspeptic and had to exist on a diet of milk and fish. Then pneumonia laid me low for six weeks. This kept me from applying for a Harkness fellowship in the USA, which would have done me a power of good. I needed liberation from the English upper-middle-class world in which I felt trapped, and from which I knew I must escape if I was ever to make anything of my life. But what was I to do? The cliffs rose sheer above me. How to climb them?

I was thrown two lifelines. The first came in a telephone call from Coldstream regimental headquarters. Would I be free, they asked, to help write the Regiment's wartime history? The task had been entrusted to John Sparrow, but his work at the Bar was leaving him little time to get on with it. I now knew John quite well, and had watched him rather enviously in the All Souls Library grappling with large boxes of regimental documents. I then had no great interest in military history as such, but was certainly interested in the Regiment and in the war, while the prospect of working with someone so agreeable and distinguished as John was very attractive indeed. John was frank: he had written one chapter of the book and made it clear that he had now lost interest. He wanted effectively to turn the whole thing over to me.

So I settled down in a relatively warm corner of the Reform Club library and began my first work as a historian; trying to discover, from dry official records and subjective personal memoirs, 'what had really happened'. The problems this presented provided exactly the discipline that I needed. Later I was to find in Clausewitz an analysis of the historian's task that coincided exactly with my own experience. First, find out what happened. Then, establish a chain of causation. Finally, apply critical judgement. Before one could interpret the past, one had to recreate it.

Once I began to fit my own experiences into the mosaic of other evidence, I realized how difficult this was. What I remembered, or thought that I remembered, did not fit with other people's memories. Documentation was uneven; voluminous on administration and logistics, it thinned out when it came to operations. People were too busy to keep full and precise records. 'War Diaries' were often written up days, sometimes weeks, after the event, when many vital witnesses were no longer available. The perceptions of participants in front-line action were distorted by excitement and fatigue. I came to realize how many narratives could be constructed from the same evidence, and to understand why I had always found military history rather *dull*. As Ardent du Picq had discovered long before and John Keegan a little after me, battle was as difficult to describe as the act of love. Military histories were thus for the most part as boring as romantic novels that avoided all mention of sex. My own work would be no better, but at least I had learned where the problem lay.

It was while I was working on this that a second lifeline was thrown. I often visited Wellington, where Maurice Allen could always offer me a bed and I could find old friends among the staff and make new ones with bright sixthformers like David Macdonald, Patrick O'Brien and John Lowe; later to make their names as dramatist, stage-designer and art historian respectively. There, as often as not, I would find John Crow, globular and pop-eyed as ever, inflicting himself on some long-suffering former colleague and his wife. (When one of them complained about his lack of pyjamas, Crow made a nightgown out of black-out material and embroidered it with a skull and crossbones which he wore about the house, terrifying visitors to whom he opened the door.) He now had a job teaching English literature at King's College, London, an establishment of which I had never heard. One day he boomed at me, through clouds of noxious tobacco smoke, 'Would you like a job?'

The job in question was an assistant lectureship in history at King's. Like most Oxford men of my generation I was hardly aware of the existence of other universities except Cambridge, and like most Londoners I hurried past the inconspicuous gateway in the Strand without noticing it. I knew nothing of the college's great reputation in law, engineering, the sciences, even history. I went to inspect it and was not encouraged by what I found: a drab neoclassical façade looking across a narrow courtyard, half still demolished by a landmine, on to the blank brick rear of the east wing of Somerset House. Still, it was only a fourpenny tube ride from South Kensington, so I decided to take the plunge. I applied for the job, was summoned for interview in May 1947, and got it, at the princely salary of £400 a year. I have never discovered what strings Crow pulled on my behalf, or what kind things were said by my referees. With a mediocre degree and no research experience, I was ill-qualified for a university post anywhere. But at that time higher degrees were exceptional, and the head of the history department was adventurous in his appointments. Two members of the department did not have history degrees at all – one had a degree in PPE (Philosophy, Politics and Economics), one in Law – while another was recruited from a teacher training college. But I was in luck, and knew it.

After the welcome notification from the registrar, I waited throughout the summer for someone to tell me what I was expected to do. I assumed that since I had been a pupil of Keith Feiling and Hugh Trevor-Roper and had been hired to replace Robert Latham (later the editor of the *Pepys Diaries*) I would teach early modern history; so I brushed up my knowledge by reading the then prime authority, Samuel Rawson Gardiner (himself a former professor at King's), and learning to read seventeenth-century manuscript in the British Museum. By late September I had still heard nothing and rang the college. The Professor, I was told, was away and unobtainable, but his secretary put me on to a senior member of the department who kindly asked me to lunch and explained that I would in fact be expected to teach not early-modern English history, but modern European history from 1750 to 1914 and lecture on the subject twice a week, starting in a fortnight's time. I would share with two colleagues a room above Aldwych tube station furnished with three desks and six hard chairs. As for tutorials – or essay-classes, as they were called – I would have to fit them in during my colleagues' absence or book a room somewhere else in the vast, ramshackle building. My Oxbridge image of tutorials conducted from a comfortable armchair in a haze of pipe tobacco was rudely shattered. This was a serious university with no time or money for frills. My own education was beginning, and not before time.

The Professor (as he was always known) did not appear until the first day of term, when he summoned a staff-meeting in his narrow, poky room lined with the Proceedings of learned societies. We were later to have our differences, but he had taken an enormous gamble in giving me my first job, and for that I shall always be grateful. He was a genial little Welshman whose talent for evasion amounted to genius. He was never there. The department was run by its two senior members, while his secretary fended off as best she could the enquiries of students who milled unhappily about in the corridor outside his room, asking what they were to do and where they were to do it. It remained a mystery to his staff where he went and what he did. He showed no evident enthusiasm for writing, teaching or even thinking about history, beyond advising us to get an article published as quickly as possible and not to let the students take up too much of our time. When a few years later Kingsley Amis published *Lucky Jim* I could hardly believe that he had not been listening at the keyhole during one of our staff-meetings.

The young are cruel and unforgiving. Basically the Professor was a kind and well-meaning man, while I must have been intolerable, with my guardee moustache, Trumper haircut, Briggs umbrella and blatant desire to get back to Oxford. When 30 years later I found myself a senior professor, I learned how with advancing years internal energy ebbs, external commitments multiply, good intentions to rewrite lectures and organize fresh seminars melt away. And I made no allowance for the war years when King's had been evacuated to Bristol, whence it had only recently returned to its bleak, bomb-damaged buildings. The effort of keeping the college afloat and re-establishing it in London must have been enormous and debilitating. The buildings were stark and comfortless, their high echoing corridors smelling of chemicals and their high partitioned rooms sparsely furnished with battered old desks and benches. It was an epitome of postwar England. The importance of the accumulated fatigue of those postwar years should never be overlooked by historians of the late twentieth century.

Only gradually did I discover what a distinguished and historic institution I had joined. Gilbert Scott's remarkably successful Byzantine chapel at its centre was a reminder of the purpose of its foundation in 1829 as a Tory counterblast to the godless and radical University College that Jeremy Bentham had established in Gower Street to spread ideological subversion. The coincidental emancipation of the Catholics by the Duke of Wellington's administration, however, led some of its wealthiest supporters to suspect that something more sinister was intended, and withdraw their backing; so the college started with a heavy load of debt on a cramped site from which it had never had the resources to expand. While it remained a centre of theological orthodoxy, a combination of penury and initiative made it take the lead in other directions, pioneering studies in medicine, engineering and law. Lyell, Faraday and Lister had all taught in the gloomy amphitheatre with its tiers of wooden benches that still served as the principal lecture-theatre. Innumerable distinguished men, and latterly women, had attended courses there; or if not innumerable, then certainly unnumbered, since a harassed college administration never kept track of them. The fact that Calouste Gulbenkian, at the time the richest man in the world, was an old Kingsman was brought to the attention of the college by the Press, too late to do much about it. As a result of this indifference to its alumni, the college still had no money, and at that time showed little interest in acquiring any. Its horizons were still those of a provincial rather than a great metropolitan university.

Nevertheless, the building pulsated with activity. In the basement were the laboratories whence came an all-pervasive smell of sulphur dioxide. In the penthouse was the pre-clinical Medical School to which large lifts transported corpses, mercifully after office hours. The *piano nobile* was occupied by the library and the spacious offices of the Principal and the theology professors. The engineers, with all their heavy equipment, some-how squeezed into the lower ground floor. The rest of us existed in such holes and corners as we could find, gradually expanding into the upper floors of the buildings lining the Strand and Surrey Street. Every incoming principal declared his intention of prising at least a wing of Somerset House from the grip of the Civil Service, but the Ministry of Circumlocution remained invincible in defence of its territory. Eventually the college was to acquire the whole of the Strand frontage between Somerset House and Surrey Street and erect the concrete monstrosity that now disgraces the site, as well as expanding prolifically south of the river; but in my day it was still squeezed into a single building: dark, cramped and hyperactive.

My colleagues were of a distinction that I only gradually came to appreciate. The Dean of the College was Eric Abbott, later Warden of Keble and Dean of Westminster. The Chaplain was Sidney Evans, later to become Dean himself and later Dean of Salisbury. Many of the science professors, such as John Randall, Eric Rideal and Hermann Bondi, were figures of world renown, and Maurice Wilkins, working away in his basement on the double helix, was shortly to join them. (His colleague Rosie Franklin I never met: women were still, incredibly, denied access to the Men's Senior Common Room and were confined to a harem of their own that most of them disdained to visit.) The humanities did not lag behind, with Geoffrey Bullough in charge of English, Leonard Palmer of Greek, Edward Wilson of Spanish, Fred Norman of German and the greatest of all, Charles Boxer, of Portuguese. Many of them had spent the war at Bletchley Park and already established a convivial society which the presence of Crow made hilarious and into which he gave me the *entrée*.

And the students were no slouches. I rapidly found that though the average Oxford undergraduate was probably brighter than the average at King's (though the bad ones were far, far worse), the hard work of the latter in face of wretched handicaps – long travel at rush-hour from suburban digs, crowded working conditions, inadequate library facilities – made them no less rewarding to teach. They could at their worse be dimly unenterprising. One girl when I asked what she wanted to do with her life replied 'Why, *teach*, of course!' in terms of such offended dignity that I never dared put the question again. And as I watched them dutifully taking notes of my lectures – lectures hurriedly put together from such elderly secondary sources as the *Cambridge Modern History* – I had a terrible vision of them teaching their own pupils from these notes, who would teach their own pupils from their notes, my platitudes and errors bounding down the generations like a destructive avalanche, sweeping away all serious scholarship in its path. But at their best they were very good indeed. From the first cohort I taught, four went on to get university chairs: Kenneth Andrews at Hull, Dennis Austin and Charles Duggan in London, and Robert Knecht at Birmingham. A few years later came Malcolm Thomis (Nottingham), Roy Bridge (Leeds), Stefan Pavlovitch (Southampton) and Valerie Cromwell (History of Parliament). For a couple of years I was able to take vacation reading-parties down to Ashmore. Then the situation hugely improved with the opening of Cumberland Lodge: a royal grace-and-favour house in Windsor Great Park that had been made available as a university conference centre, and to which we were encouraged to take students at weekends to talk about history or anything else we considered important. It was comfortable, in lovely surroundings, though the fact that the nearest pub was a mile away was a mixed blessing. I booked as many weekends there as possible, eventually became a trustee, and still regard it as a Great Good Place. Certainly it provided much-needed haven during those drab postwar years.

Meanwhile, what about my own research? Equipping myself to teach the whole range of modern British and European history did not leave much time for it, but I thought I knew what I wanted to do. Were there, I wondered, any doctrinaire Republicans in the Long Parliament who were concerned not to reform the monarchy but destroy it? If so, where did they get their ideas from? Were they merchants who looked across the sea to the Netherlands, or Italianate aristocrats who took Genoa or Venice as their model? It was a good subject: it has since been definitively handled by scholars like Blair Worden, but then it beckoned invitingly. The Calendar of Venetian State Papers seemed a good starting-point, as indeed did Venice itself. Great good fortune enabled me to rent an apartment in a Venetian palazzo during the summer of 1948, where I spent the mornings dutifully turning over papers in the Frari. But the lure of convivial friends coming to stay, the need to prepare lectures for the coming year and the infinite excitements of Venice itself were too much for my concentration. I returned with a head full of happy memories and notebooks virtually empty.

For serious historical study I had to go not south to the Mediterranean but north to the Public Record Office (then still in Chancery Lane), the British Museum and the Institute for Historical Research. Such was my Oxford insularity that I had never heard of the Institute, and I doubt whether my Oxford tutors had either. But there, in a wing of the University Senate House, beautifully equipped with printed sources and secondary works to supplement the British Museum just across the road, all the luminaries of the London History School and their graduates gathered: Sir John Neale, Joel Hurstfield, Lilian Penson, R.H. Tawney, Charles Webster, Bernard Lewis, Hugh Seton-Watson, Alfred Cobban, R.A. Darlington; a constellation rivalling if not surpassing any in the country. I was awestruck. My Oxford superiority-complex withered in the face of such an array of talent – and such *professionalism*. I am afraid that I still thought of the study of history as an agreeable occupation, and nothing at Oxford had indicated otherwise. In London it became clear that it was a great deal more than that. It was hard, grinding work in the archives; work resulting in articles that, if they survived the ferocious judgement of one's peers, might slightly enhance or correct knowledge of a single corner of the past; articles that, after a decade or so, might accumulate into a solidly authoritative book and would enable one to climb, slowly and painfully, an academic ladder leading eventually to a chair in a respectable university and fellowship of the British Academy. Like war in Clausewitz's definition, history in London was a serious means to a serious end.

Somehow by the grace of God I was to achieve both a chair (four in fact) and fellowship of the Academy, but at the time I was by no means sure that I liked the prospect before me. In retrospect I am not sure that I was wrong not to like it. There was then a drabness about the Institute, an absence of the sparkle that was to develop a few years later around the magazine *Past and Present*, or that my cousin Geoffrey Elton was to kindle in Tudor history once he escaped from London to Cambridge. The place was still dominated by the micropolitics of parliamentary history made mandatory by Neale and Namier. (Not that Namier liked the place much. Once we were together in a lift that, when we pressed the button for it to go up, firmly started to go down. 'Ach! I had forgotten', remarked Namier in his thick central-European accent: 'This is the only thing here that has a mind of its own.') There were too many 'God Professors' and their obedient acolytes: anxious young men and women whose conversation in the common room revolved entirely around promotions and jobs. I briefly attended a seminar on seventeenth-century social history conducted by the redoubtable R.H. Tawney. The old boy sat like a sleepy lion at the head of the table while his pupils timidly read him papers about, as it might be, land-tenure in Rutlandshire in the 1620s; to be rewarded, if he woke up in time, with a friendly grunt and a reference to a manuscript collection they had missed. There was no controversy, no 'impact of thought on hot thought'. Could I reasonably expect it? But if I could not expect it, did I really want to 'make it' in this world at all, with the only consolation for years of ill-paid drudgery being that I might one day become a God Professor in my turn? My visits to the Institute became increasingly rare. When I did attend their evening meetings, I usually went on afterwards to the most louche club I could find in neighbouring Soho, to spend the rest of the evening drinking in thoroughly unsuitable company.

But this was the great consolation of the University of London. It was *in London*. There were temptations that I should have resisted and did not, but also opportunities to be grasped. Unlike our great rival University College, King's did not wither in the grey deserts of Bloomsbury. A step out of the college gate and we were in the roar of the Strand. To the east lay the law courts, Fleet Street and the City – a city still largely devastated by war, round whose bombsites and churches I was able to wander during my lunch-hour. A few minutes to the north lay theatre-land, and to the west Westminster and Whitehall; discrete but contiguous worlds on whose resources I felt that the college should be drawing, but from which it then held rather primly aloof. In those worlds my friends and contemporaries were beginning to 'make it' with the prospect of far more glittering prizes ahead of them. They all seemed to be working far harder than I was, in the City, at the Bar, in Fleet Street or in Whitehall, and having much more fun. They were meeting pretty, intelligent girls and marrying them – a process I watched with detached approval tinged with melancholy, for I had long since realized that such a life was not for me.

I still spent much of my time in non-academic company. Dicky Buckle had reappeared and galvanized London with his superb exhibition about Diaghilev. He established himself in a top-floor flat in Covent Garden and introduced me to the *hautmonde* of ballet and some of the *demi-monde* as well. I enjoyed this immensely, but thanked my stars that I had declined to join him in a world where I would never have been tough enough to survive for a week. Another such was Dan Farson, companion and biographer of Francis Bacon. Our mothers had been close friends, we had played together as little boys and he had followed me to Abinger and Wellington. His world, I discovered, was also not mine. He took me to the Colony Room, where the formidable Muriel Belcher took one look at me and screamed, 'Keep him away from the bar! Keep him away from the bar! He's a copper's nark; I can smell 'em a mile off!' Not even wild oats, I thought ruefully, could root themselves in my barren soil.

I was still living at home, partly to save money, partly because I felt an obligation not to desert my ageing and not very happy parents. But I also took a room in a nearby house in Elm Park Gardens where my old Abinger friend Perry Worsthorne was leading a cheerful *vie de bohème*. The house was rented furnished from Major-General J.F.C. Fuller, the famous military historian, whose name at the time meant nothing to me. My predecessor as Perry's lodger had been my Oxford contemporary Adrian Earle, whose name was beginning to mean all too much. Moving to London, he had left behind him a trail of weeping girls and missing valuables. By the time I arrived, there was little left in the house that had not been firmly nailed down. Breaking-point had come when Perry returned unexpectedly early one afternoon to find Adrian supervising the loading into a removal van of a valuable marquetry desk. 'Riddled with woodworm', Adrian explained glibly. I promised that my offences, if any, would at least be different in kind, so we cheerfully cohabited, giving rather good parties, until Perry decided to marry the pretty French girl who lived upstairs and our shared bachelor freedom came to an end.

Meanwhile, the problem increasingly presented itself: had I chosen the right vocation? I enjoyed teaching and knew that I was a good lecturer. The more I read, the more interested I became in the patterns and challenges presented by the past, especially during the transformation of European society that had occurred during the past century and a half that I had not yet learned to call 'modernization'. The centenary of the 1848 revolutions enabled me to focus my lectures on nineteenth-century Europe, the nature of nationalism and the problem of revolution. But professional recognition and promotion lay only through research, in which I was less and less interested, within a professional environment that I found less and less attractive. It was not too late to switch to publishing, or journalism, or even the Bar; all alternatives that I was seriously considering when a challenge came that compelled a decision.

In spring 1950 I received a note from the Principal of the college, inviting me to become warden of 'The Platanes', the college's student hostel in Camberwell. I had little idea where Camberwell was, save that it was in south London, in those days *terra incognita*. (P.G. Wodehouse, himself a south-Londoner, had once pointed out that for anyone wishing to escape his enemies and creditors south London, not Africa or India, was the place to go. You were always likely to run into old acquaintances on the Limpopo or in Peshawar, but you could lurk undiscovered for ever in Penge, Peckham or Tooting Bec.) It would mean exile or near-exile from friends and family, but also the chance to break away from a lifestyle that was dissipating my energies, and to decide what kind of person I wanted to be. I realized that if I turned the job down I was not serious or worth taking seriously. So I accepted. I had one last summer holiday in Nice and Corsica with two dear friends: Paul Dehn, the poet and film critic, and his friend, Jimmy Bernard, the composer, whose sparkling lifestyle in Chelsea embodied all that I was leaving behind. Then on 1 August 1950 I drove south across the Thames as if it were the Rubicon, and made my way through the screaming trams via the Elephant & Castle and the Walworth Road to Camberwell and Champion Hill.

It was the best decision I ever took. The hostel (or 'hall of residence', as such establishments were beginning grandly to be called) consisted of two large Victorian houses in Ruskin-land, a leafy lane on the crest of Denmark Hill. To the north one looked across the whole bowl of London to the heights of Hampstead beyond. To the south the land dipped into the green vale of Dulwich and rose again to the heights of Sydenham, once crowned by the Crystal Palace. The students were for the most part tough, hard-working young men from the Midlands and the North reading sensible subjects like engineering or medicine or law. The place had been badly run down during the war and there was still an enormous amount to do to make it habitable. After five years I was more than ready for responsibility again. In the evenings, as the students settled down to work, the whole place seemed to purr with warm, quiet life and I felt a sense of almost ecstatic content. This, I felt, was what I was meant to be doing.

I thus became for a time *adscriptus glebae*, as dedicated to my charges as a fellow of an Oxbridge college or a master in a good boarding-school. I ceased worrying where I was going: I was quite happy to be where I was. I did not entirely escape the melancholy of exile. On foggy autumn Saturday afternoons I went for lonely walks round Peckham and Dulwich, masochistically absorbing the *cafard* of the London suburbs. On summer evenings before supper I looked down over London and thought of all the parties, all the romantic adventures that I was missing as my life ticked inexorably on towards 30 and beyond. But my exile was comfortable. I had a pleasant flat. I still saw something of my friends and I dutifully went to supper with my parents at Egerton Crescent every Sunday evening. I persuaded the college that they might make some money by letting the buildings in vacations for conferences or tourist groups – we were among the first people to get in on this expanding racket – and extorted a substantial grant to refurbish the place. I hired pictures for the public rooms. I restocked the garden, largely with plants from Ashmore, which the family sadly abandoned in 1952, the parents being too old and the rest of us too busy to keep it up. I installed a bar, introduced a Christmas dinner and concert (experience in wartime sergeants' messes came in useful here) and an annual summer ball. On the whole, though I say it who shouldn't, I did the boys rather well.

It could not have lasted. Agreeable though it was, this activity was a distraction from the main business of my life, my historical work, on which I was making no progress whatever. I had completely lost interest in the Long Parliament and everything associated with it. I had scrambled a little up the cliffs and now seemed stuck again. Was it too late for me to do something else?

Then suddenly, in the spring of 1954, the college authorities threw me the biggest and most unexpected lifeline of all.

7

War Studies

In 1853 the distinguished theologian and social reformer Frederick Denison Maurice had been expelled from the chair he then held at King's College for the heretical views he expressed about the nature of divine punishment. Many years later, in 1918, his grandson, Major-General Sir Frederick Maurice, had to resign as Director of Military Operations and retire from the army for writing a letter to the *Daily Telegraph* expressing equally heretical views about the prime minister's interference in the conduct of operations on the Western Front. It was thus largely as a belated act of atonement that, when in 1927 the University of London decided to follow the example of the University of Oxford and create a chair of 'Military Studies', King's College adopted the post and invited General Maurice to fill it. Maurice held the chair for only a few years before moving on to become Principal of the Working Men's College (later Queen Mary College) in the Mile End Road, but the department remained in being, running staff courses for officers of the Territorial Army, until it was dissolved at the beginning of the Second World War.

The decision to revive and expand military studies, so far as I have been able to discover, was the work largely of Professors Sir Charles Webster, Lionel Robbins and Sir Keith Hancock, all of whom had been involved at some level in the conduct of the last war or the writing of its history. It was agreed among them that the whole subject needed to be reconsidered, to make it both a serious academic study and one commensurate with the scope of twentieth-century warfare in its totality. For this it was agreed that a retired soldier, however eminent and intelligent, would not be the right man. They needed someone more attuned to the university environment, although military experience at some level would obviously be an asset. Webster had his own candidate for the job, a young ex-RAF officer, Noble Frankland, who possessed not only a DFC but an Oxford D.Phil. Frankland was Webster's collaborator in writing the *Official History of the Combined Bomber Offensive*, a work demanding not only professional skill but also considerable moral courage to state conclusions highly unwelcome to the Air Ministry. Bunny Frankland possessed both these qualities in abundance; but he would hold the post at the London School of Economics, where

Webster held a chair of International History, and where all the necessary ancillary subjects, such as economics and the social sciences, were already flourishing. But King's was reluctant to relinquish its prescriptive right to the appointment, and in me it had an at least plausible candidate. After six years I knew my way around the university; I had a faintly military image – that improbable figure Captain M.E. Howard, MC, Coldstream Guards, still hovered helpfully around – and I had published a work of military history, of a kind: Howard and Sparrow's *History of the Coldstream Guards 1920–1946* had appeared in 1951 and been respectfully noticed. How, I was asked, did I feel about the idea?

Well, I really didn't know. Although I had enjoyed writing the regimental history, it had given me no taste for military history as such. I had seen the book as a graceful farewell to arms rather than the beginning of a new relationship with them. My view of military history had been formed at Wellington, shaped by the fat red volumes of Fortescue's *History of the British Army*, Gurwood's edition of Wellington's Despatches and Edmonds' *Official History of the Great War* in the college library, where they lay behind glass doors unopened and unread – certainly not by clever sixthformers working for an Oxford scholarship. But if I took this job I would be my own man. I could escape from the narrow confines of the history department, whose meetings, held in the Professor's cramped little room to decide the precise grade of beta to be awarded to Miss Smithers, I found increasingly depressing. I could make something of it, I thought. Give it a go, said my friends. So when the offer came through in the spring of 1953, I accepted.

The first thing I asked for, and was granted, was a sabbatical year to learn my new trade. There was a lot of reading to do – if not Fortescue, then certainly Clausewitz – and I had now to learn German properly. No longer was it possible, as it had been for my brother Tony before the war, to go over to Frankfurt and live with our German cousins: sadly, there were no German cousins left. Indeed, Germany itself, eight years after the war, was in no condition to accommodate casual visitors. But there was always Austria, which I had not quite reached from Italy in 1945. Peter Heyworth, an old friend from Oxford who was learning the trade of music critic, of which he was to become so formidable a master, had just returned from Vienna. He recommended a hotel, a teacher and a number of genial friends. So off I went for the summer on a train that bore me deep into central Europe to a Vienna still under control of the Four Powers. I reached the city late one evening feeling like Mr Issyvoo arriving in Berlin, apprehensive and excited.

Vienna was still the city of Graham Greene's *Third Man* and had not yet become the soulless tourist-trap that I was to revisit a quarter of a century later. My hotel, the König von Ungarn, was shabby but welcoming, built round a courtyard in the shadow of the cathedral and, with its rooms named after the great imperial families – Windischgrätz, Schwarzenberg, Liechtenstein – it still held echoes of imperial grandeur. My own room overlooked the courtyard of the house where Mozart had written *Figaro*. The Opera House had not yet reopened, but every night in the Theater an der Wien, stars of the magnitude of Lisa della Casa, Sena Jurinac, Anton Dermota and Erich Kunz gave performances of Mozart and Verdi of a quality that transcended anything I had heard before or have experienced since. I went daily to a charming young *Lehrerin* who tried to recall for me long-forgotten elements of German grammar. I found my way to the archives of the old imperial army, meticulously kept from the muster-rolls of Wallenstein to the staff conferences of Conrad von Hotzendorff; the only army, as its guardians explained to me proudly and sadly, to survive solely in its records. I explored every inch of the old city on foot and, by bus, much of the Wienerwald and the Danube valley. From the cathedral tower I looked over the plains to the south and east, over which the Turks had advanced to the walls of the city in 1683. Well yes, I thought, I might make something of military history after all.

Then I returned to London to begin my new life. The doldrum years were over. My health cleared up. There were now not enough hours in the day to do all that needed to be done. Five years earlier in Egerton Crescent I had prayed despondently for guidance as to what to do with my life and for the capacity to do it. Now I reckoned I had both. The college decided very wisely that I could not hold my new post in combination with my war-denship, which meant – since I had no intention of remaining in the debilitating tranquillity of the suburbs – adjusting myself again to the pressures and distractions of the metropolis. I returned to South Kensington, partly because it was less trouble and partly so that I could keep a filial eye on my parents. There I found a flat in Onslow Square which seemed to me, with its endless vistas of Italianate porticos, to be the epitome of stuffy bourgeois respectability, but was conveniently accessible.

The London to which I returned had now been transformed. This was the 1950s. The gloom of the 1940s had been banished. Affluence was beginning to return to the country under the benign economic stewardship of R.A. Butler and Hugh Gaitskell. We had been cheered up by the beautifully planned and executed Festival of Britain, whose site was only five minutes' walk across the river from King's, and by the associated fun-fair in Battersea Park. There had been the accession to the throne of a beautiful young queen. The media wrote excitedly about a new Elizabethan age (more accurately than they knew, for once again we were, as we had been then, a power of the second rank, teetering on the verge of bankruptcy and punching far beyond our weight in international affairs).

Ladies bold and rich enough could be seen in the West End wearing the opulent dresses of the New Look. Their male counterparts wore suits with tight trousers and long, full jackets, brocade waistcoats and curly-brimmed bowler hats – though this fashion (except for the hats) caught on more successfully among working-class youths, Teddy (i.e. Edwardian) boys, who for the first time had money to spend. The sombre mansions of South Kensington, which had been requisitioned first to house refugees from Gibraltar and then Irish navvies to work on the bombsites, were being repainted and converted into upmarket flats, and the side-streets sprouted boutiques and restaurants to service them. A prewar elegance had briefly returned to the London stage to flourish for a few years with the musicals of Julian Slade and Sandy Wilson, the wit of Flanders and Swann, the romantic idylls of Anouilh and Christopher Fry, and the 'well-made plays' of Terry Rattigan. It did not last long: mocked by Angry Young Men, challenged by the cheerful proletarian vulgarity of the Beatles and the Rolling Stones, it was to be swept away in the revolting sixties. But it was nice while it lasted, and I have to admit that I found South Kensington a pleasant change after Camberwell. It was certainly a relief to know that when, as occasionally happened at weekends, neighbours gave late-night parties that spilled out into the street, I did not have to go out and read the riot act, which had been one of my less welcome duties at The Platanes.

My father died, suddenly and peacefully, the following winter, and with him there disappeared the last traces of that solid, mahogany order in which I had grown up. We buried him at Ashmore one cold January afternoon, and moved poor Mamma into a flat a few doors from mine. There she lingered in elegant unhappiness for another 20 years, surrounded by her lovely but uncomforting possessions, looked after by a succession of housekeepers and by her sorely tried daughters-in-law. When at last she died in 1977, we buried her ashes with my father at Ashmore. As their tombstone records, their lives between them spanned exactly a hundred years, 1877–1977. What years!

Now I had to create my own order. I found to my joy that Julian Brown was living in digs round the corner and persuaded him to move in with me. He was at the time working in the Western Manuscripts Department of the British Museum, but was later to join me at King's as Professor of Paleography, and he provided a stable and reassuring presence until he left to get married some six years later. Then Mark James came, first as research assistant, then as indispensable and irreplaceable companion.

*   *   *

Perhaps it is true of anyone who makes a success of their lives that in youth professional activities form a background to the interesting if turbulent events of private life, but with the onset of middle age the process is reversed. From now on, this record must be not of who I was but of what I did; of being rather than becoming; and I am afraid that in human terms it will be far less interesting. It may be saved from complete tedium by the happy fact that my curriculum vitae was not that of the usual academic. I was to have a more varied and eventful professional life than I had ever conceived and one that I could not possibly have planned. I was drawn forward in a series of unpredictable moves made possible only by arbitrary good luck. The Italian gift of *fortuna* was to be bestowed on me in abundant measure.

Unfortunately the change in my fortunes led to a prolonged and unhappy quarrel with the head of my department. He did not regard it as a change at all. In his view, although the focus of my research may have altered, I remained a full member of the department and under his control, not only lecturing but also teaching and examining as departmental needs required. This I would not accept. As I understood it, the university had provided the college with the money to enable me to do a special and quite demanding job. Membership of the History Department I regarded as an administrative formality. My old post had anyway been filled by a new appointment, a brilliant young man from Cambridge, Gareth Bennett, who was to go on to become a fellow of New College, Oxford, and kill himself in tragic circumstances 30 years later. So I refused to do anything in the department except lecture on the history of war. It was only after the Professor retired in 1961 that I was appointed to an independent readership with my own department, and two years later I got my own chair. It was a stupid bureaucratic wrangle that reflected credit on neither of us, and one which in retrospect I greatly regret. Still, if I had not stood my ground, the Department of War Studies might never have got off the ground at all.

All that lay in the future when I returned from Vienna in autumn 1954. I had now to learn how to be a military historian. To my surprise I found that the Institute for Historical Research had an excellent military history collection, bequeathed to it by the first Professor of Military History at Oxford, Spenser Wilkinson. With its help I set about compiling a huge bibliography which has, I am afraid, lain neglected in a cupboard ever since. I consulted the only other academic in the field, Spenser Wilkinson's successor at Oxford, Cyril Falls: a spruce little Edwardian figure who had written a kindly review of *The Coldstream Guards* and now sent me a long letter of friendly advice. In particular, he told me to read Edward Meade

Earle's book *The Makers of Modern Strategy*, which I did. By following up its references I started to build up a corpus of knowledge. Gradually it became clear what a huge and fertile field I had been set to cultivate and how very little had as yet been tilled – at any rate by British historians. The history of war, I came to realize, was more than the operational history of armed forces. It was the study of entire societies. Only by studying their cultures could one come to understand what it was that they fought about and why they fought in the way that they did. Further, the fact that they did so fight had a reciprocal impact on their social structure. I had to learn not only to think about war in a different way, but also to think about history itself in a different way. I would certainly not claim to have invented the concept of 'War and Society', but I think I did something to popularize it.

In addition to acquiring a broad basis of knowledge, I had to write a book. That was made clear to me with Yorkshire frankness by Charles Webster, who was the true godfather of War Studies in London. 'Not just a few bloody articles', he insisted: 'a proper book'. That was what I had always wanted to do. But what should it be about? Certainly not the seventeenth century, that cul de sac in which I had been trapped since the age of 16 and from which I could now escape with honour. The Napoleonic period seemed to have been flogged to death by operational military historians. (I was of course entirely wrong about this, as David Chandler was soon to show.) The First World War was too amorphous and complex a topic on which to cut my teeth. But in between, what had happened to the conduct of European warfare, between the battles of Waterloo and the Somme? It was a period dominated by the grey and shadowy figure of the Prussian Helmuth von Moltke, whose victories between 1866 and 1870 had transformed the balance of European power in a matter of months. But how had he done it?

The Franco-Prussian War of 1870 thus seemed tailor-made for my purposes. Several thousand books had been written about it before 1914, as I discovered to my alarm, but practically nothing since. Many were available in the library of that venerable learned institute for the armed forces, the Royal United Services Institution in Whitehall; a treasure-trove ten minutes' walk from King's, little-used and largely unexplored even by its own members. So, wearing a bowler hat and my Brigade tie, I called on the librarian, Brigadier John Stephenson, an energetic and intelligent soldier but one whose historical interests, like those of most of the Institute's members, were confined to the British armed forces. I found him in his shirt-sleeves weeding out all the literature dealing with the development of warfare in Europe in the nineteenth century: French, German, Italian, Russian, the publications of the French and German general staffs, military memoirs, technical studies of weapons-development, campaign atlases; hundreds of volumes, most of them not disturbed since 1914 and, so long as they remained there, unlikely to be again. The RUSI took little persuasion to dispose of them to King's for a purely nominal sum, where they became the nucleus of the War Studies Library and the focus of my own research. Here was a wonderful field so far neglected by historians: the development of military thought in the generation before 1914. The German army as a political entity was beginning to attract interest – Gordon Craig was already at work on his great work *The Politics of the Prussian Army*. But the wars themselves had lain neglected for half a century. For the first time in my life I knew exactly what I had to do.

So I had a book to write, with most of its sources easily available. Even more remarkable, I had a publisher. An acquaintance from Oxford, Tony Bland, had joined the college at the same time as myself as a lecturer in the Law Department. (Another contemporary in that department was Norman St John Stevas, an improbable bird of paradise among us dingy owls.) Tony and his wife Deirdre rapidly became close friends and took me with them on idyllic summer holidays in Cornwall. Later, what seemed a perfect marriage tragically disintegrated when Tony moved to the University of Sussex and was caught up in the madness of the 1960s; but for the 25 years that the couple were together they provided me with much happiness. Deirdre's brother, the publisher Rupert Hart-Davis, was already one of my boyhood heroes: his Reynard editions of English classics, with their fine buckram bindings and exquisitely designed typefaces, I had eagerly collected as prizes at school. Rupert visited us in Cornwall, watched me at work on *The Franco-Prussian War*, and offered to publish the book when it was finished. He then acted as not only publisher but also editor. For weeks he kept me on the end of a telephone late into the night, scrutinizing the text and knocking it into shape. Thanks to him the book when it appeared was a pleasure to look at and to hold. Thanks to him it was reviewed by all the right people in all the right places. And I have no doubt whatever that it was thanks to him that it was awarded the Duff Cooper Prize and my name became known in all the right quarters. Amazingly, it is still in print and sells respectably, though, less amazingly, it has never been translated into French or German. Perhaps the France of de Gaulle's Fifth Republic did not want to be reminded by an Englishman of their humiliations, while the Germany of Konrad Adenauer's Federal Republic was as unwilling to recall its military triumphs as were the French their military disasters.

More to the point, I was able to establish the German wars of unification as a new 'special subject' in the London History School, and attracted undergraduates of the calibre of Geoffrey Till and John Gooch, who were to become noted historians in their own right. Others like Peter Simkins were to join the staff of the Imperial War Museum, which my erstwhile rival but now firm friend Noble Frankland was transforming from an antiquarian backwater into a prime centre for the study of twentieth-century history. I also initiated a one-year Master's course in 'War Studies' involving not only the history of war but military sociology, the laws and ethics of war, economics of warfare and nuclear deterrence; to which the education branches of the services began to send outstanding young officers, including Tony (later Major-General) Trythall from the army and Tony (later Air Vice-Marshal) Mason from the Royal Air Force. Graduate students began to appear from other universities: Brian Bond came from Oxford, John Rae (via Harrow) and Wolf Mendl from Cambridge, Paul Guinn from Harvard, above all Peter Paret, of whom more later, from Berkeley. Brian Bond and Wolf Mendl were to join me as lecturers and devote the rest of their professional careers to teaching in the department. Grants from the Ford Foundation enabled me to invite over American academics like Richard Rosecrance and Morton Halperin to teach and exchange ideas. There was among us all the cheerful camaraderie of pioneers, the more so since the college could only provide us with the most primitive of accommodation. I set up my own seminar at the Institute for Historical Research and gradually realized to my alarm that I was well on the way to becoming a God Professor myself before I was even 40.

But it was not my job simply, or indeed primarily, to turn out military historians. Charles Webster and Lionel Robbins had emphasized to me the importance they attached to the eclecticism of War Studies. I had to interest the economists, the international lawyers, the social scientists, the international relations specialists, even, if possible the scientists. So, carefully divesting myself of regimental tie, bowler hat and umbrella, I crossed the Strand to the London School of Economics. There I discovered a new world, in comparison with whose effervescent turbulence King's seemed funereally sedate. I found a host of new friends and potential collaborators, mainly in the Department of International Relations: Charles Manning, Geoffrey Goodwin, Martin Wight and, in a younger generation, Hedley Bull and the historian Donald Cameron Watt. Economists like Alan Peacock were interested and supportive. Even further afield, though for me geographically nearer home, was the Imperial College of Science and Technology in the Exhibition Road, in whose shadow I had grown up, and whose students now inhabited the sombre mansions in Prince's Gardens past which I used to go on my way to play on the steps of the Albert Memorial.

There the redoubtable P.M.S. Blackett held the chair of Physics. Blackett's *Military and Political Consequences of Atomic Energy*, published in 1948, had been the first serious analysis published in England about the implications of nuclear weapons for warfare. He was delighted to learn of my endeavours. Tall, handsome, looking every inch the naval officer he had once been, he came to lunch with me in King's and sent my stock soaring among my scientific colleagues. To show the flag in the university and the world, I arranged, in the autumn of 1955, a course of public lectures on 'War and Society' that included seminal contributions by Martin Wight on War in International Relations, Richard Titmuss on War and Social Policy, and Blackett himself on Scientists and the Conduct of War. The BBC was interested and broadcast abbreviated versions of them, with an introductory talk by me. This I followed up with a series on civil–military relations, published as *Soldiers and Governments*. By the early 1960s 'War Studies' was established and flourishing.

*   *   *

In addition to all this, I found myself involved in two further demanding activities. The first was within the university itself. I could not have got War Studies off the ground at all if there did not exist, as an inheritance from the prewar era, its own board of studies on which sat Webster, Robbins and other interested giants who pointed the project in the right direction and put their weight behind it. Each board of studies was represented on the Arts Faculty board, and it was thought appropriate that I should be the War Studies representative. This would normally have been a sinecure, since the faculty board normally nodded through decisions taken by the subject boards before they went up to the Senate, where they were nodded through even faster. But these were stirring times. The university world was in turmoil. A report by Lionel Robbins had recommended not only the creation of new universities but also sweeping reforms of the syllabuses of existing ones, involving the creation of 'bold and exciting' new degrees. This was exactly what I had myself been doing, but the other boards were not happy with the idea. In consequence debates on the faculty board were long and acrimonious. Largely because I did not have the same responsibilities as my colleagues who had to run large departments, I was eventually elected Dean of the Faculty and had to keep them all in order.

During the four years that I occupied this exalted post, I learned much about my academic colleagues. They fell into three categories. The first, and by far the most numerous, wanted only to be left alone to get on with their work. But they were like hermit-crabs: if you were foolish enough to tread on them, they nipped painfully. The second were intelligent and public-spirited, understood the problems and were positively helpful in solving them. Finally there was a tiny but inescapable minority of menacing nuisances who expressed their egos by causing trouble. The problem was how to avoid antagonizing the first group, to enlist the support of the second and to neutralize the third. I also learned a lot about chairmanship, largely through observing my predecessors. The first essential, I discovered, was to be complete master of one's brief, which meant spending the previous evening carefully reading the agenda. The second was to permit any contentious issue to be discussed only for a limited time in plenary session before being referred to a subcommittee that contained those who had expressed the strongest views, including the menacing nuisances; and if possible squaring them beforehand over a good lunch. But most important of all, not to be afraid of silencing the most vociferous of one's colleagues in mid-flow. You might make one enemy, but you made a host of friends.

I must admit that I rather enjoyed all this, and hope that I made more friends than enemies. Less enjoyable were other high-powered committees to which I found myself appointed in the college and the university. One was on the future of King's itself: should it remain on its constricted site, or boldly move out to the suburbs, perhaps to join its hospital on Denmark Hill? Given the huge advantages of our central situation, which I have already described, the whole idea struck me as lunatic, but our scientists and engineers, impossibly cramped in their accommodation, understandably thought otherwise. The decision was ultimately taken to stay and rebuild on the Strand. I am sure it was correct, but wish – as must anyone who now walks past the college building – that it could have been made at a time when architects had recovered from their disastrous obsession with concrete as a building material, and that the college had had rather more money at its disposal.

As for the university, I found myself on one of its innumerable navel-gazing committees to decide what should be done about its structure. Some of the larger members – University College, Imperial College, the LSE – regarded the University of London as an irrelevant nuisance. They wanted to declare their independence, as ultimately Imperial College was able to do. Other colleges – Westfield, Bedford, Queen Mary, Royal Holloway – were too small to contemplate such a step, which would also be disastrous for the specialist schools and institutes like the School of Slavonic and East European Studies, the School of Oriental and African Studies and the Courtauld Institute, all jewels in the university's crown. King's lay somewhere in the middle, so I found myself championing the cause of the small institutions and defending the unitary university. No solution was found in my time, and opinions are divided as to whether a satisfactory one has been found since.

As a reward for all these labours, I was expected to attend degree-giving ceremonies in the Albert Hall. There a string band of the Welsh Guards

endlessly scraped their way through Elgar's *Pomp and Circumstance Marches*
as the graduands filed past our Chancellor, the Queen Mother. She hooded
the higher doctors, gave diplomas to the PhDs, shook hands with the
Masters and beamed happily at the bowing Bachelors. After some three
hours of this we would adjourn for tea where she chatted cheerfully until a
lady-in-waiting had almost physically to drag her away. 'Alas!' she apol-
ogized, 'I must be off to dine with the Benchers of Lincoln's Inn. I *do* hope
that they won't keep me up too late.' We would learn next day that she had
kept *them* up until well after midnight. One day I was to be hooded myself,
with the skill of a cowboy lassoing a steer, by her granddaughter, the
Princess Royal. It takes a woman to do this kind of thing really well.

*   *   *

The second activity was, quite properly, my own writing. In 1958, while in
the last stages of *The Franco-Prussian War*, I was approached by Professor
Sir James Butler, the editor of the official history of the Second World War,
who wondered whether I would take on a volume in the series that had
already had a rather unfortunate history. It would deal with 'Grand Strategy', the higher direction of the war, in 1942–43. It had originally been
allotted to a regular soldier, with lamentable results. The next author had
abandoned it after six months to take up a chair in South Africa. The third
was now moribund. The whole enterprise seemed doom-laden, but would I
try to rescue it?

This demanded reflection. I had intended to follow *The Franco-Prussian
War* with a study of the impact of technology on military theory and
practice between 1870 and 1914; what would now be termed the 'modernization' of war. Butler's offer would mean a complete change of direction.
But the subject was fascinating. I would have access to material that, as
matters then stood, would not become available to the general public until
the 1990s. I would be able to interview the senior commanders and political
leaders, many of whom were still alive. I would also be paid quite well,
which was not unimportant in meeting the rent for Onslow Square. But
I obviously needed the college's permission for this moonlighting. I
approached the Professor, who was still my nominal superior. The poor
man, by this time thoroughly fed up with my unorthodox activities, said it
was out of the question. Equally fed up, I appealed to the Principal, Peter
Noble, a genial and hardheaded Scot, who overruled him. So I went ahead,
as much out of defiance as anything else.

I am still not sure that the decision was wise. Given all my other activities,
the official history volume occupied me for most of the 1960s, though this
was celerity itself compared to the performance of some of my colleagues on

the project. As I feared, it did distract me from the kind of war-history where my interest now lay. But there were great compensations. Most of the necessary documents, including all Churchill's papers, were housed in the bowels of what was then the Ministry of Defence, in Storey's Gate, and I was allotted as my workroom a cubbyhole that had been Churchill's private secretary's office in the Cabinet War Rooms that still existed in the basement. In principle these were open to the public; but since this fact had never been given any publicity, they were visited only occasionally by parties from the Old Dominions who knew about it through their High Commissioners. I was also allotted a wonderful research assistant, Patricia McCallum, who had served in MI6 during the war. There we were completely undisturbed, working on Churchill's papers in Churchill's own office in surroundings quite unchanged since the events I now had to chronicle and explain. So complete was the wartime atmosphere that when I finished my daily stint and went out into the London evening, the first air-raid sirens seemed to be wailing over St James's Park.

Eventually tidy-minded Cabinet Office officials insisted on moving us to a drab office-block opposite St James's Park underground station. When some years later I returned to Storey's Gate to rescue some notes, I was appalled by what I found. The place had obviously been looted. Some respect had been shown to the main offices – Churchill's bedroom, the map-room, the Cabinet meeting-room – but even there, many small objects had disappeared, while in the warren of small rooms adjoining, practically nothing had been left. I reported this to my bureaucratic boss, but it was no longer his responsibility. More effectively, I mentioned it to Bunny Frankland, on whose Board of Trustees at the Imperial War Museum I now sat, and suggested that the museum might come to the rescue. Bunny had already performed miracles, not only in getting the museum itself up and running, but also in creating an 'outstation' at Duxford for the Royal Air Force, and in saving *HMS Belfast* from destruction and arranging for it to be moored at Tower Bridge as a permanent exhibition. If anyone could save the Cabinet War Rooms, it was he. He could, and he did. Now, enlarged by the Churchill Museum, they are deservedly one of the most visited tourist sights in London.

I also found myself in the company of the higher Civil Service. As a member of the Cabinet Office Historical Section, I could lunch in the Cabinet Office Mess, then just upstairs from my burrow in the basement. There I met old friends from Oxford, Ian Bancroft, Derek Mitchell, Robert Armstrong, young high-flyers who were now moving into positions of serious responsibility, and heard all the gossip. These were the dying years of the Macmillan administration. Of immediate concern was the reorganization of the armed forces and creation of a seriously centralized Ministry of Defence by Duncan Sandys and Peter Thorneycroft. Of this I had a view from the stalls and was to make myself something of an expert. But of broader concern was the imminent change of government in 1964 that would bring Harold Wilson into office. So far from dreading this, the mandarins longed for it. Harold Wilson had been one of them. Most of them had, like him, read PPE or economics at Oxbridge, rather than Greats like their predecessors. They looked forward to the reforms and rationalization that Labour promised, and greeted the Labour victory of 1964 with evident satisfaction. So did I, largely because it brought Denis Healey to the Ministry of Defence. But to explain why this gave me such pleasure I must now describe another dimension of what was now becoming an impossibly crowded but increasingly fascinating life.

8

Strategic Studies

I have not so far dealt with the impact that world affairs were making on my life. Immediately after the war they did not have much effect. For a few years, it is true, the world situation seemed so uncertain that I half expected to be recalled to the army again, and so valued every moment of unbroken nights spent between cool sheets. We watched bleakly the onset of the Cold War, but were more concerned with the cold and shortages at home than with events overseas. Not until 1951 did we finally escape from rationing and the need to get emergency ration-cards from an elderly dragon in the local Food Office whenever we went away for a weekend. My visit to Venice in 1948 coincided with the beginning of the Berlin Blockade and of what looked unpleasantly like civil war in Italy. After arriving there I scanned the newspaper headlines apprehensively and wondered how I would get home again. The Korean War provided the headlines for much of my time at The Platanes, but the fighting was over before I felt the need to take a profes-sional interest in it. With the explosion of the first thermonuclear weapons in 1953, however, the chilling facts about nuclear war penetrated into everyone's private life. Now, if only briefly, we were all frightened. For-tuitously my appointment as Lecturer in War Studies at King's had just been announced. I found myself fending off demands from journalists down the road in Fleet Street or even closer at hand, the BBC World Service in Bush House, to answer questions or even give talks about matters on which my ignorance was, after all, no greater than anyone else's.

I also found myself in demand as a book-reviewer, mainly of the war memoirs that were now pouring out of the presses. This also began with a Wellington connection. The assistant literary editor of the *New Statesman* at the time was T.C. Worsley, who had taught there shortly before my time (his book *Flannelled Fool* gives a hilarious account of his highly unorthodox career) and whom I had met later at Oxford through Talboys. I always found him a grim schoolmasterly figure in spite of his flamboyantly homosexual lifestyle, but he kindly steered a few books in my direction, and his successors John Raymond and Janet Adam-Smith did the same. They were followed by Terry Kilmartin at the *Observer*, and eventually by Jack Lambert at the *Sunday Times*. I acquired the habit of reviewing up to a book a week; reading them in the evenings, writing my 800 words on Sunday mornings. This went on for about 25 years. Most of the books I would have to have read anyhow; it was a wonderful discipline; it paid; and above all it brought me into contact with Basil Liddell Hart.

I have written elsewhere about my relations with this great but maddening man; at once a monster of egocentricity and one of the kindest people I have ever met.* His greatness lay in the application of a very powerful mind to the study of a single subject, unwearyingly and for half a century. He had none of the depth or comprehension of a Clausewitz. Rather he resembled Jomini, the young Swiss who brilliantly grasped the essence of Napoleonic manoeuvre when barely out of his teens and spent the rest of a long life elaborating on and illustrating a single idea. Like Jomini, Liddell Hart's mind was penetrating but narrow. He had no interest in war as a protean phenomenon interacting with the societies that fought it. For him it was a matter of operational skills that largely consisted in applying the lessons he himself taught. But he can be quite appropriately mentioned in the same breath as those nineteenth-century masters, and as a master he hungered for disciples – intelligent young people who were prepared to listen to him. He was bitterly disappointed by Oxford's failure to elect him, rather than Cyril Falls, to their chair of History of War, but it was quite understandable: not only was he personally unpopular for his attacks, however well-deserved, on British military leadership in the Great War, but his prewar writings also seemed discredited by events. In 1940 he had been notoriously defeatist. There were indeed times when he seemed to resent the fact that the Germans, who seemed so successfully to have applied his operational principles, had not won the war. By the mid-1950s, however, he had been largely rehabilitated in the public mind. He had mellowed considerably, and possessed an inexhaustible stock of knowledge and ideas he was anxious to share with kindred spirits.

In the autumn of 1954 I received a kind letter from him about one of my book reviews. Once he had learned what I was up to at King's, he invited me to stay at his home near Wolverton in Buckinghamshire – a house whose pleasant domesticity was masked under the grandiose title 'Wolverton Park'. There *fortuna* struck once more. I fell ill, and a one-night visit was prolonged for a week. The kindness of my hosts transformed a social disaster into an experience of sheer delight as Kathleen plied me with food and Basil (as they quickly became) brought up papers from his archives until my bed was covered with them. After I left we began a correspondence that continued until his death. It would have been still more voluminous had he

---

* See *The Cause of Wars* (London 1983), p. 198.

not entertained me so often and had we not been able to talk so much. Gradually I was able to develop a connection between Liddell Hart and King's that was ultimately consummated when, after his death, his books and papers came to the college and formed the nucleus of the Liddell Hart Centre for Military Archives.

The benefit I derived from knowing Liddell Hart extended far beyond what I learned from him personally. He introduced me around: to pre-historic figures like Leslie Hore Belisha, still rubicund and jovial in spite of his political disappointments; to distinguished British soldiers like Brian Horrocks, whose charisma was already being exploited on television; to equally distinguished German soldiers like the urbane aristocrat von Senger und Etterlin, against whose armies I had fought in Italy ('May I give you a word of advice?' he said, when I mentioned this: 'Next time you invade Italy, do not start at the bottom'); to rising young British officers like Mike Carver and Peter Gretton; and to Israeli heroes like Yigal Allon.

Some I met at his home, some at a dining-club over which he presided, the Military Commentators' Circle. In addition to more specialized meetings, the Circle held an annual dinner at which it was addressed by the military good and great. One such was held during the Suez operation in the autumn of 1956, when the Chief of Air Staff, Sir Dermot Boyle, assured a generally complacent audience that all was going swimmingly. Suez I regarded as an unmitigated political disaster, whatever the military outcome, and I said so forcefully, rather enjoying the role of *enfant terrible*. Basil beamed approvingly, but did not commit himself.

It was not just the spirit of contradiction that made me speak out. Suez caused me real anguish, as it did so many others. For the only time in my life I joined a demonstration in Trafalgar Square. There I felt a total interloper. The crowd consisted mainly of people who could have worn demonstration campaign-medals extending back at least to the Jarrow marches, but who were really to come into their own a few years later with the foundation of the Campaign for Nuclear Disarmament. It was a distinct culture of its own, and they regarded me with as much distrust as had Muriel Belcher in the Colony Room. So I went on a solitary walk round and round Hyde Park one grey November afternoon, trying to come to terms with the event. It was not so much that the affair marked the end of Britain as a Great Power: it marked our end as a *good* power, one that could normally be expected to act honourably. It was for me what Munich had been for a slightly older generation and Iraq would be for a younger; but whereas Munich and Iraq were understandable if deplorable acts of *real-politik*, the sheer irrationality of the Suez adventure still fills me with melancholy amazement.

In any event, it was the end of an era. After that for a generation, under the dingy leadership of Harold Macmillan and Harold Wilson, Britain simply ceased to try in foreign affairs; abandoning its global responsibilities, following in the wake of an erratic American leadership, scrabbling belatedly to join the European enterprise, and getting the worst of every possible world. The 'flip-side', it must be said, was the creation of a standard of living for the bulk of its citizens beyond the wildest dreams of their grandfathers, if not indeed their fathers. Perhaps de Tocqueville was right in doubting the capacity of democracies to pursue consistent and successful foreign policies; but his countryman Raymond Aron was equally right when he remarked ruefully, when I met him at a conference in Italy, that the English people had regressed from being Romans to Italians in a single generation. *My* generation, I thought bitterly.

*   *   *

So I found myself swept out of my academic backwater in the Strand into the turbulent seas of current affairs, or at least the study of current affairs. I became a member of Chatham House, a body of which my mother and my Uncle George had as good Liberals been founder-members and some of whose meetings I had attended as a boy in the 1930s. The director at that time was the war-hero Monty Woodhouse, whose exploits with the Greek Resistance recalled those of T.E. Lawrence with the Arabs, but who, like Lawrence, found it hard to adjust to peacetime life. A dry, rather remote figure, he did not conceal his boredom with the whole enterprise and left much of the administration to his deputy director, a job that had happily been landed by Bunny Frankland before his transfer to the Imperial War Museum. Bunny welcomed me on board, and before long I found myself acting as rapporteur to a study-group set up to examine an idea that was enjoying fashionable currency at the time, 'Disengagement in Europe'. This examined current proposals for some kind of neutralization in Central Europe, ranging from a demilitarized belt on either side of the 'Iron Curtain' to the wholesale neutralization of Germany itself, together with the East European states of Poland, Hungary and Czechoslovakia. The leading spirit in this venture was the secretary of the Military Commentators' Circle, Eugene Hinterhoff, a sad, hard-working Polish ex-officer who was labouring mightily to restore links between his country and the West. He was to be badly disappointed by the sceptical tone of my report, but it was not sceptical enough for the formidably intelligent Marshal of the Royal Air Force, Sir John Slessor, on whose advice Chatham House decided not to publish it. But among the group's members was the defence correspondent of the *Observer*, Alastair Buchan, who angrily sprang to my defence and persuaded Allen Lane to publish the report as a 'Penguin Special'; thus gaining it a far wider readership than I had dared to expect. On the strength of this *opuscule* I now found myself regarded as an expert on international relations, especially the German question, about which I pontificated with great confidence on the BBC and elsewhere.

While I was working at Chatham House, another group was studying the implications of nuclear weapons for the conduct of war. Naturally I cultivated its members. Pat Blackett, the most distinguished, I already knew. Denis Healey, the Labour spokesman on Foreign Affairs, I already knew of: a jovial ogre with a ruddy butcher's face, a musically gentle voice and a truly penetrating mind. The others were Richard Goold Adams, an intimidatingly smooth Wykehamist who after flirting with journalism had gone into business, and Rear-Admiral Sir Anthony Buzzard, former Chief of Naval Intelligence, an obsessive schoolmasterly figure whose ideas about 'graduated deterrence' provided the driving force behind the study. They were to produce a pamphlet *On Limiting Nuclear War*, and were indirectly to cause another major development in my life.

Given my Chatham House connections, I was not surprised early in January 1957 to receive an invitation to a conference at the Bedford Hotel, Brighton, to discuss 'The Limitation of War in the Nuclear Age'. But I was surprised at its provenance, the London office of the Commission of the Churches on International Affairs (CCIA). This sponsorship, I was to discover, had resulted from the influence that Tony Buzzard, a devout Christian as well as an unwearying lobbyist, had been able to bring to bear on the Bishop of Chichester, Dr Bell, one of the few churchmen to have spoken out against the Allied bombing of Germany during the war. I was also surprised to be asked to chair one of the committees, admittedly a small one concerned with questions not of substance but procedure, to wit, 'Where do we go from here?' I was a little disappointed not to be allotted to one of the three main committees where great men – politicians, churchmen, servicemen, journalists – were discussing more fundamental issues, but flattered to be made chairman of anything – I was after all still a mere lecturer – and I revelled in unaccustomed power. ('One moment, Admiral, I think we should hear what Sir Henry has to say.') The most formidable figure on the committee was Sir Arthur Salter, a nut-like little man who had dominated Whitehall through two world wars and whose control of shipping had been instrumental in winning both. It was largely his ideas that I presented as our conclusions at the final plenary session on that dismal Sunday afternoon, as the sea heaved greyly outside. We should, we suggested, try to establish some kind of institute or association to study military problems in the same broad and independent fashion that Chatham House studied international affairs. This was agreed. A collection was taken to fund the initial steps, and a committee was duly set up. The chairman of the conference, Sir Kenneth Grubb, a driving little man dressed always in black coat and striped trousers who was also the chairman of the CCIA and of everything else one had ever heard of, inevitably became its chairman. The delightful and efficient conference organizer, the Revd Alan Booth, who ran the CCIA London office, became secretary. The membership consisted of the original Chatham House group with the omission of Blackett, who was too busy, and the addition of me.

There followed a series of meetings, some in Dick Goold-Adams's office in Duke of York Street, some in Alan Booth's office in Bryanston Street, some in Denis Healey's room in the House of Commons, where we slowly hammered together what was to become the Institute for Strategic Studies (ISS). Denis Healey charmed money out of the Ford Foundation. (He initially asked for $10,000, but they never gave less than $100,000, so he had to settle for $150,000 spread over three years.) Alan, Dick and I acted as a kind of triumvirate working out structures and procedures and selecting a director. There was not much problem about this: Alastair Buchan, if he would do it, was the obvious man. As defence correspondent of the *Observer*, he was one of the leading military commentators in Britain. As their former correspondent in the USA, he knew anyone of any consequence in Washington, and as an Old Etonian and son of John Buchan, the statesman and novelist, he could find his way round the British establishment as well. He was a melancholy, brooding figure whose thick fair hair made him look younger than his years, and prematurely aged face considerably older. Blackett helped to find us offices in the building of the Royal Society of Arts in the Adelphi, conveniently situated between Fleet Street and Whitehall, and even more conveniently five minutes' walk from King's. The Institute's subsequent headquarters in Tavistock Street and Arundel Street was even closer to the college. As 'strategic studies' developed at the Institute, I was able to embody it in the Master's degree at King's, cultivating both in fruitful interaction.

Although Kenneth Grubb remained chairman of our council and Alan Booth our secretary, we quickly found that we could not sustain our obligation to study both the political and the moral dimensions of our subject, as had been the original intention. Few of us shared the belief of the Campaign for Nuclear Disarmament that the moral dilemma created by the invention of nuclear weapons could be solved by simply abolishing them, but none of us could ignore the profound moral problems created by their possession, let alone their use. So a less well-known body came into being, with Bishop Bell as its president and Alastair as vice-president, entitled

CCADD (Council on Christian Approaches to Defence and Disarmament), with links to similar bodies in Europe and the USA. The existence, as I rapidly discovered, of an infinite number of 'Christian approaches' to the subject justified the use of the plural 'approaches': the problem of relating theology to politics was no easier in the twentieth century than it had been in the time of Constantine. So I had to add St Augustine to my reading-list as well as Clausewitz.

When Alastair died, tragically early, in 1976, I was asked to take his place as a vice-president of CCADD, and had to make up my mind whether I was really a Christian at all. I decided with many qualms that I probably was, and accepted. The Christian doctrine of the 'Just War', as refined by Aquinas and the rest of them, certainly provided as good guidance through the nuclear minefield as we were likely to get. About the application of that doctrine it has proved possible for Christians to argue as ferociously with one another as we have about every other moral question; but at least we no longer kill one another about it.

*   *   *

At about the same time, my interests were being tugged in yet another, if related, direction. I have already described the contacts I had made with the International Relations Department at the London School of Economics with Martin Wight and his younger colleague Hedley Bull; serious scholars deeply unhappy with the status and nature of their subject, then the prey of pacifist ideologues and maverick lawyers, and both trying to reintegrate it into the great traditions of Grotius and Vattel. Another such was the Cambridge historian Herbert Butterfield, who was in touch with a similar group of scholars in the USA. There the Rockefeller Foundation had sub-vented a high-level committee, containing such luminaries as George Kennan and Reinhold Niebuhr, to discuss the problems of world order in the nuclear age. Rockefeller now expressed an interest in supporting a similar body in Britain. Butterfield and Wight undertook its organization. On the strength of the articles and reviews that I was beginning to write, I was invited to join as a specialist on nuclear problems. Wight and Bull contributed their knowledge of international-relations theory – Wight's first paper bore the dispiriting title 'Why is there no International Theory?' – Butterfield and his former pupil Desmond Williams, then teaching in his native Dublin, furnished expertise in diplomatic history, while depth and weight was provided by the philosopher Donald Mackinnon – a charming man but one whose discourse I found almost unintelligible. Others came and went. Butterfield was at pains to invite practitioners in the field of international relations, who tended to be former pupils from Peterhouse who had attained eminence in the Foreign Office. One such was Adam Watson, clearly destined for the highest honours in the service, but who became so fascinated by the theory of his subject that he was eventually to resign and make a new and equally distinguished career as a Professor of International Relations in the USA.

This committee met three times a year in the Master's Lodge at Peterhouse to read and discuss papers that, although intellectually of the highest quality, sometimes seemed rather remotely related to our designated topic – if indeed we *had* a designated topic, which was not always clear. For much of the time I was out of my depth, though flattered to be thought capable of understanding any of it. When Butterfield retired from Peterhouse, the meetings became spasmodic. When he, and later Martin Wight, died, the committee became moribund. We were able to revive it in the 1970s at Oxford, where Hedley Bull joined me as Professor of International Relations and I could provide a venue at All Souls. Eventually we acquired a certain status in the academic world as 'The English School', rather as if we were a group of avant-garde painters; or rather *arrière garde*, distinguished by our roots in traditional theory and history from the 'behaviourism' and abstraction that characterized American teaching of the subject. If we did indeed have any influence in the academic world, I think we did a great deal of good; but I remain astonished to have found myself in such august company.

*   *   *

By this time I had a clear idea of what we were trying to do, both at King's and down the road at the ISS. As I expressed it in a rather pompous letter to *The Times*:

In most fields of social and political activity – public health for example, education, social welfare, economics, foreign affairs – there exists a large and well-informed body of public opinion, usually grounded in the subject by academic study, that acts both as a check and a goad on governmental action and provides when necessary a source of expertise. This is not the case in the field of defence. Outside the armed forces themselves there is no community of well-informed laymen capable of or interested in developing any kind of expertise on the subject. Public debate is left very largely to passionate but ill-informed ideologues of the left, and equally passionate and barely better-informed supporters of government policy, often themselves retired service-officers, on the right. The operational expertise of the armed forces can not be replicated beyond their ranks, nor should it be. But at the strategic level – what military forces were needed, how they should be raised and equipped, how they should be used as an instrument of national policy, above all what national policy should be – the opinion of an educated laity is indispensable; and it is entirely possible to form an intelligent opinion on these matters without access to highly classified information. Public opinion of some kind there is bound to be, and it will make itself felt at the ballot-box. Better that it should be well-informed than not informed at all.

That had been the thinking behind the establishment of the Department of War Studies at King's. The ISS took it a stage further. Nuclear weapons, and the threat of total annihilation that they brought with them, demanded a total reconsideration of the nature of war and peace; how to wage the first and maintain the second. This, we felt, should not be left entirely to officials in the Foreign Office and Ministry of Defence. We thus saw our first task as being to collect and circulate to our members as much relevant information and comment – at that time primarily American – as we could lay our hands on, through our journal, whose bleak title *Survival* indicated our view of the seriousness of the situation. Secondly, we should try to compile reliable statistics of weapons, especially nuclear weapons, on both sides – this was the time when wild reports of a non-existent 'missile gap' were being circulated by hawks in the USA to influence the presidential election. Thirdly, once we could afford it, we should engender inhouse research of our own. Finally, we should try to lure officials, uniformed and otherwise, out of their self-imposed purdah in Whitehall to engage in dialogue.

This was not easy. Had I at that stage read Kant, I would have been able to quote in our support one of his specifics for perpetual peace: that academics should leave bureaucrats to run the country, but that bureaucrats should listen to what academics had to say. I doubt whether this argument would have made much impact, but fortunately there were people in authority who already saw the point. Pre-eminent among them was Marshal of the Royal Air Force Sir John Slessor, he who had been so dismissive of my *Disengagement in Europe*. He was one of the most intelligent of our wartime military leaders: an airman who, unlike most of his colleagues, realized that air power was of little significance unless exercised in close association with surface forces. He was also one of the very few who had thought through the significance of nuclear weapons, and if he had not invented had certainly popularized the concept of 'nuclear deterrence', which he introduced into British defence policy in 1951, some three years before it was accepted by the US Joint Chiefs of Staff. His book *The Great Deterrent*, published in 1957 after his retirement, was, with the exception of Blackett's *Political and Military Consequences of Atomic Energy* and Liddell Hart's even more perceptive essay *The Revolution in Warfare*, the most important study of the subject yet published in Britain. Like them, he welcomed the foundation of the ISS as a forum where such thinking could be carried forward. The presence of these three eminences on our council gave the Institute credibility from the outset. Slessor's example encouraged senior officers from all three services to contribute to our seminars, though few could listen so patiently and respond so courteously as he did to brash young academics half his age and with none of his experience.

At a lower level in the official hierarchy, though no less effective in influencing it, was Michael Palliser, a friend not only from Wellington but also from Oxford and the Coldstream. His career in the Foreign Office was to take him through punishing stints as Private Secretary in Downing Street to Harold Wilson when Marcia Falkender was his political adviser, and Permanent Under-Secretary in the era of Margaret Thatcher, but nothing shook his unruffled calm. At that time, 1958, he was head of the Policy Planning Staff in the Foreign Office, and he needed little persuasion to sign up with the ISS and get his colleagues and successors, especially John Thomson and John Barnes, to do the same. The infection spread to their colleagues in the Ministry of Defence, Frank Cooper, Arthur Hockaday and Michael Quinlan. There were other more shadowy figures who furnished us with the information that made it possible to provide the statistics that gave *The Military Balance*, our annual report on international armaments, credibility from the beginning. In fact the relationship with Whitehall could not have been happier. Seldom can bureaucrats have listened so courteously to academics, and academics have basked so gladly under the happy illusion that their ideas were being taken seriously in the corridors of power.

*   *   *

None of this would have been of the slightest consequence if the ISS had not been taken seriously in the USA. There strategic studies had been born when the first bomb had fallen on Hiroshima, and come of age with the first thermonuclear explosion at Bikini seven years later. As early as 1945 Bernard Brodie had written: 'Thus far the chief purpose of a military establishment has been to win wars. From now on its chief purpose must be to avert them. It can have no other purpose.' Understandably, the defence chiefs of the USA did not agree. They had seen no problem in integrating the atomic bombs dropped on Hiroshima into their armouries in order to deal with a war with the Soviet Union that seemed imminent at the time of the Berlin Blockade in 1948. In 1949 the Soviets acquired their own nuclear capacity, which was sufficient to keep the war that broke out in Korea the following year limited to 'conventional' forces. Then in 1953 the USA exploded a thermonuclear device of such terrifying power that it was hard to see how it could be related to what was now seen as the major problem confronting 'the Free World': Soviet 'indirect aggression', of which the Korean War was seen as an example.

In 1954 John Foster Dulles, the American Secretary of State, declared the intention of his government to retaliate against any Soviet aggression by means, and at places, of its own choosing. Within a year the Soviets had developed their own thermonuclear capability. Worse, in 1957 the successful launch of the manned spacecraft *Sputnik* indicated that they had out-distanced the USA in what was becoming known as 'the Space Race'. The USA thus seemed vulnerable as it had never been before. Could it now use its nuclear weapons at all without fear of retaliation – or, worse, pre-emption? Could it be relied on to use them in defence of its European allies? Could 'limited' wars be fought, such as that in Korea, without the use of nuclear weapons, and if so, how could those limits to be agreed and communicated? Was limited *nuclear* war possible? Finally, was nuclear disarmament possible, and how could it be enforced?

On all these, and cognate subjects, a flood of literature had been pouring out of the USA during the last years of the 1950s, by writers such as Brodie himself, Herman Kahn, William Kaufmann, Henry Kissinger, Klaus Knorr, Oscar Morgenstern, Paul Nitze, Robert Osgood, Thomas Schelling, Jacob Viner and Albert Wohlstetter. We saw one of our first tasks at the ISS as being to familiarize ourselves and our members with what these pundits were thinking. Next, we had to contact them and persuade as many as possible to attend a conference in the summer of 1959, at Oxford. The topic was what would later be called 'extended deterrence': the credibility, or lack of it, of the American 'nuclear guarantee'. Could the Americans be relied on to use nuclear weapons against the Soviet homeland in the event of an attack on Western Europe by Soviet conventional forces, when the Soviets could retaliate in kind against the USA? Alastair persuaded a remarkable number of these pundits to attend and himself acted as rapporteur.

The book that resulted – *NATO in the 1960s* – makes ironic reading today. It concluded that NATO could remain viable only if its European members were prepared, individually and collectively, to spend far more on their conventional forces than had hitherto been politically acceptable, and if some form of nuclear force under joint NATO command could be established in Europe. The same recommendations were to be made, in some form or other, for the next 30 years, and were still being made when the Cold War came to an end. The problem of 'extended deterrence', the readiness of the USA to risk nuclear retaliation against its own territory by initiating nuclear war in defence of its European allies, provided material for innumerable conferences. Britain and France found their own solution by developing their own 'nuclear deterrents' (though how independent the

British deterrent was, once it relied on purchase of US submarine-based missiles, remains a matter of opinion). But what about the Germans? If West Germany were not provided with some credible guarantee of American nuclear support, might not the Soviet Union woo or intimidate her into neutrality by a promise of reunification – or, worse, might she not insist on developing nuclear weapons of her own? And faced with these possibilities, how could NATO possibly hold together at all?

I must admit that I was always sceptical about the reality of such a threat. West Germany was full of American forces and their families. The idea that any US government would simply write these off in the event of a Soviet attack, nuclear or otherwise, or that any Soviet government would gamble on their doing so, seemed to me very remote indeed. But I was always easily out-argued, not so much by the American 'defence intellectuals' as by the formidable intellects of our own Foreign Office and Ministry of Defence. None the less, these arguments gave me the opportunity of attending at least two conferences a year on the topic, which hugely and agreeably extended the range of my own friendships and helped to create on an international level exactly the kind of 'civil society' of defence intellectuals that we were trying to build up at home.

The French initially, during these early years of de Gaulle's Fifth Republic, were predictably sticky. We found that the directorates of their government-funded institutions could be as obdurate and unfriendly as their Soviet counterparts. But there were free spirits who from the beginning refused to toe the Gaullist line, and over the years they multiplied: André Beaufre and François de Rose, Pierre Hassner and Dominic Moïsi, Thierry de Montbrial and Jean-Louis Gergorin, François Heisbourg, and above all the incomparable Raymond Aron, all brought powerful and independent minds to our debates. With the Germans a comparable sodality was already being built up at the annual Königswinter conferences, to which I found myself invited partly on the strength of *Disengagement in Europe* but largely, I suspect, on the recommendation of Dick Crossman, who was one of the founders and with whom I was now on terms of close friendship. (About him I could write much more. He was a dear man; but the country owes to Harold Wilson a deep debt for keeping him well away from the Foreign Office and the Department of Education, the two ministries that he really coveted and where he could have done deep and irreversible harm.) The transnational links established at Königswinter, as we sloshed back the Rheinwein late at night and toiled up the Drachenfels early in the morning, extended far wider than the defence community, but they strengthened the links we were establishing with Karl Kaiser, Theo Sommer, Uwe Nehrlich, Christoph Bertram and, most usefully of all, Helmut Schmidt.

If 'extended deterrence' provided an excellent excuse for holding such regular conferences, so did the topic of disarmament, or rather 'arms control', as the more sophisticated learned to call it. This was the subject of the next conference the ISS organized at Oxford in 1960, which was if anything an even greater success than the first. It was a topic in which the new Kennedy administration was showing considerable interest, and we were exceptionally lucky in persuading Hedley Bull to act as rapporteur. The text he provided for discussion, later published under the title *Control of the Arms Race*, was to become a classic. Hedley was an abrasive young Australian who had no time for the woolly cant that well-meaning liberals had accumulated around the topic over the past half-century, and to watch him deftly despatch their sacred cows was a sheer joy. We could not reinvent the world, he argued: we live inevitably in a world of mistrustful sovereign powers, and the best we could do was to make it possible for them to mistrust one another a little less. It would not be too much to say that his little book revolutionized thinking on the subject. It should still be the point of departure for both academics and bureaucrats.

Anyhow, the Ford Foundation liked what we had done with their three-year grant, and gave us more. In 1964 we became the International Institute for Strategic Studies (IISS), and extended our range yet further. As we did so, I extended my own interests, experiences and, above all, travels.

9

The USA

In the spring of 1960 the Ford Foundation gave me a generous grant to tour the USA and visit the universities and institutions where strategic studies were beginning to sprout. I was to visit the States frequently thereafter, but since this was my most comprehensive tour and I kept a diary, it is worth reporting in full.

Cynics would now say that I was being brainwashed, but if this was so it proved very effective. I already knew something about American history. I had taken the 'special subject' on the origins of the Civil War when I was at Oxford; partly because even then I realized the important part that the USA would play in the postwar world, but partly also, I am afraid, because all the sources were in English. Nevertheless I was as ignorant as were most Englishmen of my generation about the astonishing diversities and oddities that underlay the bland uniform culture with which the movies had made us familiar from birth.

The first culture-shock came on the evening I arrived in New York. Ah, New York! Jazzy New York, unsleeping New York, Bernstein On-the-Town New York! My host was Arthur Hadley, a notable journalist with a fine war-record whom I had met at the Brighton conference. On my first evening he took me to dine at the Century Association, and that opened my eyes to the diversity of American culture. There was not a stick of furniture to be seen from later than the early nineteenth century. Portraits of grave ante-bellum statesmen graced the walls and antique silver the table. An exquisite dinner was served by dignified, elderly black stewards wearing white gloves. (Many later visits have persuaded me that this impression could not have been strictly accurate, but that is the way it seemed at the time.) That was not the image of New York, or indeed of the USA, I had in my head. I was quickly to learn that somewhere, most likely New York itself, I would find whatever image of America I or anyone else had in their heads. Next morning Arthur took me to breakfast in a diner where the delicious coffee, crisp bacon, two eggs over easy with hash browns introduced me to another, more familiar America. But the apparent uniformity of the country, and the ceaseless rhetoric used to support it, was essential to hold together a people who were in fact infinitely diverse.

I learned much else during those six weeks. The first revelation was that everything in the USA was not just bigger, but usually better than at home.

So it should have been: not only were Americans more numerous and richer than we were but their wealth and hospitality also attracted the greatest world authorities on any topic one cares to mention, whether they were there on prolonged visits or as permanent immigrants; an immigration greatly increased by the Jewish diaspora of the Nazi era. Whatever truth there may have been during the Second World War – and even then there was precious little – about the British playing Greeks to the American Romans, there was certainly none now. The Americans had little to learn about the world from us or anyone else, and anything they needed to learn they had plenty of experts of their own to teach them – if they cared to listen.

The second revelation was that they took their responsibilities for world leadership with a seriousness that, coming from a post-Suez Britain sunk into ironic self-flagellation, I found awe-inspiring. And the third was that, deeply interested as they still were in Europe, they had equal if not greater concerns with their neighbours in Latin America and even more with the Far East. (The fact that all this came as a surprise betrays the depth of a parochialism that was, I am afraid, all too typical of my generation of Englishmen.) But all these interests, and all this expertise, was forced into the straitjacket of the Cold War. By all but a tiny number of experts, the Soviet Union was seen in the USA as a force of cosmic evil whose policy and intentions could be divined simply by multiplying Marxist dogma by Soviet military capacity. The view that 'the Soviets' were *Russians*, with fears and problems of their own derived from past history and present weakness, and might be dealt with as rational adults, had to wait for Henry Kissinger's advent to office a decade later before it made any impact on American policy. That is not to say that when I advanced this view it was not courteously heard and intelligently discussed, nor that it did not find a measure of agreement in sympathetic quarters in Washington and New York; but a fourth thing that I learned about the Americans was the sheer ferocity of their political system, and the lengths to which political activists would go to silence and humiliate their political adversaries. In this respect at least, nothing seems to have changed in 40 years.

The spring of 1960 was a particularly interesting time to be in the USA – though it is hard to think of any moment in my lifetime when American politics have *not* been interesting. These were the last months of the Eisenhower presidency which had set the mood of the 1950s. Eisenhower's emollient rule had calmed the turbulence of the McCarthy era and created the peaceful, wealthy, self-satisfied society immortalized by the paintings of

Norman Rockwell; a society against which in the 1960s the young would react with as much savagery as had the European revolutionaries of 1848 against the smug *biedemeyer* world that had bred them. This tranquil regime had been badly shaken, as we have seen, by the Soviet launch of *Sputnik* in 1957, which threw the American public into one of their periodic fits of panic in which it becomes difficult to make the voice of reason heard at all. It was widely believed not only that the Soviets were ahead in 'the Space Race', but also that they had established a lead in Intercontinental Ballistic Missiles (ICBMs) and that the territory of the USA now lay at their mercy.

The Eisenhower administration knew this to be nonsense, but this knowledge derived from intelligence overflights of Soviet territory by U2 aircraft whose very existence they denied; until the Russians very inconveniently shot one down on the eve of a summit conference at Paris, thus giving the then Soviet leader, N.S. Khrushchev, the opportunity publicly to humiliate Eisenhower personally and the USA in general. Hawkish Republicans and ambitious Democrats descended like vultures on the wounded administration. 'The missile gap' became the *leitmotiv* of the Democratic presidential candidate J.F. Kennedy, who should have known, and did know, considerably better. The electoral contest was well under way when I arrived in New York, and a pretty dirty one it proved to be.

*   *   *

Thanks to the Ford Foundation, and thanks even more to the personal introductions provided by Alastair, who seemed to know everyone worth knowing, my time was well spent. In New York I gave a dinner-talk to the Council on Foreign Relations (far grander and more dignified than its British cousin Chatham House) about the British attempt to maintain its nuclear status by purchasing a ballistic missile, Skybolt, from the USA. (This was my first experience of those American meals, worthy of Alice in Wonderland, where, after a hurried starter, one was called on to speak and watch course after delicious course being devoured by the audience until by the time one sat down there was nothing left.) I visited that grandest of defence correspondents Hanson Baldwin in his office at that grandest of newspapers the *New York Times*, who expressed guarded doubts about the missile gap. Brian Urquhart, an Oxford contemporary of Alastair's who was already principal aide to the Secretary-General of the United Nations, gave me a conducted tour of the UN building, including a debate in the General Assembly where the Saudi delegate was denouncing Western immorality. I renewed contact with my cousin Walter Eberstadt, who had fled with his family from Hamburg to Britain, where he had first been interned and then allowed to fight with the British army, which he did with great distinction.

He had finally settled in the USA and was now a partner in Lazard *frères*. He told me that the American space industry was not doing too well, owing to the enervating effect of the climate in Florida and California where it was principally sited (air-conditioning, be it noted, was still in its infancy). More significantly, he believed that the pressure for rearmament from the military–industrial complex was so strong as to be irresistible, whoever won the election. Finally I visited the Institute for War and Peace Studies at Columbia University, which I saw as a role-model for my own miniscule department if I could raise any money. There I met, among others, Sam Huntington, already famous for his book on civil–military relations *The Soldier and the State*, who invited me to dinner the following evening to meet, among others, a young Polish specialist in Soviet Studies from Harvard, Zbigniev Brezinski. Unlike most Americans but like all Poles, Zbig *did* know quite lot about Russian history, and did not like what he knew. It was to show 20 years later when he became National Security Adviser to the Carter Administration. I found him, as I have found so many Poles, slightly bonkers but perfectly charming.

And so to Washington, which I found to be a city at war. Officers in uniform thronged its streets. On the first evening in my hotel we were entertained at dinner by a male-voice choir singing what they announced as 'The Badlim'. This proved to be the Battle Hymn of the Republic. As they thundered out the lines 'As He died to make men holy, let us die to make men free' I wept as freely as anybody (I always do), but could not help wondering how nuclear weapons could 'make men free' in any meaningful sense of the word. I received copious briefings in the Pentagon: one from an air force general who had no time for 'limited wars' or 'arms control' but favoured massive retaliation 'and then some'; one from a scholarly and intelligent army general, 'Tick' Bonesteel, a Rhodes scholar and Oxford contemporary of Alastair's, who spent two hours explaining to me the whole spectrum of American defence policy; and one from the navy that consisted of a very impressive plug for the Polaris submarine-launched missile that was just coming into service and would, they argued convincingly, transform the whole nuclear balance. It was not clear that the officials of the three services had any idea of, or interest in, what the others were saying. I was grilled about British defence policy by sceptical officials of the State Department. I was given lunch at the Metropolitan Club by the great Walter Lippmann and invited to a grand Georgetown dinner-party by Joe Alsop, clever, cantankerous, malicious, where I disgraced myself by arriving half an hour early but sat next to his far nicer brother Stuart, who had served with the British army in Italy. I was given a quiet and productive lunch at the Press Club by Henry Brandon, the *Sunday Times* correspondent and an intimate of the Kennedy family. On the Hill (as I rapidly learned to call it) I was courteously received by Senators Fulbright and 'Scoop' Jackson. The latter found me a seat in the public gallery of the Senate for a debate about the extension of 'civil rights', where senators from Southern states were speaking with as much indignation about infringement of 'states' rights' as their ante-bellum predecessors. Senator Kennedy put in an appearance; a tall, handsome, suntanned figure whose *jeune premier* looks seemed more suited to an old-style musical comedy star than to the serious business of being President of the USA. I lectured at the National War College on 'The Dilemmas of British Defence Policy'; a lecture that, with minimal updating, I continued to give to a variety of audiences, military and academic, for the next 25 years. I visited the Johns Hopkins School of International Studies and met those founding fathers, Arnold Wolfers and Hans Morgenthau. And, not least in importance, I made contact, as an 'official historian' of the Second World War, with my American colleagues, especially Maurice Matloff and Forrest Pogue, and felt bilious with envy at the magnificent resources they had at their disposal which they so freely placed at mine.

By this time I had learned something more about the Americans – the reckless generosity of their hospitality. One or two of my historian colleagues invited me to their homes simply so that I could put my feet up and relax. 'I can't imagine what it must be like', said one of them sympathetically, 'half your time spent in a hotel room, the other in being polite to people.' And, he might have added, drinking too much. It was an era, now thank God almost forgotten, when Americans were still getting Prohibition out of their systems by simply knocking the stuff back in enormous quantities. Outside New York and Georgetown, an evening's hospitality might consist in up to three solid hours' drinking whisky or dry martinis before adjourning, all appetite now totally destroyed, to a meal consisting of salad and an enormous steak (indifferently cooked by one's host) with nothing to accompany it but coffee. Wine was then for wimps. The only time my veneer of courtesy really cracked was when, in the middle of one such meal, my hosts started teasing me about British cuisine. I must by then have drunk about six large whiskies, and retaliated in kind. It was an occasion that I prefer to forget.

Evenings like that tended to multiply when I headed south and west. From Washington I set out on a four-week safari embracing Chapel Hill and Duke Universities in North Carolina, RAND Corporation in Los Angeles, San Francisco, Madison Wisconsin, Columbus Ohio, Harvard, MIT, Dartmouth College, West Point, and so back to New York; visiting either defence research institutes or universities where strategic studies of some kind were being carried on.

I was driven to Chapel Hill by Louis Morton, principal official historian of the Pacific War, now teaching at Dartmouth College and on much the same fact-finding tour as myself. It took six hours. Once we were over the Potomac we were in the South, and its poverty, wildness and lack of cultivation became clear almost at once. The scrubby woods and corn-patches round Richmond could have changed hardly at all since the Civil War. South of Richmond it was even worse, trees falling and rotting in shallow swamps, wooden shacks scattered in barren fields of red clay. The march of civilization was evidenced by roads being scooped out of the wilderness by huge bulldozers, with billboards, filling stations and motels already lining their sides. 'A prodigal, wasteful civilization', I wrote rather primly in my notebook, 'How I long for the neatness of Europe, the land precisely apportioned, the fields meticulously cultivated by generations who have lived on them for centuries and had to make them fruitful! Here settlers have raped the soil and casually moved on, leaving an exhausted wilderness.' But when at last we reached Chapel Hill, we found the South of romance: large gracious houses with pillared porches scattered among lawns and blooming cherry and dogwood. I was put up at the Carolina Inn, elegant with faux antique furniture, and entertained by Robin Higham, who was that rarest of creatures, an English immigrant, and son of David Higham, my literary agent in London. Robin drove me over to Duke University, a Gothic pile built in the 1920s with tobacco money set in a glorious arboretum, and introduced me to Ted Ropp. Ted was a brilliant teacher who published virtually nothing in his lifetime; his doctoral thesis, on the French navy in the nineteenth century, was famous among scholars long before it was posthumously published. Between them they ran classes in military history and intended to set up a national security programme. We exchanged views, and I gave talks to their colleagues and students on 'Problems of European Defence'; my alternative and equally hardwearing party-piece. In my notebook I described the audience as 'relaxed young men in open-necked shirts and trousers'. Shirts? *Trousers*? When did jeans and t-shirts come in?

Then the long flight to the West Coast; for the first time always an adventure for Europeans. 'Fly-over country' my New York friends called it. 'Looking-glass Land' I preferred, with the total regularity of its chess-board square fields and its square towns. When it grew dark we saw only the lights of the towns in straight criss-cross lines with clusters of red neon in the centre. Yes, I know that this is now a familiar sight to every British tourist, but to me it was new and astonishing. O my America! My New Found Land!

Los Angeles was hell. In many ways it still is, but then it was worse. The small and sleazy downtown area was surrounded by an infinite wasteland of bungalows (often no more than shacks), superstores, fast-food joints, filling-stations and used-car lots, criss-crossed by freeways from which it was unwise to stray. There was an elegant fringe on the hills to the north – Pacific Palisades, Bel Air, Hollywood – where the movie stars lived and from which one had the romantic view of the city lights so familiar from dozens of 1930s films. The rest was soul-destroying. I was hosted by a former research assistant to Basil Liddell Hart, who kindly offered me hospitality, but who proved to be a melancholy divorcee living in a small downtown apartment with a single double-bedroom that I had to share. On the first day he showed me round the town, including a visit to Disneyland that was sheer joy. The next day was Easter Sunday. He judged it too hot and everywhere to be too crowded for us to go out at all. We stayed indoors all day and relays of his friends came to visit us, drinking whisky from three in the afternoon until long after midnight. Kind as my host was, I swore never to visit Los Angeles again unless to stay with someone I knew, and with my own transport. I kept my promise, and on subsequent visits have enjoyed myself a great deal more.

Next day I visited RAND Corporation at its glitzy headquarters near the beach in Santa Monica. RAND ('Research And Development') had been set up by the US air force after the war to keep together the civilian scientists, economists and sages who had served it so well in wartime, and who were now largely focusing on the problem of deterring, if necessary fighting, and surviving nuclear war. They included some of the cleverest men I have ever met: Charles Hitch the economist; Andy Marshall, who was to mastermind American defence policy for the rest of the twentieth century, Harry Rowen, Jim Digby, and of course Albert Wohlstetter, of whom more later. They were overwhelmingly from the hard sciences: mathematicians, physicists, economists, systems-analysts, engineers. I talked to them about British defence policy; they talked to me about second-strike forces; we talked to each other about limited war and arms control. All complained bitterly about what they saw as the flabbiness and lack of leadership of the Eisenhower administration. Most of them were to be recruited into the Kennedy administration a year later by Robert McNamara and descended on Washington, busting with fresh ideas.

I was immensely impressed, but not altogether happy. For one thing, RAND seemed like a monastery inhabited by clever theologians, who both by temperament and (even more) by location were quite remote from the real affairs of the world. I had already formed the impression that the USA was a different planet, but California belonged to another galaxy. This impression was strengthened by a research project being carried out by some of the Randsmen about how long it would take to reconstitute Los Angeles after a nuclear war. Not long, they reckoned. They were possibly right, if anyone was mad enough to want to do anything of the kind. But how could one ever reconstruct Paris, London, Rome, or Madrid?

Further, the Randsmen seemed to be falling into the error of their predecessors of the Enlightenment era (against which Clausewitz had reacted so vigorously) of assuming that everything connected with war could be quantifiable and so making quite unrealistic calculations. They left out friction, the contingent, the unforeseeable, all the things that really mattered. They reduced the infinite complexities of world affairs, in particular of relations with the Soviet Union, to 'bean counts' of nuclear weapons. (One particularly ludicrous assumption was that, because the Soviet Union had lost 20 million dead in the Second World War, they would be prepared to risk comparable losses in an attempt at 'world conquest'). The most trenchant of RAND's critics was indeed one of their own, Bernard Brodie, a naval historian who had been enlisted under the guise of a political scientist. Bernard's dissatisfaction with the work of his colleagues led him to study Clausewitz, which was to prove instrumental in his powerful support for the publication of the new translation that Peter Paret and I were to set on foot a few years later.

Bernard Brodie's great antagonist at RAND, and indeed everywhere else, was Albert Wohlstetter. Albert and his equally able wife Roberta became personal friends, and we remained so for as long as we avoided discussing nuclear strategy. Albert was the most charming and civilized of men, who behind the façade of a gastronome, bibliophile and general bon viveur had a mind like a steel trap. He was a mathematical logician by training, and it showed. His basic assumption, common to so many of his countrymen, was the insatiable hostility and total ruthlessness of a Soviet Union bent on world conquest, that would run any risk to achieve its ends. 'Realism' in his view consisted in worst-case analysis. He used this to convince himself and everyone else of the vulnerability of the USA to nuclear attack, which could be overcome only through huge increases in military expenditure. He was, and remains even after his death and the end of the Cold War, a highly influential figure in American politics, many outstanding 'neoconservatives' having studied under him at the University of Chicago. Much of what he said and did was salutary in dispersing muddled and wishful thinking, but regrettably he conducted his controversies with a ferocity strangely at odds with his debonair personality – a ferocity that, alas, his pupils have imitated. There was always, it was once said, a distinct odour of burning when Albert was around.

Neither Bernard nor Albert were at home on this, my first, visit to RAND. Nor was Herman Kahn, that grotesque and globular figure who was about to publish his study *On Thermonuclear War*, an essay on what he accurately called 'thinking the unthinkable' that must have done wonders for the recruitment of the Campaign for Nuclear Disarmament. The cold-blooded, almost casual manner in which he discussed the level of 'megadeaths' to be expected if nuclear weapons were used, and the various levels of nuclear conflict to be expected, created a *succès de scandale*. But was he wrong, I wondered? Should not somebody have been thinking about such things? Anyhow, it was a relief to leave RAND Corporation and fly north to San Francisco.

My reaction to San Francisco was that of any paid-up European: here at last was a real city, beautiful, civilized, sophisticated, innocently wicked. I felt that it was, like Brighton, somewhere to spend a weekend rather than make one's home. Still, after Los Angeles it was bliss. I visited Berkeley, but although the political scientists and historians received me politely, none seemed very interested in strategic studies. Although I was taken to see the famous nuclear accelerator on the top of the hill, I was more occupied in admiring the superb view of San Francisco harbour than in trying to understand what they were doing there. On the campus students were actually drilling, sweating uncomfortably in the archaic uniforms of the ROTC, reminding me that this was a nation that believed itself to be at war. To find any serious intellectual interest in military affairs I had to take the bus out to Palo Alto and visit the Stanford Research Institute and the Hoover Institute for War, Revolution and Peace on the campus of Stanford University. The first was a yet more glitzy version of RAND, carrying out research for the military–industrial complex in Silicon Valley just up the road. The second had for the past 40 years been the destination of an unhappy procession of Russian emigrés, including Alexander Kerensky who had only recently died, so the black view of the Soviet Union that prevailed there was predictable. Between them, these two establishments made RAND seem a nest of doves.

All in all I was beginning to wonder whether the so-called 'Atlantic community' really extended as far as California, so it was a great relief to find myself flying east again. I touched down at Madison, Wisconsin, and Columbus, Ohio, both of whose universities had received pots of money to promote strategic studies and did not quite know what to do with it. I ended up at Cambridge, Massachusetts, and there I felt at home again. Not only was there a thriving strategic studies community along the Charles River, but the subject was also being discussed there in terms that I understood and by people with whom I felt an instant affinity, even if I did not agree with them. I was put up at the Brattle Inn, run by two New England female dragons who treated me like a drunken sophomore. Harvard Yard was full of clean, quiet young men with jackets, ties and short haircuts, almost indecently polite and gentlemanly (Oh, the fifties!). I attended a lunchtime seminar addressed by Dean Rusk, then president of the Ford Foundation and not yet Secretary of State, who explained, in the wake of Eisenhower's recent débâcle at Paris, why presidents should not attend summit-meetings. I visited the Center for International Affairs, then run by Bob Bowie, former Assistant Secretary of State to John Foster Dulles, to whom he bore a startling resemblance, and a young professor, Henry Kissinger. Henry had already made a considerable reputation with his book *Nuclear Weapons and Foreign Policy* and was now working, he told me, on a study of Bismarck; which gave us more interesting things to talk about than limited nuclear war.

Then I journeyed along the Charles River to the Massachusetts Institute for Technology and a dinner-party where I met Walt Rostow, with whom I discussed the bombing of Germany and the analysis of its results that he had helped to write; Arthur Schlesinger Jr, whose *Age of Jackson* I had fortunately just read, and others who then meant nothing to me but whose names were to loom large in the Kennedy administration. The next day was spent discussing arms control, largely with scientists such as Max Milliken, Jerome Wiesner, Bernard Feld, Ithiel Poole, and others whom I was to get to know better at the Pugwash conferences, of which more later. During the course of my visit I also met, and talked to, Tom Schelling and Joe Nye. All I found to be deeply humane men, with a well-founded dread of nuclear war (especially among the scientists who understood exactly what it meant), but also an understanding of the problem of power, and a mistrust of the terrible simplifications perpetrated by their Californian colleagues as strong as my own.

All these names may mean little to future generations, but to mine they meant much. If I drop them here it is not out of vanity (although I did feel, and continue to feel, great pride at being able to count so many of them among my friends) but because they were at that moment waiting in the wings for the curtain to rise on the Kennedy administration, in which they were to hold positions of influence (always excepting Kissinger, who was biding his time) and do so much to mould American policy throughout the coming decade. Seldom can a ruler have collected around him a group of such intellectual brilliance. It was an era that was to end in disaster thanks to Vietnam, of which few of them had then ever heard; but at least it did not end in nuclear war.

Somewhat reassured, I continued my journey south through the white clapboard villages of New England, each with its prettily spired church or meeting-house, to Dartmouth College; gracious Georgian buildings full of tough, ski-mad young men on whom Diego Rivera's subversive murals in the library seemed to make little impression (but perhaps they seldom visited the library). There I met up again with Lou Morton and discussed with his colleagues Eugene Lyons and Laurence Radway the problem of military education. Then by train down the broad, forested Connecticut River valley, Dvorak's *New World Symphony* echoing in my head, until at nightfall I came to Newhaven and Yale.

Once there had been a flourishing strategic-studies seminar at Yale under Arnold Wolfers, but for some reason the then president had closed it down. There were now only scattered historians to talk to: Hans Gatzke, Hajo Holborn, George Emerson, Paul Hammond. I was whisked through establishments that were one day to become part of my life – Mory's, the Elizabethan Club, the Sterling Memorial Library – almost without noticing them. The magnificent neo-Gothic campus only brought to my jaded mind Denis Brogan's unkind comment: 'It only shows what the Goths could have done if only they had had the money.' But by then I was very tired. There was one more visit, to West Point, a baronial pile romantically situated on a bend of the Hudson River, where I learned about their education programme and talked to an instructors' seminar about NATO. Then, richly freighted with knowledge and experience, I caught the plane home.

∗   ∗   ∗

As one of the first Englishmen – at least civilian Englishmen – to travel in the States and talk about defence questions, I brought back enough invitations from universities, research institutes and military academies for a return visit to keep me going literally for a lifetime. But I was to return far sooner than I expected.

In the autumn of 1961, after Kennedy had won the election and my new friends from RAND and the Charles River were ensconced respectively in the Pentagon under Robert McNamara, and the State Department under the aegis of Mac Bundy, formerly Dean of Harvard and now National Security Adviser to the President, I was invited to attend a conference of the Pugwash Association (or Movement, as some preferred to call it) at Stowe, Vermont.

'Pugwash' had been founded a few years earlier and named after the country estate of the wealthy Canadian who hosted and financed it. (The unfortunate association of the name with one Captain Pugwash, a pirate in a popular British comic strip, meant that the enterprise was never taken so seriously in the United Kingdom as it deserved.) Its founders were primarily Western scientists, many of them conscience-stricken about the part they had played in the invention of nuclear weapons but all quite properly terrified at the possibility of nuclear war and anxious to promote the cause of disarmament by establishing contact with their Soviet colleagues. Some may have fallen into the category of Lenin's 'useful idiots', but by no means all. Western governments had been paying at least lip-service to the idea of GCD (General and Comprehensive – for some 'Complete' – Disarmament) ever since the foundation of the United Nations; but towards the end of the 1950s the possibility of more limited measures, at least to prevent the possibility of 'unintended' nuclear war or the proliferation of nuclear weapons, was being taken more seriously in government circles. The concept of 'disarmament', with all its unfortunate prewar implications, was yielding to that, more respectable, of 'arms control'. The subject was already, as I have indicated, a topic of hot debate at RAND and MIT during my visit in the spring of 1960; and the following winter Kennedy, while still president elect, permitted some of the leading participants in that debate to test the water by accepting invitations to attend a Pugwash meeting in Moscow.

I gather that they got very little joy out of it. It was clear to all except the useful idiots that the Soviet government regarded this as a God-given opportunity for 'peace' propaganda. Their delegates were prepared to discuss nothing except General and Complete Disarmament, and that as total and rapid as possible. Questions about inspection and control of arms reduction were brushed aside. Proposals for practical limited measures were ignored. On the Soviet side the discussion was dominated by bureaucrats whose status as scientists was obscure. The really distinguished scientists they fielded, who included such world-famous figures as Kapitza, Tamm and Tupolev, gabbled embarrassedly through scripts evidently written for them but otherwise remained silent. The Soviet line was that anyone who did not sign up to GCD, and a final communiqué endorsing it, was by definition a warmonger and saboteur and had no place in 'the movement'. It was not a good beginning.

None the less, the Americans persevered. To get Soviet scientists into the same room as their Western colleagues, at least listening to Western views, was seen as a crack in the Iron Curtain. Western scientists, or most of them, could be relied on not to accept a role as unwitting tools of Soviet propaganda. Indeed, the more they heard of it, the less likely this would be. So a return match was arranged for September 1961, and US allies were encouraged to join in. The secretary and moving spirit in Pugwash (to beg the question whether it was a Movement or not) was Joseph Rotblat, an émigré Pole who had worked on the Manhattan Project and regretted it ever since. He was a saintly figure and, like most saints, a great deal shrewder than he appeared. Pat Blackett (who was certainly not a useful idiot) took me to see him, and persuaded him (and me) that no harm would be done by taking me along. My role, as I saw it, would be to hold my own in the political arguments with the Soviet apparatchiks, who were no more scientists than I was, thus freeing the real scientists on both sides for more fruitful discussions. Thus it was that I found myself in the company of such great men as Pat Blackett himself, William Penney, John Cockcroft, Solly Zuckerman and Rudolph Peierls, together with their equally eminent American colleagues in the placid surroundings of the Vermont hills just as the leaves were beginning to turn.

We were housed in great comfort in a village surrounding a well-equipped conference centre. The Americans had also sent 'political scientists' like Henry Kissinger and Bob Bowie who gave as good as they got. Utterly stymied on GCD, the Soviets had to listen to sometimes recondite proposals for arms control emanating from RAND, and there were times when they had my sympathy. They were at a disadvantage: although simultaneous translation facilities were provided for plenary sessions, there were none for the smaller groups where more intimate discussions were intended to take place; so the Russians had to cluster in bewildered groups round the translators who were themselves often at a loss to know what the Americans were talking about. But I came away with two very strong impressions. The first was that the Russians were just as frightened of us as we were of them. *Sputnik* may have scared the hell out of the Americans, but the huge growth of the US air force and ballistic missile programme worried the Soviets no less. The Soviet superiority in conventional forces in Europe may have worried the West, but the revival of German armed forces and their embodiment in NATO evoked in the Russians terrifying memories of a kind that we could only guess at. Of course, Soviet government propaganda played on these fears for all they were worth, but they were real, and had to be taken into account. A coach tour had been arranged on our free afternoon to show our guests the beauties of New England, but on their return one of them sighed in broken but understandable English: 'How fortunate you are, to live in a country that has never been invaded!' None of this convinced me that the combination of Soviet armed forces and ideological hostility did not present the West with a serious problem; but it was a problem, as I began to emphasize in my own writings, rather than a threat.

My other impression, a more sombre one, was how little the British now mattered. We were fielding our 'A team'; scientists as fine as any in the world. They spoke with enormous authority. What went on in private discussions I have no idea, but in plenary sessions they were almost ignored. The Russians and Americans were interested only in one another. We might occasionally clarify issues, but that was all. Those on our team who felt that we might provide a weighty and independent voice were sadly disillusioned. The Soviets did not even try to separate us from the Americans, and the

Americans were politely uninterested in anything we might have to say. Whether we liked it or not, we were living in a bipolar world.

I continued to attend Pugwash conferences for another ten years or so, during which they gradually changed their nature. Even the Soviets grew bored with talking about GCD. An increasing number of scientists from the 'Third World' were invited to attend, who rightly insisted that attention should be focused on the problems of their own regions and refused to attribute these simply to 'Western imperialism'. After the Arab–Israeli War of 1967, the Palestine issue confused the clear confrontation of the Cold War and refused to go away. But my clearest memory is of a conference at Sochi in 1969, a year after the Soviet invasion of Czechoslovakia, when the Western delegates unanimously demanded that this should be placed on the agenda and the Soviets tried every trick in the book – including putting up a wretched Czech delegate who begged us to avoid the topic – to stop us from talking about it. We sat up all night negotiating the wording of the final communiqué. This was the only time that anything of the kind has ever happened to me. I was surprised to discover how easy adrenalin, fuelled by righteous indignation, made it. By 5 a.m. we had worn the apparatchiks down. But I thanked my stars that I had not decided to be a diplomat.

*   *   *

Back to the USA. After the Stowe conference there were too many visits to record, all of them interesting, most of them pleasurable. Whenever possible I began them on a Friday by flying to Washington DC, where an old friend of Alastair's, Murat Williams, would pick me up at Dulles airport and drive me to his farm near Charlottesville, where I relaxed in his pool under the shadow of the Blue Ridge Mountains. Next day he would escort me round one of the nearby Civil War battlefields, and in the evening would invite in some of his neighbours who, plentifully fuelled by bourbon, would fight the battle all over again. Alternatively I would fly to New York and make straight for the Oyster Bar at Grand Central Station, the most wonderful restaurant in the world, to strengthen me for whatever ordeals lay beyond the Hudson. Most of the visits were brief, action-packed and enjoyable; lectures or conferences at universities or military colleges (especially the Army War College at Fort Carlisle, where on a bitterly cold day in early March we were escorted along the Gettysburg battlefield from end to end with frequent icy stops to learn details of the tactics on both sides). A longer and immensely enjoyable stay was four months spent in Washington at the Woodrow Wilson Center for Visiting Scholars in 1984, when Mark was able to come with me. Murat found us a tiny house in Georgetown, just round the corner from Joe Alsop, Henry Brandon, Kate Graham and all the glitterati. President Reagan had just determined to provide the USA with a comprehensive system of ballistic missile defence, officially known as the Strategic Defense Initiative but immediately dubbed 'Star Wars', which gave us plenty to argue about over their dinner-tables. Later there would be Yale, which I shall come to; but earlier, in 1967, there had been a rather less happy visit, when I spent six months as a visiting professor at Stanford University.

*   *   *

It was not a very happy time for me personally. I was experiencing what was probably a kind of male menopause in my own life, largely because it was not clear whether my relationship with Mark would survive his decision to take a teaching post in Ghana, which happily it did. It was certainly not a happy time for the USA: a huge billboard on the freeway outside San Francisco proclaimed 'LET'S WIN IN VIETNAM AND GET OUT!' And it was emphatically not a happy time for Stanford itself. When I tell Stanford alumni that I spent some time teaching there, they tend to muse and enquire 'Was that the year they attacked the ROTC block? Or when they burned down the think-tank?' Arrangements for my accommodation had broken down, so I had to spend my first weeks in a dreary hotel in Palo Alto. I don't think I had ever felt so lonely and unhappy.

Things improved. Some of the students in my class learned of my plight and with typical kindness fixed me up as a faculty resident in one of the dormitories. This was not luxurious – two rooms with no washing or cooking facilities – but I was so touched by their kindness that I was glad to accept. Even better, my fellow-countryman Robert Rhodes James was also there as a visiting professor with his delightful family, and they took me under their wing, inviting me to good English Sunday lunches and to trips *en famille* to the Monterey peninsula. (Robert, I should say in parenthesis, was a brilliantly clever man who started his career when still an under-graduate by writing the standard life of Lord Rosebery and ended as an MP, taking in a clerkship in the House of Commons and a fellowship at All Souls on the way, but without ever quite finding his niche.) I rented a Ford Mustang convertible, in which I persuaded the more goodnatured of my pupils to escort me on trips to Yosemite, Big Sur, San Simeon and the redwoods north of the Golden Gate Bridge. Finally, I had an introduction to the retired historian Marshall Dill, a member of a very old and grand San Franciscan family, who offered me hospitality at weekends, and showed me all the variegated aspects of that bizarre but enchanting city.

At Stanford I was teaching classes on European history for Gordon Craig, who was on sabbatical leave. In addition I took on a military history seminar at the University of California at Davis, where Peter Paret (also on sabbatical) was teaching, and where he had persuaded Basil Liddell Hart to accept his first and only academic appointment. Peter and Basil were strongminded men with ideas of their own who did not get on at all well, but between them they had created a wonderful seminar. Davis was also rather a wonderful place, what I saw of it: not so much the Best-Western motel which was all that I saw of the town, or the seminar room which was all that I saw of the campus, but the student beer-cellar to which we adjourned after class, where I found the kind of *gemütlichkeit* that I so badly missed at Stanford. There such a spirit perhaps existed in the fraternity houses, but there seemed little feeling of community within the university as a whole, although in terms of facilities it wanted for nothing. Nor were the fraternity houses all happy places. Most of the 'student unrest' that was seething throughout my time seemed to arise in these centres of conscience-stricken bourgeoisie; certainly not from dormitories such as that in which I lived, full as they were of hardworking kids, many of them black, who wanted only to get on with their lives.

Anyhow, six months were more than enough, and when the time came I was counting the days to release as if I were a small boy at school. I drove north through some of the most beautiful countryside in the world to Vancouver, which was certainly one of the most beautiful cities in the world. There I took the train to Montreal to see Expo '67. Unfortunately I chose the northern route that passed through the Rockies at night, and then spent two long days chugging through scrubby birch forests where the visibility was seldom more than a hundred yards. All I had to read was Raymond Aron's monumental *War and Peace among Nations*. I read it all through, twice, finding myself at the end of it both wiser and better informed; but that was hardly the point of the trip. Anyhow, the exhibition, when I got there, was enormous fun, and sent me home in happy mood.

What I learned from all these visits, as I have said earlier, was the infinite diversity of Americans under their carapace of genial friendship and hospitality. There were indeed some whose visceral need for an enemy to enable them to display their virility sometimes terrified me and still does. Such people seemed more at home when their country was at war than when it was at peace. But there were many whose solid wisdom and common sense, combined with the kind of genuine idealism that in Britain had become the object of post-imperial irony, made me grateful that the USA was a superpower. I learned that there was little point in a foreigner railing against American foreign policy, whatever it might be, when the Americans made a far better job of doing it themselves. What we could and should do, I maintained then and maintain still, was to stay on board and add our voices to their internal debates, if only to encourage those with whom we agree.

10

Whitehall

There were in my time three archetypes in the academic world, all pretty odious. One was the 'God Professor': the permanent head of a department who condescended to lecture once a week and whose staff had been hand-picked from a court of dependent servile graduate-students. The second was the 'Airport Professor', more likely to be found in airport lounges en route to international conferences or to give well-remunerated lectures at the other end of the world than on the home campus. The last was the 'Consultant Professor', usually an economist, more often to be found in Whitehall sitting on or chairing government committees than in exercising a duty of care to students.

By the 1960s I was developing the worst characteristics of all three. To do myself justice, I had to be a God Professor in my tiny department, otherwise it would not have existed at all; though I did devolve as much responsibility as I decently could on to my longsuffering colleagues, Wolf Mendl and Brian Bond. I also spent far too much time in airports: the global contacts I developed through the IISS tugged me all over the place, though mainly, as we have seen, to the USA. But by the time I retired I had lectured in venues as diverse as the Netherlands, Germany, Italy, Switzerland, Poland, Russia, Israel, South Africa, India, Bangladesh, Iran, Sri Lanka, Singapore, Australia, New Zealand, Japan and South Korea. About my adventures and mis-adventures on these trips I could write another and far more entertaining book, and may well do if I am spared. Since most of them took place during vacations, my teaching suffered less than my research. I tried to keep to a schedule of two weekly lectures for undergraduates, one weekly graduate seminar and a fortnightly session with each of my graduate students. It was not enough, and all I can say in my defence is that there were others whose record was even worse.

None of this would have mattered so much, however, if I had not allowed myself to become a Consultant Professor as well: a role into which I let myself be drawn partly through curiosity to see how the country was governed and partly through the illusion that I could do something to improve it. The Foreign Office had set up a Disarmament Research Unit, mainly to read and comment on the flood of material produced by

American think-tanks. I was wise enough to turn down the offer of a post as inhouse academic adviser that was to be filled, far more appropriately, by Hedley Bull, but I wrote memoranda for the Foreign Office and sat on their Disarmament Advisory Committee. This body was taken more seriously by some ministers than others, many of whom saw it mainly as a device to keep Labour back-benchers quiet. Our only perk was a large lunch after our meetings, usually at Lancaster House. 'Ah', said Osbert Lancaster when I told him about it, 'Eating for Peace.'

More serious was my work for the Ministry for Defence, where Denis Healey reigned for six eventful years, from 1964 until 1970. Denis had already thought more seriously about the problems of nuclear strategy than anyone else in the country, and was not prepared to leave the making of defence policy in the hands of three armed services who were often barely on speaking terms with one another. Their leaders were possibly the finest our country has ever produced, tried and tested as they had been in the greatest war we have ever fought. Some were men of exceptional intelligence, who would perhaps not have joined the services at all if they had not foreseen the coming of the war. But they were above all tribal chiefs, and were not prepared to see their own service worsted in the struggle for a share of a shrinking budget. For seven years after the war, they had been allowed to go their own way, producing a series of shoddy compromises redeemed only by the strong but brief leadership provided by Jack Slessor in 1951–52. The Ministry of Defence consisted of little more than a secretariat bequeathed by Winston Churchill, effective so long as Churchill was in charge but otherwise quite incapable of controlling three ferociously independent ministries. Harold Macmillan's brief tenure as Minister of Defence in 1954 revealed to him a situation that as prime minister he set out to remedy. Through two tough successors, Duncan Sandys and Peter Thorneycroft, and the cooperation of the supremely self-confident Louis Mountbatten (who as chairman of the Chiefs of Staff Committee had the advantage of being equally detested by all three services), he knocked together the heads of the service chiefs, and in 1962 created a single ministry to which all three service ministries were effectively subordinated.

From my burrow in the basement of the office-block at Storey's Gate, then shared by the Cabinet Office and the Ministry of Defence, I followed all this with fascination. It was clear even to me that effective unification could best be achieved not by putting the three services into what they contemptuously called a 'mud-coloured uniform', but by unifying the bureaucratic framework within which they functioned. The power of the civil servants was enormous. With few exceptions, the military staff in Whitehall served for only two or three years before returning to various levels of command within their own services. But their civilian colleagues spent their entire careers in their ministries and knew far more about them than did the military. Under the old regime, those civilians had devoted themselves with total, sometimes almost fanatical, loyalty to the parent ministries – the Admiralty, the War Office, the Air Ministry – within which they spent their lives. They united when necessary against their old enemy the Treasury, but as often as not they spent their time fighting one another. Now they were amalgamated in a single body ultimately responsible to a single master, the Permanent Under-Secretary of the Ministry of Defence, and the path of promotion might take them through all three of its now subordinate ministries. They were identified by function – policy, logistics, procurement, manpower, finance, weapons-development – rather than by service, and their uniformed colleagues had to follow suit. Denis Healey found that he still had gigantic battles to fight. He had no military staff of his own, and when he created one (the Programmes' Evaluation Group) it nearly spelled professional death for the brilliant young officers he selected to serve on it. But he was in charge, and let everybody know it.

At a very low level I was able to provide Denis with some marginal help, less in the field of defence policy than of officer education; less glamorous, admittedly, but not unimportant. My own brief military experience gave me an entirely spurious credibility with the services, and at least enabled me to understand, and to a large measure to sympathize with, the basic tribalism that made any kind of rational organization – especially of the army – so difficult. My civilian qualifications were respectable. I was, it will be remembered, Dean of the Arts Faculty at London University at a time when we were wrestling with the demands of the Robbins Report for the expansion of higher education by creating new universities and enlarging the scope of degrees within old ones. In that capacity I was also involved with a body called the Council on National Academic Awards, which was extending the right to give degrees to bodies concerned with further, as well as higher, education. The object was to enlarge the proportion of the population possessing degrees from the existing 4 per cent, if not to the 50 per cent that was one day to be the target of the Blair administration, then to something less derisory.

The interest of the services in officer education was twofold. One was to ensure that the very high-grade education provided at their technical colleges – Manadon for the navy, Shrivenham for the army, Cranwell Engineering Department for the RAF – should not fall below that of their civilian counterparts. The other was that the education given at the cadet colleges at Dartmouth, Sandhurst and Cranwell should also be brought up to degree standard, so that on retirement their alumni could compete in the job-market with civilians possessing better paper qualifications. The Ministry of Defence was chiefly concerned to eliminate the redundancies created by the existence of six service colleges. Denis Healey himself hoped at least to mitigate service tribalism at an early age. The Treasury simply wanted to save money. I was invited to look into the situation and make recommendations. My colleague was the Chief Inspector at the then Ministry of Education, Cyril English, who was not only an expert on technical education but also a delightful man. We were provided with an office in the new ministry building on the Embankment and a secretary. The secretary was also provided with a secretary. The secretary's secretary was provided with an administrative assistant who provided us all with cups of tea, and we were left to get on with it.

We spent the first half of 1966 visiting the colleges. Cyril had little difficulty with the technical colleges, but the cadet colleges, Dartmouth, Sandhurst and to some extent Cranwell, presented more of a problem. There the cadets spent two years being knocked into shape and indoctrinated into the mystique of their service; learning to be soldiers, sailors and airmen. This for all of them meant being mercilessly chased on the barrack-square; for the soldiers, ceaseless cleaning of kit and all-night exercises; for the sailors, messing about in boats; and for the airmen, doing their preliminary flying training. Such academic education as they received barely got beyond sixth-form level, and the award of a degree was out of the question. So Cyril and I came up with what seemed a really neat idea. The three cadet colleges should remain where they were, doing what they did for a year. For a second year the young officers of all three services should all go to a central Royal Defence College for a year of more academic study, which might either be extended for a further year and lead to a degree, or provide the basis for continuing education with their units on the lines of the Open University. Both the cadet colleges and the technical colleges would be combined in a Royal Defence Academy, a degree-giving body with its own central faculties. The tri-service Royal Defence College would be located in the magnificent setting of the Royal Naval College at Greenwich, already host to a course for young naval officers, which could become the nucleus of the kind of tri-service body that we planned.

At first all went well. The Chiefs of Staff welcomed the idea in toto. I suspect that so long as the ethos of their respective services was firmly established in the first year by the traditional means in the traditional environment, they did not mind too much about the rest. But then the rats got at it. Greenwich proved too small to house the tri-service college we had in mind, so the navy rather lost interest. The location was transferred to Shrivenham, which suited the army and the RAF, both of whom had been rather worried that Greenwich might be too near London for the moral welfare of their cadets. Then the RAF lost interest, because the timing of their flying training could not be made to fit with the needs of the other services. (The cadets at the US Air Force Academy in Colorado did not even see an aircraft for three years, but they, we were told, were different.) The financial estimates, of course, escalated horribly. The headmasters consulted were contemptuous of the whole idea of the services providing their own degrees, and insisted that the function of academic study in the service colleges should be what it had always been: to cram the brightest cadets to enter the traditional universities. So the idea faded away. Each service went its own way. The RAF opted boldly for an all-graduate entry. The navy sent its best and brightest to the universities and did not worry too much about the others. And the army?

The army was left to me. I was asked to recruit an academic advisory council to help reshape 'academic studies' at Sandhurst so as to produce, if not a degree, then a diploma that would be recognized in the world of further education and might be adopted as a foundation course by one of the neighbouring universities. I hopefully recruited a professor of politics from Reading, a professor of education from Surrey, headmasters from both the private and public sectors and an Oxbridge college tutor, and got down to it. We stayed down at it for seven years, from 1968 until 1975. Then we were wound up, having accomplished nothing at all.

The academic staff at Sandhurst were enthusiastic and cooperative. Theirs was not a happy lot. Most were teaching at a level well below their academic capacities, in an environment far from sympathetic to academic study. In the pecking order the director of studies ranked well below the regimental sergeant-major. They were well enough paid, but had few career opportunities. They contained some very distinguished military historians indeed, notably David Chandler, Christopher Duffy and John Keegan, but they were working in isolation from the rest of the historical profession, and both parties suffered. The commandants were distinguished soldiers on their way up who had been ordered to help us and very loyally did, but their own commitment to the idea varied. They had the disconcerting habit of bringing to our council meetings at least two very large dogs which slept contentedly under the table but whose attention-span ran out after an hour. The commandants were responsible to the Director of Army Training, who in his turn was responsible to the Adjutant General. Like lemons in a fruit-machine, all was well if you could get three sympathetic figures lined up. But as soon as this happened, one of them would change, and his successor took at least six months to read himself into his new job. By then he would have some bright ideas of his own, and we were back to square one.

In any case it was a complete waste of time from the very beginning. There were two routes by which officers could enter the army. One was as a regular officer via a two-year course at Sandhurst. The other was with a short-service commission via a five-month course at Mons Barracks, Aldershot, where I had learned my own rudimentary military skills. But there was a backdoor. Once they were given short-service commissions, young officers could transfer to the regular list. That was what anyone with half a brain naturally did, and what the colonels of their regiments naturally advised them to do. As a result, candidates for regular commissions were dwindling alarmingly. The obvious answer was to close down Mons, send everyone to Sandhurst on a one-year course, and forget about serious academic study. This solution was indeed so obvious that the Army Board had decided in principle to adopt it in 1967, a year before the Academic Advisory Council was set up, but nobody had thought fit to tell us. The decision to implement this decision was not made for another five years, which was just long enough for us to set up an academic programme that the co-location of the two establishments now made completely unworkable.

Those of a less kindly and tolerant disposition than myself might accuse the army of setting up our council simply to satisfy the demands of their political masters without ever having any intention of implementing its recommendations. In retrospect I am more sympathetic to their problems, both of officer-recruitment and of decision-making. This was not the only area in which the peacetime services, without any deadline to meet or shareholders to pacify, could go on prevaricating about non-urgent decisions as minister succeeded minister and lemon succeeded lemon in the fruit machine. Theirs is not the only ministry in Whitehall where this happens – or rather, used to happen. After all, this was the mid-1960s. I have no doubt that since then all the problems that we had to tackle have been solved, at Sandhurst and everywhere else. I can only hope that the Howard–English Report, though now deservedly forgotten, may have helped to clear out some dead wood and make that improvement possible. I wrote the whole thing off to experience, and the army gave me a consolation prize in the shape of the chairmanship of the Army Education Advisory Board: a post that involved doing virtually nothing but looked good on my c.v.

*　*　*

By this time I had finished my volume in the Official Histories, which I expected nobody to read and suspect that few people ever have. But somebody did, and to my amazement it was awarded, in 1973, one of the first Wolfson history prizes – the largest cheque I have ever handled. At the celebratory lunch I sat next to Sir Isaac Wolfson who, after a long silence, asked, 'What are you going to do with the money?' I did not yet know, so I asked his advice. 'Put it in a Portuguese bank', he said very firmly. This may or may not have been good advice at the time, but since a year or so later there was a revolution in Portugal, I am on the whole glad that I did not take it. Instead I went with Mark on a round-the-world tour. My Quaker genes, blast them, forbade me from relaxing on a Bali beach, though we did visit Bangkok and Hong Kong. But I attended a conference in Canberra, and spent a week at Stanford with Peter Paret, putting the finishing touches to our translation of Clausewitz's *On War*, of which more anon. We also worked on a revision of Edward Meade Earle's great work *Makers of Modern Strategy*, and Peter introduced me to an incredibly bright graduate-student who would, he thought, write a good chapter for us on Soviet Military Thought. She did, and went on to yet higher things: her name, Condoleezza Rice. We were to meet again, as we shall see.

*   *   *

But my days as an official historian proved far from over. After completing my Grand Strategy volume I was co-opted on to a committee to consider publication of a series of 'Intelligence Histories' to deal with the hitherto ultra-secret activities of British Intelligence and security services during the war; primarily, of course, the code-breaking at Bletchley Park. About these I still knew little. I had, as an official historian, been 'indoctrinated' – that is, sworn not to reveal anything about code-breaking that I came across in the course of my researches. But the documents made available to me had already been so effectively weeded that, although I knew that code-breaking was taking place, I had no idea of its effectiveness and the vital part it played in the Allied victories. In retrospect I can see that to write the history of the war without mentioning it was like writing *Hamlet* without the Ghost. If the officials of MI5 and MI6 had had their way, their activities would remain secret to this day, but the pressure for revelation was becoming too great. ULTRA in general, and deception in particular, were after all the huge and unsung Allied successes of the war, without which none of the other successes would have been possible; and many of those responsible for those successes who were not regular members of the security services thought it high time that their story was told.

One of those was my old tutor J.C. Masterman, who had played a critical role in deception operations. One afternoon he invited me to tea and placed in my hands a little pamphlet that turned out to be his signing-off report to MI5, later to be published as *The Double-Cross System*. This told the whole story of the use of double agents to build up in the minds of German intelligence a picture of vast Allied armies, first in the Mediterranean and then in the United Kingdom, awaiting their chance to invade. 'Should this be published?' he asked. 'Yes', I replied emphatically, 'but won't they try to stop you?' 'They probably will', he answered, 'but I don't think they will prosecute me, and they certainly can't prosecute the Yale University Press.' They couldn't, so the book duly appeared and caused predictable consternation in Whitehall. Some years later I found myself at dinner sitting next to Sir Alec Douglas-Home, who had then as Foreign Secretary been in official charge of the security services. He was also a Christ Church man, so naturally conversation turned to Masterman. 'Do you realize', asked Sir Alec, 'that they actually tried to make me lock him up? It was that book of his, of course. But lock up the best amateur left-hand spin-bowler in England? They must have been out of their minds. I soon put a stop to that, I can tell you.'

So Masterman survived: 'I have been a pillar of rectitude all my life', he remarked, 'so I think I was entitled to do one really naughty thing.' But I could see why Whitehall had been so outraged. The dyke of secrecy had been breached. Enterprising American journalists widened it further, insiders became increasingly indiscreet, and it was absurd to try to keep the secret any longer. Nobody saw this more clearly than the chief of the security services Sir Dick White, who was also, as it happened, a former pupil of Masterman's. Gentle, courteous, eminently civilized, Dick would have filled the role of head of the Secret Service in a novel by an old-fashioned lady novelist to perfection, but in the real world he seemed almost too good to be true. Unlike his colleagues, he also understood the value to the security services themselves, who had recently had a very bad press, of having their wartime successes made public. I suspect that without his constant pressure, the official intelligence histories would not even have been written, let alone published.

The steering committee agreed that there would be five volumes, three dealing with intelligence – overwhelmingly the activities of Bletchley Park – one with security, and one with deception, which involved both intelligence and security as well as military operations. Professor Harry Hinsley, who had been at the heart of code-breaking since the beginning of the war, assembled a team to write the first three volumes; Anthony Simkins, formerly of MI5, would do the fourth; while the fifth volume was allotted to Peter Fleming, a professional writer and flamboyantly heroic figure who had himself been involved in deception operations throughout the war. Then, alas, he suddenly died, and the beady eyes of the steering committee turned on me. I was already a member of the team. I was *persona grata* with both the armed forces and the Cabinet Office. I had a good track record of publication. So why not?

For me there was every reason in the world why not. I had now moved to Oxford, hoping to escape the toils of the metropolis and produce some serious academic work. It was made clear to me that there could be no guarantee that my volume, once I had written it, would ever be published. I should have said no. But as ever I was weakminded. The subject itself fascinated me. I had an adolescent longing to find out how the intelligence services actually worked during the war – how spies spied and how they were caught. I was promised a parking permit on Horse Guards Parade (posterity can have no idea of the importance of such a privilege in the closing decades of the twentieth century). Above all, my old assistant Pat McCallum, who now revealed that she had been at the heart of the deception team, would be there to help me. So I said yes.

There was one snag: I had not been cleared for security at the necessary level.

In case the reader has been wondering, I should make it clear that whenever I was invited to do a job for the government, I always pre-empted trouble by warning the officials concerned that I was gay. They were men of the world and took it in their stride, though it may have made them exercise their discretion in ways of which I was unaware. But my work would now involve access to the Crown Jewels, so I had to be interviewed in depth by MI5. 'This is very much a matter of course in your case', said the kindly old man who conducted the first interview, 'just to make sure that you aren't a Soviet agent, or a drug addict, or a homosexual, or . . .' 'But I am homosexual', I interrupted. The poor man blushed deep crimson. I felt very sorry for him. He rallied bravely, and took down the sordid details of my life that I went on to give him. They then sent round a formidable young man wearing an MCC tie to explore further. They apparently already had a file on me, dealing mainly with my visits to conferences behind the Iron Curtain, and with my having lent my flat when I was in the States to a close friend in the Colonial Office who had come unstuck after a nasty scandal in Sierra Leone. They also had a file on Mark, who when doing research for his geography degree had asked for maps of a settlement on the Danish coast that was in a NATO prohibited area. None of this seemed to worry them very much. Then my interrogator asked, 'How well did you know Guy Burgess?'

The answer was, not very well. He was certainly an acquaintance. He had been the lover of an undergraduate whom I had known slightly at Oxford, and come down to parties where he dazzled us with his wit and worldliness. After the war, when I was working in the library at the Reform Club, he was underemployed at the Foreign Office and would drift in during the morning. We would occasionally drink together, usually at my expense ('terribly sorry old boy, but . . .'). When he disappeared he owed me at least five pounds. All this I explained to my interlocutor, who listened politely and then said, 'Do you remember writing him this note?'

I did. Fortunately it was perfectly harmless, even addressed 'Dear Burgess'. I think it was an apology for intruding into a conversation he was having with some minor diplomat at the Reform. It had turned up when they searched his flat, and it was probably then that they opened a file on me. I was immensely impressed with their competence, and told them so. They were prepared to take my word that my acquaintance with Guy went no further, and let me through.

Like the Grand Strategy volume, my deception history took a ludicrously long time to finish. I began it in 1972 and it was not complete until 1979 (five years of free parking in Central London). I was then summoned to an interview by my old friend Robert Armstrong, who had by now climbed to the top of his own slippery pole to become secretary to the Cabinet. He told me with great embarrassment that the prime minister, Margaret Thatcher, had decided that it would be 'inappropriate' to publish it. Apparently she had always been unhappy about the decision of her Labour predecessors to sanction publication of the series. Now she had been confronted by the news, not only that Anthony Blunt (Professor Sir Anthony Blunt KCVO, Keeper of the Queen's Pictures, Director of the Courtauld Institute, *crème de la crème* of the Establishment) had been spying for the Soviet Union for the past 40 years, but also that MI5 had known all about it for the past 15 of them. Understandably she felt that the less the world knew about the activities of the security services, the better. It was too late to stop the publication of the Hinsley volumes, but she could, and did, stop mine.

In fact Blunt does not appear by name in my book, but he had certainly been an active member of the deception team. Probably his greatest contribution had been to recruit his friend, the picture-dealer Tomas Harris, who became the case-officer for the great double-agent GARBO. I knew Blunt quite well as a fellow professor in London and slightly in private life. I had always enjoyed his company, and was as amazed by the revelation as everyone else. Naturally I was disappointed by the Prime Minister's decision, but could not complain. It had always been made clear that publication of my volume would be at the discretion of the government, and I had been paid reasonably well for writing it. It was put on the shelf for ten years. By the time it was published, virtually all its revelations had been leaked to freelance writers by elderly participants who were quite properly anxious to see their achievements made public before they died. That also I wrote off to experience.

*   *   *

In spite of this rude rebuff, I enjoyed good relations with Margaret
Thatcher. Early in 1980 she invited me to lunch at Chequers for a discussion
about arms control. I think I must have been recommended to her by my
old friend Hugh Thomas, a man whom I had always admired for his guts in
resigning from the Foreign Office over the Suez crisis and for his amazing
fertility as a historian of the Iberian world. He was now one of her *éminences
grises*. She had come to office at a critical moment in international relations,
and she very sensibly realized that she needed all the advice, official and
unofficial, that she could get.

Posterity may well wonder why the situation looked so serious in the
early 1980s. The USA was in one of its periodic fits of panic. It had not
recovered from humiliation in Vietnam. More recently it had suffered a
severe setback by the overthrow of its *protégé* the Shah of Iran, the impri-
sonment of its diplomatic team in Teheran and the disastrous failure of the
attempt to rescue them. In spite of ongoing Strategic Arms Limitation Talks
(SALT), the Soviet Union was formidably building up both its nuclear and
naval strength, and the capacity of the USA to deter an attack on Western
Europe, or even on its own homeland, seemed more than ever in doubt. In
1979 Soviet armies had occupied Afghanistan. This was seen in Washington,
like the invasion of South Korea three decades earlier, as the first step in a
programme of deliberate military expansion. (The British, who had their
own experience of Afghanistan, were more relaxed about it.) President
Carter, with some reason, was mercilessly criticized for failing to provide an
adequate response. In the USA a group of hawks formed a well-funded
Committee on the Present Danger, consisting largely of pupils and associates of Albert Wohlstetter, who urged the breaking off of arms-control
negotiations and massive rearmament. Mrs Thatcher was temperamentally
inclined to agree with them. The Foreign Office was not. Not surprisingly,
the Prime Minister sought further opinions.

It was nice being back at Chequers again, and I could not resist the
temptation to boast of my experiences there 30 years earlier, and those
memorable film-shows. At lunch Margaret Thatcher skilfully combined the
role of prime minister and materfamilias: Denis was there, being affable;
their daughter Carol (my neighbour at lunch) was bright; and their son
Mark turned up unexpectedly in a noisy sports car, dressed like a 1930s cad
in pinstripe suit and suede shoes, forcing a last-minute rearrangement of the
placement. Hugh Thomas was there, one or two other academics, some
Foreign Office officials, and Peter Carrington (then Foreign Secretary).
Gosh, I thought, I've made it. After lunch we sat round a log-fire which the
Prime Minister replenished in the intervals of taking notes while we tried to

answer her crisp and pertinent questions. Apparantly I did not disgrace myself, because she asked Hugh to set up a small committee to draft independent recommendations for the conduct of British foreign policy consisting of myself, Leonard Schapiro and Elie Kedourie.

Leonard was a leading expert on the Soviet Union, Elie on the Middle East. Both were deeply pessimistic. The Soviets were on the march, thought Leonard, and as determined as ever on world conquest. Elie believed that the Middle East was already a lost cause. I was sceptical on both counts, though I had to defer to their greater expertise. I certainly believed strongly in the need to preserve credible deterrence, but thought this possible without accepting the worst-case analysis being peddled by the Committee on the Present Danger. They believed that the recently concluded Helsinki Accords had been a defeat for the West by 'legitimizing' the Soviet control of Eastern Europe. I believed that it might prove a mortal wound to the Soviets by opening the region up to Western influence and ideas. We patched together a totally incoherent document that deserved to go straight into the waste-paper basket and probably did.

I continued to be invited to Chequers seminars and always found the Prime Minister friendly and courteous. But she was not easy company, lacking as she was in any sense of humour and increasingly impervious to new ideas. On occasion she could be really alarming. Once she invited me to dinner at Downing Street, together with Hugh Dacre (as my old tutor Hugh Trevor-Roper had then become) to discuss the text of a speech she was due to deliver to the United Nations. She had obviously had a hell of a day and was in a vile temper. There were about ten of us there, all civil servants apart from Hugh and myself. I sat on her right, and her manner of conducting the conversation was to go round the table clockwise and bully each guest in turn. 'Well, Sir Edward', she would ask some wretched *fonctionnaire*, 'and when are we going to get some good news from your department for a change?' Eventually she came round to Hugh Dacre, who was sitting opposite her. 'Well, Lord Dacre', she asked, 'and when can we expect another book from you?' 'Well, Prime Minister', Hugh replied rather loftily, 'I have one on the stocks.' 'On the stocks? *On the stocks*? A fat lot of good that is. In the shops, that is where we need it!' Fortunately by the time she got round to me, she had run out of ammunition; or perhaps she knew better than anybody why there was no book forthcoming from me. As I looked at that perfect profile, that peach-like complexion, that immaculate golden hair, I thought how lucky we were that the checks and balances of the constitution prevented her from having the whole lot of us taken out and shot on the spot.

11

Oxford

We have now got rather ahead of ourselves, and must backtrack to the 1960s.

I was so busy during that notorious decade that I was barely conscious of the huge cultural transformation that was going on around me. Not even the invention of sexual intercourse, as Philip Larkin described it, neatly sandwiched as it was between the *Lady Chatterley's Lover* verdict and the Beatles' first LP, penetrated into my busy life. I did not realize that *My Fair Lady* was to be the last in the line of great musical comedies that had been opened for me 30 years earlier with *Mr Cinders* and was now to be replaced by the giant and interminable spectacles of Andrew Lloyd-Webber. I was only dimly aware that the light music and jazz with which I had so happily grown up – Louis Armstrong, Benny Goodman, Cole Porter, Irving Berlin, Jerome Kern – was now being consigned to the back shelves for connoisseurs of the antique, in favour of pop and rock music of a kind that required different sensibilities than my own to appreciate; indeed that the gentle discipline of dancing as I had known it was giving place to what I can only call a Dionysiac riot. But even I noticed that men were gradually ceasing to wear hats, unmistakeable badges of status if not of class. The military short-back-and-sides haircut that had been mandatory for nearly a century was disappearing, as was the wearing of ties. Young men grew beards and allowed their hair to curl romantically over their ears and down their necks. Their seniors (including me) experimented cautiously with side-whiskers. This was no mere matter of fashion: the tectonic plates of society were shifting. The stability of the 1950s, so welcome to my own generation after two decades of nightmare, was now seen by the young as stuffy and oppressive, condemned by the followers of Herbert Marcuse as 'frozen violence' or 'oppressive tolerance'. Nor had the violence always been frozen or the oppression tolerant. Rebels were finding good causes in Latin America, in Algeria, in Northern Ireland, above all in Vietnam. The times, they were a-changin'. Or was it simply that I was growing old?

Meanwhile, I had one further involvement with the Ministry of Defence which was to prove of greater importance to me than any other.

As part of his campaign to create a public opinion as well educated about defence as it was about economics, Denis Healey planned to strengthen the links between the armed forces and the universities, and set up a committee under his Permanent Under-Secretary, Sir James Dunnett, to see how this might be done. I cannot remember whether I was formally a member of that committee, but I spent a lot of time with it and helped to shape its recommendations. These were for a two-way traffic. The Ministry of Defence would finance a number of 'Defence Fellowships' for senior officers, who would spend a year at a university writing a thesis under the supervision of an appropriate academic It would also finance 'Defence Lectureships', academic posts relevant to defence questions. in universities willing to host them. Lectureships were created in such topics as Soviet Studies, Defence Economics, International Relations, International Law and Ethics of War, modelled on the courses that we were already teaching at King's. One academic body that responded positively to this invitation was All Souls College, Oxford. This was highly appropriate, since it had taken the initiative 60 years earlier, after the Boer War, in creating the first academic post in military studies, that had since matured into the Chichele Chair of the History of War. What political manoeuvring lay behind the college's decision to create the post I do not know, and have never liked to ask. But one evening in the autumn of 1966, after an IISS seminar in London, I was approached by Professor Max Beloff, a fellow of the college and a loyal supporter of the IISS, who urged me to apply for it.

There were many reasons why I should be interested, but nostalgia for Oxford was no longer one of them. I had grown out of that long ago. I had acquired a deep affection for King's and felt for London itself the sentiment so well expressed by Dr Johnson: it contained all that life could afford. But life, enjoyable though it was, was becoming too complicated. I was doing too much. I was becoming known as a competent administrator, and to my consternation was receiving invitations to consider vice-chancellorships or the equivalent. If I remained in London, there seemed little prospect of my ever doing any serious work again. I was drinking rather too much; and, perhaps most important, my stable domestic base was threatened, as I have written earlier, by Mark's decision to take up a two-year teaching-post in Ghana. I did not relish the prospect of living in London on my own. I felt some qualms about leaving my department so soon after its establishment, but it was thriving in the excellent hands of Wolf Mendl and Brian Bond, and I felt that I could not contribute a great deal more than I had already. So I declared my interest in the Oxford post and warned the Principal of King's. In response to his request for advice about my successor, I suggested Laurence Martin, one of the few British scholars with an international reputation in strategic studies who then held the chair of International

Relations at Aberystwyth. I then set off for the sabbatical term at Stanford that I have described earlier. I went by sea on a cargo ship via Panama, romantically conscious that I was leaving an old life behind and was about to begin a new one.

It was not, however, to be as easy as that. Nothing connected with Oxford ever is. On arriving at Stanford I found a letter with the news that the college had decided to elect to the post not me, but Laurence Martin.

It was an entirely justifiable choice. I was a military historian, and the college already had a military historian on its strength in the shape of the Chichele Professor, Norman Gibbs. What could I provide that he could not? Laurie Martin was a political scientist who had studied at Yale with the doyen of strategic studies, Arnold Wolfers, and would have brought an entirely fresh approach to the subject. Had I been a fellow of the college, I would certainly have voted the same way. I can't deny that the news made me miserable, but the misery was shortlived. A few weeks later came the news that Laurie had turned down the post, and it was offered to me.

Again, I have never enquired into the history of all this. I suspect that the support given by John Sparrow for my candidature may have alienated some junior fellows, among whom he was far from popular, as we shall see. But I also suspect that he made it very clear to Laurie that the post was a temporary one, financed for only five years by the Ministry of Defence, and there could be no assurance that the college would take responsibility for it after that; which understandably gave Laurie, a family man, second thoughts. Be that as it may, my election to All Souls left the chair at King's available to him, so everybody was satisfied.

All these tergiversations meant that I could not take up my fellowship until autumn 1968. Meanwhile, I was able to provide one more service for King's. Peter Noble was due to retire as Principal, and I was put on the search committee to find a successor. It was generally agreed that, excellent as Noble had been in many ways, his qualities were better fitted to a great civic university than to a metropolitan one. A staunch Aberdonian, he had developed few contacts in the London world. In a period when fund-raising was becoming increasingly important for universities, this was judged a drawback. We needed someone with more 'dining-out' power, and better contacts in Whitehall.

The first name that came to my mind was my old friend Edward Boyle, who was now Minister for Education in Harold Macmillan's administration. We had grown closer over the past few years, largely through a common interest in Glyndebourne. Indeed, some five years earlier he had invited me to chair the Commission on Primary Education that was eventually to be taken on by Lady Plowden. This was an utterly crazy suggestion to make to someone like myself who not only had no children of his own but was unlikely ever to have any, and thank heavens I had the wit to refuse. Edward seemed a long shot, but I suspected that, still deeply unpopular with elements of the Conservative Party because of his resignation over Suez, he was not likely to go much further in politics, and knew it. Indeed, he showed more interest than I had expected but, as he explained to me over a sumptuous lunch at the Connaught, the timing was not right. A few years later he accepted an invitation to become Vice-Chancellor of the University of Leeds, so my diagnosis had not been at fault.

With Edward ruled out, who was there? We agreed that we needed above all a figure who would keep the college in the public eye, hold his own in the political infighting in the university and knew his way about the corridors of Whitehall. A senior civil servant? A city tycoon? But why not a soldier?

Once that possibility was mooted, though half the committee dismissed it as ludicrous, I knew exactly the man. Several times over the past few years I had been taken out to lunch by distinguished senior officers, for me figures of awe, who enquired diffidently about the possibility of administrative posts in the university world after their retirement. Shan Hackett was in an altogether different class. I had come across Shan (aka General Sir John Hackett, GCB, DSO and Bar, MC – to say nothing of MA and B.Litt. Oxon.) in several capacities at the Ministry of Defence. He was a clever, twinkly, energetic little man, far from popular with colleagues, who regarded him as too clever, and political masters, who thought him too independent, but much loved by all who had served under him. He had several times expressed to me his hopes of returning to academic life. An alumnus of New College, where before the war he had completed a B.Litt. thesis on Saladin, he claimed to regard his military career simply as '40 years' absence of mind'. I suspect that he had his sights set on the wardenship of his old college, but his manifold talents were far more appropriate for London. When I mentioned his name to the search committee, there was a stunned silence. Then the Professor of Chemistry, Donald Hey, asked, 'Wasn't he Commandant at Shrivenham [the Royal Military College of Science] a few years ago?' I was able to confirm that he was; which unleashed an encomium that bore all before it. 'He knows how to deal with professors', concluded Hey grimly.

While Shan in fact was not very successful in dealing with professors, showing them little of the deference they expected, he certainly knew how to deal with students. His appointment was announced when he was still serving as Commander-in-Chief, British Army of the Rhine. The then president of the Students' Union and his girlfriend were on a walking tour in the Black Forest. Shan had them picked up in his official car to spend a

weekend giving him a tutorial on his future duties. Although student dis-
orders were reaching a climax when he arrived in the Strand, throughout
his tenure of office King's remained an oasis of peace – except when he
himself took command of the revolutionary armies and led them on a
demonstration to Whitehall demanding bigger grants for students and
higher salaries for principals. He was a lovely man.

*   *   *

So in Michaelmas 1968 I shifted my base to Oxford. 'You will find', warned a
contemporary who had taught there for the past 20 years, 'that things have
changed since your time. The buildings are cleaner and the undergraduates
are a great deal dirtier.' Certainly the buildings were cleaner. Thanks largely
to the generosity of American alumni, the dingy grey stone that I recalled
from the 1940s had now been burnished to mellow gold and pristine white,
providing an appropriate background to the television films that were being
shot there almost continuously for the two decades of my residence. As for
the undergraduates, my friend had been unfair. They were not dirtier, but
they were certainly different. They no longer wore the grey flannel trousers,
tweed jackets and ties that had been *de rigueur* for my own generation. Now
they dressed in jeans (preferably scuffed and torn), t-shirts and sandals, and
the grander they were, the more farouche their appearance. They no longer
decorated their rooms, as we had, with Medici reproductions or hunting
prints, but with posters proclaiming that Che Guevara lived. They no longer
called themselves undergraduates, but students. And when I arrived they
were in a state of revolt.

What they were in revolt about was never quite clear. Like their counterparts in Paris and Berlin (but unlike those in the USA for whom Vietnam
provided a very specific cause), Oxford students were inspired by a visceral
reaction against authority as such, rather than anything specific that
authority was doing. The fact that in Oxford they had nothing much to
complain about made their predicament all the more frustrating. The only
authorities with whom they came in contact were normally their tutors, for
the most part genial and understanding people whom it was difficult to
suspect of sinister designs. 'The University' was the enemy; but what and
where was the university, and how could one attack it? Even the dons found
it difficult to find its dingy offices, hidden away as they were in an anon-
ymous block somewhere behind Wellington Square. The Vice-Chancellor
still possessed a rather splendid study in the Clarendon Building opposite
the Bodleian Library, so they occupied that; but the incumbent Alan Bullock
(a tough Yorkshireman of irreproachable working-class antecedents) simply
shifted his base. The university building with which undergraduates were

most familiar was the Examination Schools in the High Street, so they occupied that as well; but in the Michaelmas term the Schools were used only for lectures, and since few undergraduates attended lectures anyway, the forces of revolution could establish themselves there without anyone really noticing. I wandered in one afternoon, all unawares, to be seized by some excited youths and hustled before a kind of Committee of Public Safety who graciously sanctioned my release. Everybody was clearly having a wonderful time.

A secondary target was All Souls itself. Nobody quite knew what went on there but it was suspected, not without cause, of being a bastion of privilege and elitism. One afternoon an army terrible with banners demanding 'Open All Souls!' descended upon us. Although normally the college was open to all comers, it was thought prudent to close the gates. They were opened to allow Dr A.L. Rowse to take his afternoon walk. 'Who are you?' demanded the ring-leaders. 'My name', he replied, 'is Rowse. For your further information, I am from the working classes – unlike, I suspect, any of you. In addition I have written some 30 books, which is more than any of you, singly or collectively, are ever likely to do. Now get out of my way.' It must be said that the main authority for this incident was Rowse himself, but it was well in character, and the crowd certainly melted away.

Leslie Rowse was certainly the most remarkable member of a community that did not lack for eccentrics. Like me, he was a bachelor living in college, so I encountered him every morning at breakfast. He would come in already talking, as if someone had wound him up before he left his rooms, and he continued talking until he returned to them. His talk consisted in denunciation of his colleagues, of the government and of the working classes ('the idiot people'), roughly in that order. To me he was always kind, possibly because I was, like him, not 'hetero'. He sat next to me at dinner on my first evening. Glaring round the table, he remarked, 'There is not a single person here with any claim to be first-rate.' He was profoundly and fascinatingly learned and could be quite charming when he wished. But if one brought in a guest who had to sit next to him, you never knew whether he would behave impeccably, insult the visitor unforgivably, or (if he was male and under 30) make a pass.

Then there was John Sparrow. John was, of course, an old friend and patron. I had eagerly looked forward to seeing more of him. But I had barely seen him for 20 years, and he had changed considerably. Then he had been a hardworking Chancery lawyer, certain to take silk, likely to be promoted to the Bench, to chair important commissions, and probably end up as a Law Lord. His election to the wardenship of All Souls altered the course of his career, while making it no less probable that he would become an important figure in the ranks of the Good and the Great. But John was that rarest of beings – a Wykehamist without a public conscience. He saw All Souls as a private shelter from a world that he found increasingly disagreeable, and devoted himself to keeping it so. He displayed no interest in the university, let alone the world of higher education in general. When his turn came to be Vice-Chancellor, he refused. When I asked him why, he hissed, 'I am not an *educationist!*', infusing the word with a degree of contempt and loathing that I found almost frightening. His misfortune was to become Warden at a time when pressure for reform of some kind, within the college as well as outside, was becoming irresistible. The favoured course was to turn it into a graduate college on the lines of St Antony's – one that he was wise to resist, the college having neither the facilities nor the space for such a transformation. He was persuaded instead to support a programme for visiting senior scholars modelled on the Princeton Institute for Advanced Studies, which itself had been modelled on All Souls. This ensured a constant stream of fresh talent through what had to all accounts become rather a muddy swamp. John accepted this and endured it stoically; showing himself at his best as a charming host to the visiting fellows, if not always to their wives.

These battles had been fought and won before I arrived, and the college was settling down fairly peacefully in their aftermath. It did so the more successfully because John made excellent appointments to the two most important offices in the college: Charles Wendon as Bursar and John Simmons as Librarian. Under their aegis, the college ran itself. John had little interest in the academic activities of its members. 'Research' was for him a word almost as loathsome as 'education'. He was himself a fine scholar and a notable bibliophile, who had burst on an astonished world at the age of 16 with an edition of John Donne's *Devotions*, but had done nothing serious since. He had a brilliant mind, as Hugh Trevor-Roper put it, that 'went straight to the periphery of any subject'. He hated decisions and devoted a superb intelligence to preventing college meetings from reaching any. He made no bones about his homosexuality; indeed, the older he became the more frankly he flaunted it. But paradoxically he disapproved of the Wolfenden reforms. For him the pleasures of the love that dared not speak its name should be reserved strictly for the elite. Talented, witty, charming, he should have ended his life respected in his profession, with a host of friends. As it was, he was lonely, unhappy, and sought solace increasingly in drink.

*   *   *

Anyhow, there I was, installed in beautiful rooms that looked out on the Radcliffe Camera on one side and Queen's College Library on the other, their peace broken only by the occasional click of croquet balls from the warden of New College's garden. After King's, where my office on the first floor of the Strand was probably the noisiest in the entire academic world, I found the silence intimidating. And what was I to do? My official title was 'Fellow in Higher Defence Studies', but what were they, and where did they fit into the Oxford syllabus? London had been a jungle in whose rich soil one could plant a walking-stick and watch it grew into a tree overnight. Oxford was an overpopulated island, every inch of which had been intensively farmed by the same families for generations. The farmers were friendly enough, but woe betide anyone who encroached on their territory.

Of nowhere was this more true than the History Faculty. 'History of War' did indeed have its place in the syllabus and its professor, but it could be studied by undergraduates only in a 'special subject' on the Napoleonic Wars. This was excellent of its kind, involving the use of diplomatic as well as naval and military documents, but difficult to broaden into the kind of 'War and Society' course that I had developed in London; nor did its teachers show any appetite for doing so. PPE (Philosophy, Politics and Economics) was more welcoming, and had no difficulty in agreeing that lectures on problems of nuclear strategy were indeed relevant to their syllabus. I was the more fortunate in that the teaching of international relations at Oxford was itself being transformed. Hitherto the subject had been synonymous with diplomatic history; more specifically European diplomatic history since 1815, with a special subject on the Treaties of 1919. The professor was Agnes Headlam-Morley, whose father Sir James had been an adviser to the British delegation at that peace conference. But she was on the verge of retirement. Her successor, in 1972, was to be no less a person than Alastair Buchan.

Alastair left the IISS in 1969, and had spent the following three years transforming the old Imperial Defence College, where senior officers of the Commonwealth had spent an undemanding sabbatical year, into a dynamic new Royal College of Defence Studies, open to all friendly nations, with a ferociously demanding syllabus. This was another initiative by Denis Healey, highly unwelcome to the Chiefs of Staff, who did their best to mitigate its consequences by appointing a 'good fighting general' as Alastair's successor. Unfortunately he was also a good drinking general and lasted only a year. In Oxford there was a powerful lobby among senior members of the university, mainly 'men of the world' like Oliver Franks, Alan Bullock, and John Redliffe Maud, who felt strongly and rightly that Oxford needed someone of Alastair's talents to do a comparable job in dragging the teaching of international relations into the latter half of the twentieth century. For undergraduates the process was already well under way, thanks to the initiative of such college tutors as Wilfred Knapp, John Dunbabin and

Christopher Seton-Watson; but Alastair set about creating a graduate school that was to attract first-rate students from all over the world, especially the USA. The time allowed him was short: he died, suddenly and tragically, four years later. Fortunately Hedley Bull was available to take his place and by the time Hedley himself died ten years later, equally tragically and prematurely Oxford had taken its proper place as one of the world's leading graduate schools in international relations.

I played some part in this, and was rewarded by being able to teach some quite remarkable graduate students: Rick Haass, Ivo Daalder and Philip Bobbitt from the USA, Azar Gat from Israel, and from Britain Christopher Coker and above all Lawrence Freedman, who was one day to take over the Department of War Studies at King's and build it into a huge empire that was virtually to monopolize the teaching of the subject for the British armed forces. There were also the military 'Defence Fellows', formidable figures like James Eberle, Tony Farrar-Hockley, Frank Kitson, and above all Nigel Bagnall, who were all to rise to the top of their respective services, and whose presence at my seminars lent credibility to our academic speculations. At the other end of the spectrum were undergraduate enthusiasts whom I encouraged to form a society, the Oxford University Strategic Studies Group, which in course of time was to prove a seedbed for further graduate students and, ultimately, teachers.

All in all, I was not underemployed; especially when, after three years, my colleagues in the Politics Sub-Faculty passed me the poisoned chalice and made me a University Examiner, which took three summers out of my life. Hardly had this finished when my equally appreciative colleagues in the Modern History Faculty realized that I was a soft touch and did the same. During those summers, when I rose at 5 a.m. to read my quota of 20 scripts a day and then sweated through the hottest two weeks of the year in the Examination Schools wearing full academic dress, I consoled myself by thinking that people in other professions had to work as hard as this every day of their working lives. But they were paid considerably more for doing so.

*   *   *

Meanwhile, I was supposed to be doing some work of my own. My Grand Strategy volume was now in the press and the Intelligence Histories were as yet only a gleam in Dick White's eye, but I had brought with me from King's a task more interesting than either. As part of the essential reading for my subject, I had studied Clausewitz's *On War*, and found it deeply impressive. I had cooperated with (it would be impertinent to say 'supervised') Peter Paret in his thesis on Prussian military reform in the

Napoleonic period, and learned from him a great deal more about Clausewitz's political and cultural background. We both agreed that a new translation of *On War* was long overdue. From King's, Peter had gone on to Princeton. There he enlisted the interest of Gordon Craig, Bernard Brodie and the Princeton University Press. Between them they organized a conference in Berlin in 1964 which planned an edited translation of Clausewitz's entire works, with Peter and I assuming responsibility for *On War*.

Of this ambitious project, only *On War* survived. My German was not remotely good enough to undertake the translation myself, and Peter did not have the time, so we recruited a retired member of the British diplomatic service, Angus Malcolm, who had already translated an important book on the Prussian Officer Corps and lived not far from me in South Kensington. Angus was the very model of a British diplomat. He had inherited the good looks of his grandmother, Lily Langtry, who had stunned the Edwardian world with her beauty. Always perfectly dressed, he had a shrewd mind, a great sense of humour, and a good ear for the English language. Working with him was a joy. Together we produced a rough translation. Then poor Angus suddenly died. By this time Peter was established at Stanford and I was at All Souls. I had hoped to persuade the college to elect him to a visiting fellowship so that we could work on the text together, but I did not as yet have enough clout to get my way. Neither email nor fax had yet been invented, so we had laboriously to exchange drafts by post. Peter was able to spend a summer in London, and I was able to visit Stanford for a week in 1973 on my Wolfson-financed world tour to finalize the text. We eventually published it in 1976.

This was the most rewarding work, intellectually as well as financially, that I have ever undertaken. Intellectually it made me realize what a superb training for a historian it is to edit a text: to live in intimate contact with a great mind, place what he wrote in context, and try to express his meaning in terms that make sense for one's own generation. It showed me how much I had missed in never having trained as a classicist or a medievalist, and how many nuances of meaning one can and, more interestingly, cannot, adequately express in one's own language. Financially I profited from the fact that the US armed forces, in the aftermath of their Vietnam débâcle, had just discovered Clausewitz and were making him required reading in all their service colleges. Whether the advent of the absurdly termed 'War on Terror' will make them consider him obsolete remains to be seen. I hope it does not, for their sake as well as mine.

Meanwhile, other obligations accumulated. The most intimidating, an invitation to deliver the Ford Lectures in English History, came in 1971. This was, and is, the Blue Riband of the British historical profession, and the invitation astonished me. I know that this may seem the most odious kind of false modesty, but I had genuinely not realized that the profession took me seriously. My performance for my first degree had been at best second-rate, and I had never redeemed it by slogging doctoral research. I had made my reputation by veering off at a tangent on a path of my own that transgressed far beyond the accepted bounds of conventional history. I had slid into All Souls by a convenient side-door, one largely of my own creation. Surely those implacable, incorruptible, unforgiving scholars who had judged my calibre so accurately 30 years earlier had always seen through me and always would? But apparantly they had not. I had, it is true, been elected to the British Academy, but this I attributed to the friends I had made as Dean of the Arts Faculty at London. The judgement of the Oxford History Faculty was altogether more formidable. But if they thought I was up to giving the Ford lectures, I had better have a go.

The only research worthy of the name that I had ever done in English history was in the archives of the Cabinet Office for my Grand Strategy volume. I decided to start there, and read through the minutes and memoranda of the Committee of Imperial Defence since its inauguration at the beginning of the century. As I did so, a pattern gradually emerged, like a developing photographic print, of the conflict between Britain's obligations to the defence of its world empire, and the problems created for her by the emergence of a powerful and hostile Germany across the North Sea; a conflict she was never able to resolve and which was to prove fatal in 1940–42, when she lost her Empire and might have lost her independence but for the intervention of the USA. It was a huge subject and needed a huge volume, or series of volumes, to do it justice; but its main lines might just be sketched in the eight lectures at my disposal. I had a go, and they were well enough received. I should perhaps have then used them as the basis for a large, deep and thorough treatment of the subject, but I did not want to be bogged down. I was happy to have opened up the subject, and the short book that I did publish, *The Continental Commitment*, was to be of some value to undergraduates, sixth-formers, and indeed the general public, until it was replaced by more thorough surveys and was deservedly forgotten.

I was next invited to deliver the Radcliffe Lectures at the University of Warwick in 1975, which enabled me to provide a digest of the lectures on 'War in European History' that I had delivered at King's in the 1950s and 60s. The students of Warwick were in a state of turmoil and occupying the offices of the Vice-Chancellor, but enough of them turned up to make my visits thoroughly enjoyable. The publication of the lectures was to make a lot of money for the Oxford University Press, and not a little for me. They were translated into 16 languages, which have enabled me at least to recognize Czech, Romanian, Estonian and Hebrew when I see them, not to mention Japanese and Chinese.

Finally in 1977 Cambridge invited me to give the Trevelyan Lectures, for which I chose the title 'War and the Liberal Conscience'. G.M. Trevelyan himself, on whose beautifully literate writing I had been brought up at school, embodied the paradox of the liberal thought that I had imbibed at home. While denouncing the absurdity and injustices of war in general, liberals have applauded it when fought in the 'just cause' of 'national self-determination'; a philosophy that produced, in Trevelyan's own lifetime, some of the bloodiest wars in history. My reading for this introduced me, rather late in life, to the political thought of the Enlightenment, and, more important, of the Counter-Enlightenment. I began to discern how the dialectic between them was to shape the history of Europe in the nineteenth century, of the world in the twentieth, and is now gaining alarming strength in the twenty-first, defying prophecies of 'the end of History'. Like *The Continental Commitment*, these lectures were a brief survey of a vast subject, but unlike my Ford Lectures, I have always regretted that I did not expand them, although I was briefly to return to the topic in a monograph, *The Invention of Peace*, some 20 years later. I would like to have another go at it now, but I doubt whether I could compete with Theodore Mommsen and write a magnum opus in my eighties.

All this, together with the Intelligence Histories, kept me busy during the 1970s; a melancholy decade after the happy madness of the 1960s, characterized at home by serious inflation, the dictatorship of the proletariat in the shape of ruthless and uncontrollable trade unions, and the reappearance of Irish republican militancy. We had to become accustomed, as 30 years earlier, to dining in London's West End to the sound of bombs offstage. Abroad, however, things looked better. The intensity of the Cold War had abated, thanks largely to the advent of moderate men in both Moscow and Washington (too moderate for the taste of Albert Wohlstetter and his disciples) and the travails of President Nixon and his associates. Talks about arms control seemed to be making some progress, while in Europe diplomats on both sides, with infinite patience, were easing open the Iron Curtain by the Helsinki Accords, which pessimists feared would lead to the 'Finlandization' of Western Europe and optimists to the 'Swedenization' of Eastern Europe. All this provided grist to the mill of the IISS and similar institutions, whose conferences proliferated. At these I gave papers which, together with the lectures I delivered to a wide range of audiences academic and military, now fill a dozen box-files which might provide material for yet another book.

In 1977 Norman Gibbs retired from the Chichele Chair of History of War, and I applied to be his successor. I would have been happy to stay as I was, but the Ministry of Defence's subvention of my fellowship was due to expire the following year and I would have been out of a job. I had to compete with my old friend and fellow Wellingtonian, Piers Mackesy, a far better scholar than myself, who had borne the burden of teaching military history in the university for the past 20 years. But his interests were considered to be too narrowly confined to the eighteenth century, so I got the post, somewhat to my relief.

My first concern was to shift the centre of gravity of the subject from the Napoleonic Wars to the twentieth century. I introduced two new under-graduate subjects. The first was on the Dardanelles campaign in the First World War, on which there was a wonderful wealth of documentation, political and military. The second was on European thinking about war and peace in the decades before 1914, in which I could introduce students to some of the ideas I had explored in the Trevelyan Lectures. But hardly had I got these under way when the chair was whisked from under me. I received a letter from Margaret Thatcher offering me the Regius Chair of Modern History.

*　*　*

For the past hundred years, ever since the tenure of the great medievalist Bishop Stubbs, the Regius Chair has been regarded as the flagship of the historical profession. It had been held by a succession of scholars, mainly themselves medievalists, all well worthy of the appointment; but it attracted little attention outside the academic world until the advent of Hugh Trevor-Roper in 1957. He and his principal rival for the chair, A.J.P. Taylor, were both highly combative personalities who were not averse to publicity and had plentiful access to it through the links with the media that they had established over many years. This made their campaign a matter of keen metropolitan if not national interest. Hugh was regarded in the faculty with not exactly affection – if he ever had an opportunity to quarrel with a colleague he took up the gauntlet with enthusiasm – but with awe at the breadth of his learning and admiration for his command of the English language, mixed with some regret that he had never produced an oeuvre quite worthy of his talents. Now he had been elected Master of Peterhouse, Cambridge, and elevated to the peerage with the title of Lord Dacre of Glanton. I think he was more delighted at the prospect of leaving Oxford, where he was now thoroughly bored, than with going to Cambridge, a university for which he had always expressed contempt. On his frequent return visits he made clear that he was not happy with his new colleagues; an unhappiness mitigated by satisfaction at the knowledge that they were even less happy with him. He briefed me about my new duties over a bottle of champagne at the Ritz; certainly the first holder of the Regius Chair ever to have done so.

Why me? I was not the first choice of the faculty, if indeed I figured as a runner at all. The favourite was quite properly Keith Thomas, a wonderful scholar whose work *Religion and the Decline of Magic* has transformed our understanding of the *mentalité* of the late seventeenth century; but there were others quite as well qualified, whom it would be invidious to list. If I had any advantage it was administrative, as cynics quickly pointed out. The university was strapped for cash. I could be transferred from the Chichele to the Regius Chair, the former could then be frozen, and it could be assumed, I am afraid quite accurately, that I would feel obliged to carry out the duties of both posts on the salary of one. In addition I was still doing all the work I had taken on in the field of international relations when I was Fellow in Higher Defence Studies, so I was quite a bargain. Finally, I was probably the only historian, at Oxford or anywhere else, of whom Margaret Thatcher, in whose gift the appointment lay, had ever heard.

Anyhow, I accepted. Some of my colleagues in the faculty expressed polite surprise, but the appointment was not seen as a public scandal. I was congratulated by my friends on having climbed to the top of the greasy pole, but in truth I felt more like Alice, who, after a series of bizarre adventures through the looking-glass, reached the back row of the chessboard and was crowned Queen. But I was not well qualified for the post. During the years that I spent struggling with problems of deterrence, mutual, virtual, extended or minimal, with first strikes and second strikes, with limited war and arms control, the nature and content of historical study had been transformed. My own generation of historians had been deeply influenced by the French *Annales* school, and talked learnedly of *mentalités*, of *la longue durée*, of 'total history', and 'history from below'. The Young Turks in the faculty were dismissing history as a 'text' that had to be 'deconstructed'. I had to catch up with them all by reading Braudel and Leroy Ladourie, which I enjoyed, and Derrida and Foucault, which I did not.

I was expected to give an inaugural lecture. I had already given two, one in London and one in Oxford, saying why I considered the history of war to be important. Now I had to explain why I considered history itself to be important. There was no problem in persuading my colleagues that they were not wasting their time in doing what to them came naturally. But why should anyone pay them to do it or subsidize undergraduates to study it at the taxpayer's expense?

Briefly, I suggested, it was because some kind of history was going to be written anyway, and it was important to get it right. Mankind could not entirely dispense with some sense of the past, and people had always invented some kind of tribal myth to account for their existence and guide their actions. Historians, rather than poets, were the unacknowledged legislators of mankind. If we were not to blunder into unwise, foolish or downright evil actions, it was important that our knowledge of the past should be as full and as accurate as possible, constantly updated and transmitted to new generations. But I took the opportunity to convey another message as well, one that I had learned from 25 years of sitting through international conferences and seminars. It was about the importance of understanding the diversity of human cultures. I have described my own frustration and alarm at finding how many influential Americans believed that they could understand and predict Soviet actions by multiplying Marxist theory by military capacity without taking into account the fact that these people were Russian, and that Dostoevsky might be a more accurate guide to their behaviour than Marx. But nearer home was the complete inability on the part of the British ruling classes between the wars to understand the ugly brew in central Europe that was to produce Hitler and bring him to power. There was no way in which one could understand these and other phenomena in international affairs unless one studied history. That was my confession of faith, and remains so.

One consequence of accepting the chair was that I had to change colleges and move from All Souls to Oriel, where the Regius Chair had been based ever since the days of Dr Thomas Arnold. Like so many changes in my life that had at first seemed unwelcome, this was one for which I soon became grateful. It was, as I soon realized, like moving from the comfort of an army group headquarters to a good county regiment in the front line. This was where the action was. The fellows of Oriel may have been slightly embarrassed by my appointment – they had just decided, very wisely, not to elect me their Provost – but they could not have been more welcoming, and the fortunate coincidence that the Bursar, Hugh Browne, was an old friend from Wellington ensured that they made me very comfortable.

College fellows ran not only their colleges, but their faculties. One of my more distinguished but unwise predecessors in the Regius Chair, Sir Charles Firth, had set out in his inaugural lecture to tell the faculty what history should be taught and how to teach it. They sent him to Coventry, where he remained for the rest of his tenure. His successors had all been college fellows themselves and knew better than to tell their colleagues what to do. They, after all, were the front-line fighters in the battle against undergraduate ignorance and indolence. They knew what could and could not be done, and on the whole did it well. Admittedly this gave them a vested interest in the status quo, but if change was to come, better that it should be by consensus than by diktat.

I found therefore that although I was welcome in my new college, it was assumed that I should take no part in the teaching of undergraduates. It was a deprivation that my predecessor, who had spent 20 years as a college tutor, endured stoically, but which I rather regretted. I had been allowed to teach undergraduates when I was at All Souls, and I found them refreshing after graduate supervisions that all too often largely consisted in counselling about their financial, marital or career problems. But this quarantine could be carried to extremes. One evening after their Schools dinner, the history finalists encountered me in the quad and jovially bore me off to join them for coffee and brandy. After that I took them to my rooms for further refreshment. The senior history tutor was outraged, and refused to speak to me for weeks. I remained unrepentant, and am glad to say that on a purely social level the undergraduates remained approachable and seemed to like being approached; sufficiently so to remind me that, whatever might be decided at the Olympian levels of Faculty and General Board and Hebdominal Council, these were the people who mattered, and the college authorities knew it.

Incidentally Oriel, like most colleges, had by now 'gone mixed' and admitted women. Perhaps it was the coldly critical regard of their girlfriends that had led the young men to abandon the bohemian hairstyles of the 1960s and even to wear jackets and ties. These were Thatcher's children, though the knowledge did not seem to depress them. I realized, not without melancholy, that I was now old enough for them to be my grandchildren.

But if he was permitted neither to teach undergraduates nor to direct his colleagues on the faculty, what was a Regius Professor for? Like other professors, he supervised his graduate students, of whom I now had a respectable number. He gave lectures; but few undergraduates attended them except Americans who seem to have, bless them, a genetic disposition for attending lectures, no doubt inherited from their forefathers and the three-hour-long sermons of such divines as Cotton Mather. Since the Americans who came my way were mainly graduates reading international relations, I stuck so far as possible to the twentieth century, and so commanded respectable audiences.

Finally the Regius, like a constitutional monarch, enjoyed an ill-defined *droit de regard* over the activities of the faculty, though one to be exercised only with great discretion. Like a constitutional monarch, he could advise, encourage, and warn; which involved sitting on every committee of the Faculty Board as well as the Board itself, and representing the Faculty on the next level up in the university hierarchy, the General Board of Faculties.

After four years, the History of War chair was 'unfrozen' and Bob O'Neill gave up the directorship of the IISS to take on both its duties and the teaching of 'Higher Defence Studies'. An Australian of boundless energy and charm, he established both on a permanent basis and attracted students from all over the world. I handed these duties over to him; but I still had to spend every afternoon on some committee or other discussing the problems either of the university, or of the faculty, or of the college. In retrospect every one of those afternoons seems to have been fine: bees buzzed in the gardens outside, the scent of wisteria drifted through the open windows, undergraduates chattered cheerfully on their way to the river, and there we were, imprisoned by our responsibility for their destinies, discussing how to spread our exiguous supply of butter over a never dwindling stock of bread. In the evening the sound of undergraduates enjoying themselves drifted up from the quad as I ploughed glumly through the agendas for the following day. The administrative chores that I had fled London to avoid had caught up with me with a vengeance.

I could not complain: I had enjoyed eleven halcyon years at All Souls, during which I had produced a respectable number of books. But when in the spring of 1987 I received a letter from Paul Kennedy at Yale, saying that they were establishing there a new chair of Military and Naval History and enquiring whether I would be interested in filling it, I did not say no.

12

Fin de Siècle

In autumn 1939 the Second World War had begun and I entered the sixth form at school to begin work for an Oxford scholarship. In autumn 1989, half a century later, the Cold War ended and I retired from the Regius Chair at Oxford with a knighthood. We had all, I reckoned, been lucky; far beyond our deserts. But history had not come to an end, either for me or for the rest of the world.

I had already experienced a few tremors that indicated that the tectonic plates of the international system were shifting. In the summer of 1986 Mark and I went on a cruise to Leningrad in the Soviet ship *Baltica*, the only Brits among happy workers from Eastern Europe being rewarded for meeting their productive norms. The sun beamed down from a cloudless sky on to a glassy sea, and there was a non-stop playing of hilarious films showing the more absurd aspects of American culture. One evening when alone on the deck I was approached by a young member of the crew who enquired, in excellent English, what was my academic speciality. When I told him, he asked whether it was true that before the war Stalin and Hitler had made a pact to divide Poland between them. I said that it was indeed true, and went on to provide further details. Was this, I wondered, some kind of 'provocation', or was the KGB, who no doubt had accurate files on me, trying to initiate some kind of seduction? (He was certainly a very handsome young man.) But I reckoned that this interpretation would be wildly to exaggerate my own importance, and it was more likely that he genuinely wanted to know. But that he should want to know, and had the courage to ask, suggested that there were serious stirrings going on, of which we should be aware.

A few months later the *Baltica* was to convey Gorbachev to meet President Reagan at Reykjavik, bearing arms-control proposals that staggered the West. Margaret Thatcher had already decided that Gorbachev was 'a man she could do business with', and had invited him to England. His entertainment included a lunch at Hampton Court to which I was invited. It was midwinter. There was no heating in the palace. Gorbachev was no doubt in his element. The rest of us nearly froze to death. The following spring the Prime Minister was invited back on a return visit, and I was summoned to a

Chequers seminar to advise her on what to expect. To my astonishment the Sovietologists present told her that she would find a country on the verge of collapse. Their diagnosis was confirmed for me when in the autumn of 1988 I attended an arms-control conference in Florence. An American delegate tabled a paper proposing, as a 'confidence-building measure', an exchange of information about expenditure on different kinds of armaments. A respected young Soviet specialist, Alexei Arbatov, replied that this was out of the question. The Soviets, he told us with exasperation, simply did not know how much they spent on armaments: their armed forces did not tell the government and probably did not know themselves. Even the notional figures provided for publicity purposes meant nothing. The most reliable figures, he said, were probably those provided in the IISS manual *The Military Balance*. It was clear that the Soviet Union was crumbling.

Paul Kennedy's invitation was timely for many reasons. At Oxford I was turning into a stale apparatchik. I would anyhow have to retire in 1990. If I cut short my tenure by a year, that would give me four years at Yale – more if I wanted – at double the salary I was earning at Oxford. So in August 1989 Mark and I set out for the New World and a new life.

Loaded as we were with baggage, we booked a sea passage on the *QE II*, and found ourselves bumped up to first class: my new title obviously had its advantages. (And its disadvantages. It was widely assumed in the States, especially by wordprocessors, that 'Sir' was a first name, like 'Duke' as in Duke Ellington.) They did not actually call it first class: in fact, the ship lacked 'class' in every sense of the word. Whereas the old *Queen Mary* had been a floating Ritz, decorated by the leading artists and craftsmen of the day, the *QE II* was a floating Holiday Inn, its décor bland, its public rooms crammed with shops and fruit-machines. Our table companions were wealthy couples who had retired early, and whose conversation revolved about the cruises they had taken in the past and those they intended to take in the future. The captain spent most of his time being photographed with the passengers, so it did not surprise us when a few months later the ship ran itself ashore off Long Island. But all was forgiven when early one morning the Statue of Liberty loomed up through the mists and we docked among the skyscrapers in midtown New York. This was the way to arrive in the USA. Kind friends met us with a van for our belongings and drove us along the interstate freeway to New Haven. I suddenly felt a rush of sheer happiness as, at the age of 67, I sloughed off one outworn life and looked forward to starting another.

We were indeed very happy at Yale, though in many ways it was not a very happy place. New Haven itself is a rundown rust-belt town that has not flourished since the early part of the twentieth century. Such charm as it had ever possessed was ruined by the freeway cutting it off from the sea. The university campus, neo-Gothic stone and neo-Georgian brick, built between the wars partly to boost the regional economy, was impressive, and contained some outstanding new buildings such as the translucent Beinecke Library. (Only sardonic Harvard men would point out that the most impressive building of all was the university gym.) The undergraduates lived, with a sprinkling of faculty members, in 'colleges' created and built in imitation of the Oxbridge model. But there were no-go areas a few blocks away, and intrusive beggars filled the streets. The students did not seem to mind much. A liberal admissions policy ensured a rich mixture of gender, race and class (the typical Yale man, it was said, was a Korean woman reading business studies), but there was still a core of handsome and self-confident young men, brought up to believe that it was their destiny and duty to rule their country, if not the world, and confident of their ability to do so. Oxford must have been rather like this, I reflected sadly, before 1914.

Less happy were the faculty members. The squalor of New Haven itself meant that they lived by preference at some distance from New Haven, in one of the pretty villages of upstate Connecticut or in Manhattan itself, and came in to the university only when duty demanded. (The president himself lived in Manhattan and resigned suddenly at the end of our last year, leaving the university accounts in chaos.) As a result, there was little sense of community life. There was no faculty club, only Mory's, an alumni club haunted by the spirits of the long-dead oarsmen whose photographs filled the walls, and the Elizabethan Club, where anglophiles could take afternoon tea. In some faculties the members barely knew one another; and in some they were hardly on speaking terms. The historians, however, were a splendid exception. We were at once made welcome by a genial community containing a high proportion of Brits: Paul and Cathie Kennedy, David Underdown, Linda Colley and David Cannadine, and Jonathan Spence. What with them and the Elizabethan Club, it was sometimes hard to remember that we were abroad at all.

I had made it clear when accepting the invitation that I would undertake no administrative responsibilities but would be happy to do as much teaching as they cared to ask. This involved more work than I had expected. My undergraduate courses focused largely on European warfare from the eighteenth century onward, but I broadened them by giving them the trendy title 'The Dynamics of Conflict'. I had assumed that the students would have some background knowledge of European history, but of course they hadn't. Why should they? Most of them were majoring in some quite different topic, engineering or law, and had never touched the subject. When asked to describe the difference between teaching at Yale and at Oxford, I would tell an apocryphal anecdote about a class to which I might have taught the origins of the Second World War. When asked whether they knew A.J.P. Taylor's book on the subject, the Oxford men would reply loftily, 'Oh yes, we did it in the sixth form.' 'What do you mean, you did it?' I would ask; 'Did you read it?' 'Well, we read *in* it ...' The Yale reply was more direct. 'No. Is it in the book-store? How much does it cost? Which pages should we read?' They would then find it, read it, and come back with some highly intelligent questions. I would also go away and read the book in question for the first time in ten years – sometimes far longer – and discover that it was quite inappropriate and long out of date. So I found myself having to compile new booklists, and work harder than at any time since I had started teaching at King's all those years ago.

But the people who really mattered were my graduate assistants. My classes were gratifyingly large, sometimes approaching a hundred, and were divided among half a dozen 'graders' who led discussions of the lectures and marked the examinations and term papers. With few exceptions they were wonderful: they reminded me of the NCOs who had made life so easy for me in the army 50 years earlier. They also drove home the sheer professionalism of American university teaching. In Britain all that was expected of doctoral aspirants was a thesis involving three years' research. In America they needed not only a thesis of equal length but also further examinations on broader aspects of their subjects, together with serious teaching experience, extending over at least four years, during which they had to finance themselves. At Oxford, where I was allowed rather more *droit de regard* over graduate than undergraduate studies, any young man or woman who obtained a first and who was encouraged to do so by their college tutors, could obtain a government grant to 'do research'. Far too many opted to do this rather than face the cold world outside. After two years both their grant and their interest often ran out. Even if they did not, the chances of the poor kids finding a job once they had got their doctorates were far from good. I used to give them all initial pep-talks (or rather anti-pep talks) warning them of this. These never had the slightest effect, apart from making me rather unpopular with their supervisors.

Thanks to the support of my graduate assistants, weekends were free to explore New England or visit New York, as well as to return home in the long summer recess. I must be frank: I no longer had any serious research project. I was in a desultory way collecting material for a history of the First World War, but that was to be pre-empted by so many excellent historians that ultimately it shrank to what was possibly the shortest history of that conflict ever written. But I was now over 70. My main concern was to cram as much enjoyable experience as I could into such life as was left to me.

In this I was helped by that insatiable American appetite for listening to lectures to which I have already referred. Thanks to the Yale Alumni Association, the Council on Foreign Relations and other such bodies, not to mention my old friends in the service staff colleges, I was able to visit every corner of the USA, and be handsomely paid for doing so. In addition I benefited from the Churchill-worship that flourishes in North America to a far greater extent than in Britain; partly because we are not good at celebrating our great men, and partly because there have been none in the USA since Lincoln whose reputation has not been highly controversial. I was able in 1990 to visit Fulton, Missouri, where in 1946 Churchill had warned that an Iron Curtain was descending over Europe, and to assure my audience that it was now being raised again. At Madison, Wisconsin, I had to eat my way through a 12-course banquet of the kind with which it was assumed that Churchill would himself have been familiar in the Edwardian era (though wisely they arranged for me to give my lecture first). But the grandest hospitality was provided in Edmonton, Western Canada, where we were provided with a uniformed ADC, a police escort from the airport with sirens blaring, and a guard of honour by cadets of the Royal Canadian Air Force, which I inspected with all the expertise acquired in the Guards' training battalion all those years ago.

Other lectures were more serious, and, like those at Yale, all had to be rewritten. The notes on the Cold War, on NATO, on arms control and nuclear deterrence that had kept me going for the past 30 years, all had to be scrapped. Tremendous events were transforming the world in which I had lived in and studied for the past half-century. Gorbachev had declared the Cold War at an end and accepted, to the consternation of the Pentagon, almost all the Western arms-control proposals. He had refused to crush the stirring reform movements in Eastern Europe, particularly those in East Germany, which culminated in the overthrow of the communist government and the demolition of the Berlin Wall. Then came the reunification of Germany and the Paris treaty of December 1991 that provided the definitive closure to the German wars that had begun in 1914. Finally, there was the collapse of the Soviet Union itself. When President Bush the elder spoke of a 'New World Order', few disagreed. When that 'order' was put to the test by Saddam Hussein's invasion of Kuwait, the 'collective security' invented by President Wilson in 1918 and hitherto regarded as a bad joke was put into practice and worked; and although the disintegration of Yugoslavia was handled with deplorable clumsiness, the conflicts in the region remained local and did not escalate, as they had in 1914, into another world war.

I had to improvise lectures about all this for audiences who, like my Yale sophomores, knew nothing of the subject and were desperate to learn. My lectures on the origins of the First World War helped explain the Yugoslav problem and those on the peace treaties of 1919–21 provided a basic knowledge of the Middle East. Even the most sceptical of my political-science colleagues had to admit that a knowledge of history was not a complete waste of time. I was able to improve my knowledge of Central and Eastern Europe by using my research funds from Yale and useful introductions from my friends in the Foreign Office to spend the summer of 1990 attending a high-level conference of politicians and intellectuals in Vienna and then driving around Czechoslovakia, East Germany, Poland and Hungary, where two things impressed me: the backwardness of the economies and the pathetic anxiety of the new leaders to catch up with the West. Life in the countryside seemed to have stood still for 50 years. We drove along almost deserted roads that had not been repaired for decades through unspoiled countryside, shabby, unpainted villages and gloomy, decrepit towns. Where rebuilding had taken place, it was in the garish modernistic style of Britain in the 1950s. Everywhere the air stank of lignite coal, and in the industrial regions of Silesia and Cracow the atmosphere was so polluted as to be barely breathable. At the Vienna conference universal euphoria was darkened by the bewilderment, verging sometimes on despair, of the East European leaders as to how to cope with the enormous economic problems with which they were now presented. But even those who were most despairing agreed that this was a wonderful moment to be alive, and so did I; though we were sometimes wearied at the incessant television performances of Smetana's *Ma Vlast* and Beethoven's 'Ode to Joy'.

Germany had not yet been reunited, but the patent incompetence of the new government in the East – some of whose ministers were in Vienna and made no pretence of knowing how to do their job – made clear that this would not take long. It was made even clearer when we spent a night in Erfurt in what was still East Germany. The final of the World Cup was being played between West Germany and Argentina. The whole town was indoors, watching it on television. When Germany won, by a penalty goal in the last minute of extra time, the town exploded. People poured into the streets, cars drove round and round with their horns blaring, and crowds roared happily over and over again '*Deutschland! Deutschland!*' Mrs Thatcher would have been very worried, but we were not. There was no trace of angst or arrogance in that cheerful noise; only of pride in and solidarity with their kinsmen over the frontier.

Sometimes it seemed almost too good to be true. That autumn I spoke at a NATO conference on military education in Rome, attended by grizzled, heavily bemedalled Russian officers who discussed with endearing frankness the problems they faced in maintaining morale in their armed forces with no enemy in sight, and with their country disintegrating under their feet. There was no trace of revanchism on one side, or triumphalism on the other: the defeated were unashamedly asking for help, and the victors were concerned only how best to provide it. As a result, the settlement that was reached seems likely to be enduring, and those responsible for it deserve more credit than they have received: especially President Bush the elder and his Secretary of State, James Baker; Mikhail Gorbachev and his Foreign Minister, Edouard Shevardnadze; Helmut Kohl and his Foreign Minister, Hans-Dietrich Genscher. President Bush in particular rose to heights of statesmanship unseen in Washington since the days of General Marshall and Dean Acheson. Unfortunately such gifts do not always run in the family.

My four years at Yale were thus happy ones, not only for me but also for anyone who had lived through the bloodstained 'short twentieth century' since 1914. I returned home with enough writing and lecturing to keep me busy into the new century. I consigned my books about NATO, the Cold War and above all, nuclear deterrence to the remote upper shelves of my library, where they now repose like volumes of medieval theology discussing the nature of the Real Presence. They might still interest specialists, but other problems of international security were more immediately relevant. A new generation of experts was coming forward to deal with them. I could lie back, so I thought, and leave them to it.

*   *   *

On 11 September 2001 terrorists hijacked four American airliners and flew two of them into the twin towers of the World Trade Center in New York before the horrified eyes of a worldwide television audience; killing some 3,000 people. A third crashed into the Pentagon in Washington. Only the heroic action of the passengers on the fourth prevented it from reaching its target, probably Congress or the White House. This terrible event was enough to prevent me, or anyone else, from relapsing into a somnolent and self-satisfied old age.

The instinctive response of an appalled USA was to hit back at anyone and everyone who could be held responsible. President George W. Bush simply declared 'War on Terror'. Responsibility was claimed by a transnational group of Islamic fundamentalists, Al Qaeda, and American retaliation against their bases in Afghanistan was prompt, spectacular and effective. But for the Bush administration this was only the beginning: '9/11', they argued, had shown that terrorists were now capable of causing such horrific damage that such attacks must be forestalled, if necessary by pre-emptive strikes against those who harboured or supported them. The 'rogue state' most likely to do so, they argued, was Iraq; and when in March

2003 American and British forces invaded Iraq and overthrew Saddam Hussein, it was assumed by a large majority of the American people that this was just such a 'pre-emptive' war.

But 9/11 had not just revealed the vulnerability of urban societies to attacks by 'non-state actors' who could not be deterred or defeated by conventional military means. Even more alarming was the light that it shed on a phenonemon of which Western societies were only gradually becoming conscious: the gradual alienation of the Islamic world – or much of it – from the culture, the achievements and the aspirations of the Western Enlightenment.

I had written a little about this in a small book *The Invention of Peace*, a year earlier, where I tried to describe how the the Enlightenment, and the secularization and industrialization it brought in its wake, had destroyed the beliefs and habits that had held European society together for a thousand years and evoked a backlash of tribal nationalism that had torn Europe apart and reached its climax with the two world wars. The victory of the West in those wars and the Cold War that followed led many to believe, with Francis Fukuyama, that history had now come to an end. The 'Third World' would, however stumblingly, follow in our path, as modernization and globalization produced there a wealthy and (Western) educated elite, a rising standard of living, and ultimately universal democracy and global governance. But the same shadow that had dogged the achievements of the Enlightenment in Europe was now extending to the rest of the world. Everywhere its impact caused as much misery and disruption as it did longevity and wealth. Few of us realized how deeply rooted was the visceral hatred of the West and all it stood for – not least among the educated classes from which we expected salvation.

The Islamic world was the worst affected. By the mid-twentieth century it had almost disappeared from the Western intellectual map. We assumed that after its defeat at the gates of Vienna in 1683 and its long retreat as the Ottoman Empire decayed and disappeared, Islam would either peacefully modernize itself under Western tutelage or remain a quaint target for tourism. The whole mighty structure that had contested with Christianity for the primacy of the world for a thousand years had become an object of amused toleration. The result had been a simmering resentment among the Muslim educated classes, which combined with the social problems created by modernization and the political confrontations resulting from Western intrusions into the heart of the Islamic world (of which Israel was only the most provocative), to create the profound antagonism that bred the fanatics who destroyed the Twin Towers, and who still hope to bring down the West in an ongoing jihad.

It was some sense of all this that made me deeply uneasy about President Bush's declaration of a 'War against Terror': a war for which the USA claimed a hunter's licence to use force anywhere in the world and the right to dispense with all the restraints of international law that they had done so much to create. At my age I should have known better, but I rushed into print with an article pleading with the USA not to regard this atrocity as warranting a 'war' to be waged unilaterally, but as a crime against the international community, to be treated as such. A primary objective of such terrorist acts, I argued, was always to provoke an overreaction from the authorities that would mobilize support for their perpetrators, and the policy of the Bush administration was likely to make matters worse rather than better. In particular, to bomb suspected centres of terrorism, I argued, was 'like trying to eradicate cancer cells with a blow-torch'.

Many other people were saying much the same thing, but my article was widely syndicated and evoked much support, not least in the USA. I had to admit that the bombing of Al Qaeda bases in Afghanistan had been very effective; but too many conclusions could not be drawn from a campaign against that isolated 'failed state'. The war that the Bush adminstration was preparing against Iraq would be in a different category. The evidence that Saddam Hussein was in any way connected with 9/11 was tenuous. So was evidence that he was rearming himself with 'Weapons of Mass Destruction' in defiance of UN prohibitions. This was in any case a matter for the United Nations to decide on the basis of their inspectors' reports, and these were at best inconclusive. That Saddam was a dictator of exceptional brutality was undeniable, but that had not prevented the USA from supporting him during his decade-long war against Iran. In any case, the 'regime change' demanded by President Bush had never been regarded as a legitimate *casus belli* in international law; while the placid assumption that Saddam's regime could be effortlessly replaced by a peaceful democracy was breathtaking in its naivety.

But it was not simply the weakness of the case for war against Iraq that forfeited sympathy for the USA even among its most loyal allies: it was the bullying style of the Bush administration, its evident contempt for doubters and dissenters. The USA, they made clear, no longer needed its former allies and no longer feared its former enemies. Like Britain at the height of her imperial power, the USA had got the ships, the men and the money too. One of the saddest experiences in my life was to see a nation for which my own gratitude, affection and admiration had been almost unbounded, become within a few months regarded with hatred by half the world and mistrust by most of the rest.

How the Americans themselves reacted to the situation I was able to see at first hand when I was invited at the end of 2002, on the eve of my eightieth birthday, to occupy a visiting chair at the Kluge Center at the Library of Congress. I felt able to accept it for only four months. I did not want to be separated for longer from my books, my garden and my cats; but it would provide a wonderful viewpoint from which to observe the onset of what everyone knew would be the next Iraqi war.

Once there, I discovered how deeply divided was American opinion, at least in Washington. My own article had been widely read and everywhere I found sympathetic audiences. But there was no real debate. The chattering classes chattered, but the administration did not pay the slightest attention. On earlier visits, whether Nixon or Reagan, Carter or Clinton had been in the White House, I had met members of the administration at Georgetown dinner-parties as a matter of course. Now, following the example of their President, they had hunkered down. Further, by 'declaring war', Bush had seized the high ground. Criticism was damped down as unpatriotic. In any case, since it was quite clear that he was determined to have his war anyhow, it was a waste of breath. However, I did seek out Condi Rice, now the President's National Security Adviser. She received me quite charmingly, declaring that she well remembered meeting me at Stanford (which I doubted) and that she was a great admirer of my work (which I hoped was true). Bright, tough, elegant, formidably intelligent, I doubt whether she shared the convictions of her 'neocon' colleagues like Dick Cheyney and Paul Wolfowitz, but she was unlikely to express any views that were disagreeable to the President. She listened patiently as I rehearsed my views. But the Middle East, she insisted, was 'a boil infecting the whole world system that had to be lanced'. I suggested that the real boil was Palestine rather than Iraq, and that the most spectacular victory over Iraq might only make it harder than ever to win the 'War against Terror'.

A month later, the war began. Whether it has yet ended is a matter of opinion. It is as if we had been dealing with a patient suffering from a cancerous growth, about whose treatment the specialists disagreed. Should he be treated with drugs, radiotherapy, chemotherapy or invasive surgery? Surgery, insisted the most powerful of the doctors, equipped as he was with the latest 'state of the art' instruments. So surgery it was. The growth was removed. Three years later the patient is still in intensive care. Whether he will survive and become a healthy member of the international community, remains a matter of considerable doubt.

*   *   *

Today the world seems in little better shape than it was when I was born into it, in the chaotic aftermath of the First World War. The twenty-first century is likely to prove no less interesting than the twentieth. But as Immanuel Kant put it 200 years ago: 'Nature does not seem to have been concerned with seeing that man should live agreeably, but that he should work his way onward to make himself by his own conduct worthy of life and well-being.' With those words I concluded my Valedictory Lecture at Oxford. I hope that someone was listening.

Lightning Source UK Ltd.
Milton Keynes UK
UKOW06n0611131115

262652UK00014B/117/P